Hitler's Great Gamble

A New Look at German Strategy,
Operation Barbarossa, and the
Axis Defeat in World War II

James Ellman

STACKPOLE
BOOKS
Guilford, Connecticut

Published by Stackpole Books
An imprint of The Rowman & Littlefield Publishing Group, Inc.
4501 Forbes Blvd., Ste. 200
Lanham, MD 20706
www.rowman.com

Distributed by NATIONAL BOOK NETWORK
800-462-6420

British Library Cataloguing in Publication Information available

Library of Congress Cataloging-in-Publication Data available

Names: Ellman, James, author.
Title: Hitler's great gamble : a new look at German strategy, operation Barbarossa,
    and the Axis defeat in World War II / James Ellman.
Description: Guilford, Connecticut : Stackpole Books, [2019] | Includes
    bibliographical references and index.
Identifiers: LCCN 2019016357 (print) | LCCN 2019019789 (ebook) | ISBN
    9780811768481 (Electronic) | ISBN 9780811738491 (cloth : alk. paper)
Subjects: LCSH: World War, 1939–1945—Campaigns—Eastern Front. | World
    War, 1939–1945—Campaigns—Soviet Union. | Soviet Union—History—German
    occupation, 1941–1944. | World War, 1939–1945—Germany. |
    Germany—History, Military—20th century.
Classification: LCC D764 (ebook) | LCC D764 E55 2019 (print) | DDC
    940.54/217—dc23
LC record available at https://lccn.loc.gov/2019016357

DEDICATION

To my grandmother, Mrs. Marian Liebermann (1917–2018).

- *Born in Vienna in the final days of the Hapsburg rule.*
- *Raised in the First Austrian Republic.*
- *Sent into exile after the Anschluss by her parents, who were forced to remain and await the grim fate of all Jews living under Nazi rule.*
- *Married a fellow Viennese refugee in England and delivered my mother into a world at war during the Birmingham Blitz.*
- *Built a successful life for her family in the New World.*

Contents

Introduction

$\mathcal{W}$orld War II was the supreme cataclysmic event in the history of mankind. It resulted in more than seventy million deaths, and the fighting raged across the globe from desert to arctic to steppe to jungle to metropolis. Entire peoples were decimated, maps redrawn, great cities reduced to rubble, and the power of the atom unleashed, which heralded the possible extinction of our species. As such a monumental event, it is worthwhile to understand why the war happened and unfolded the way it did and influenced the world that emerged from its ashes.

It is difficult to believe that after more than seventy years and the publication of a vast number of scholarly volumes regarding World War II that there could be anything of import yet to write about the conflict. However, I believe that a few of the most important events of the period have been overlooked or misinterpreted. This volume will attempt to shed new light and analysis on two of the most crucial points of the war and argue the following:

(1) That the Nazi Third Reich's attack on the USSR in 1941 was not a doomed act of madness or hubris as many historians now conclude. Rather, it was a logical gamble that maximized Germany's chance of achieving its war goals and came extremely close to success. Other options presented to Hitler were considered and correctly discarded as unlikely to lead to victory. In November 1940, the German dictator offered his Soviet counterpart a deal to prevent or delay a conflict, but Stalin spurned the opportunity. Ideology, geographic ambitions, and a scramble for economic resources meant that war was probable between the two totalitarian powers once the buffer states between them had been ripped away. Hitler calculated that an attack

1

on the USSR in 1941 was the time most likely to result in a Nazi victory
and hegemony for his nation over northern Europe.

(2) That Germany's failure to conquer the Soviet Union was primarily
due to other than the most commonly believed reasons. The defeat was not
a result of a military that was too small to perform the task, a diversion in
the Balkans that delayed the invasion, a severe Russian winter, the Nazis'
evil ideology, or Hitler's refusal to listen to his generals and direct the focus
of the invasion on an early capture of Moscow. No, the primary reason for
the USSR's eventual triumph was a failure of Axis diplomacy. Germany
failed to gain the offensive actions it needed from its allies, Finland and
Japan, to achieve victory. As a result, all three went down to defeat. Had
Hitler engaged in committed diplomatic and military coordination with
his partners, it is difficult to see how the USSR could have survived.

To understand the two points above, we must understand why the
war occurred. Most historians agree that the cause of World War II was
the militarism and expansionist aims of Italy, Japan, and Germany. Without Germany's support, Italy and its ineffective military would never have
been able to wage a conflict of great import and geographic scope. Without
Germany's 1940 land victories over France, the Netherlands, and Britain,
it is unlikely that Japan would have been able to achieve such smashing
triumphs prior to its fiery ruin. Thus, it was the power of Germany that
allowed a handful of regional grievances and conflicts to become a world
at war. So, what were Adolf Hitler's goals? Answering that question will
tell us why World War II happened the way it did and, to a great extent,
it was the decisions made by the German dictator from 1939 to 1942 that
shaped the twentieth century world that followed.

There are several competing theories as to why Germany sparked the
conflict known as World War II. Was it to right the wrongs of the Treaty of
Versailles after a great war in which both sides were equally at fault? Was it
to refight and win World War I? Was it to exterminate the Jews and other
peoples despised by a warped Nazi ideology? Or was it even bigger than
that? Was it an outright attempt to conquer the world?

This book argues that Hitler's goals become clearer when viewed from
a geopolitical viewpoint and with an analysis of his published writing. Simply stated, he wished to secure Germany as the dominant nation in northern
Europe and have it achieve Great Power status. Hitler was a murderous
megalomaniac, but his declared objective for Germany was *Lebensraum* or
"living space," not conquest of the entire planet. After all, he was willing to
assign great swaths of the globe to his allies, demanded no territory of the
British Empire, and endeavored to avoid disputes with the United States.

This does not mean a realization of his goals would be peaceful. At a minimum, France and Poland would have to be militarily defeated and forcibly dismembered. If Britain, the USSR, and the United States opposed Hitler's plans, as was likely, then the dramatically larger combined GDP and populations of these enemies would overwhelm the Third Reich. Thus, to achieve his objectives, Hitler had to find a way through diplomacy, bluster, and strategy to keep these three Great Powers from combining against Germany.

Despite an evil, false, and genocidal ideology, Hitler's territorial goals were effectively the same as those of Germany in World War I. For over a decade, he played an exquisitely successful strategic game and came remarkably close to achieving a sustainable victory. Evaluated in this light, World War II looks significantly different compared to the common belief that the Nazis were striving for nothing less than global conquest. The Molotov-Ribbentrop Pact of 1939 becomes obvious from a German point of view. It needed to defeat its enemies sequentially, as it could not stand against all of them at once. The invasion of Russia in June 1941 also appears significantly more rational and well timed: it was a calculated gamble rather than a great mistake. What otherwise would seem to be uncharacteristic forbearance shown by Hitler toward the belligerence of the United States and President Roosevelt is clearly logical under this analysis.

There are entire books dedicated to enumerating long lists of Hitler's mistakes.[1] Of these errors, the consensus is that the greatest was the German attack on the USSR on June 22, 1941. Consider the following quotes regarding the invasion from esteemed historians Ian Kershaw, Niall Ferguson, Drew Middleton, Joachim Fest, Norman Rich, and William Shirer:

- "The decision looks like a death wish for himself and his nation."[2]
- "It is a truth almost universally acknowledged that the attack on the Soviet Union was Hitler's fatal mistake."[3]
- "Hitler's decision to invade Russia was the product of the convictions and illusions of the dictator's demonic psyche."[4]
- "The decision to attack the Soviet Union even before the war in the West was decided has often been viewed as one of Hitler's 'blind,' 'puzzling,' or 'hardly comprehensible' resolves. . . . His decision to launch the war in the East at this particular time resembled an act of desperation."[5]
- "The German attack on Russia in 1941 has been called the greatest blunder of the Second World War."[6]
- "The destruction of the Soviet Union came first. . . . This, we can now see, was a staggering blunder."[7]

The majority of German casualties took place in crushing defeats in the East, so a conclusion that the invasion was a mistake seems reasonable. Nevertheless, Part I of this book will respectfully argue a different opinion: that an analysis of geopolitics, German war aims, and facts on the ground show that the invasion of the USSR was not a mistake. It was a gamble, yes, and a huge one at that, but one in which the odds were calculated and distinctly in Hitler's favor. Yes, Germany lost and the USSR won. Nevertheless, Hitler seized on the moment that maximized his chance of victory and minimized Stalin's. German military power was at its height, while that of the Soviet Union was at a low point. Germany started the invasion brimming with confidence and with willing allies ready to commit blood and treasure to the cause. The USSR was alone, ringed by enemies, and seething with internal dissent in the wake of the murder of millions of its citizens in Stalin's purges and mass forced starvations. Germany's position versus its larger eastern neighbor was starkly more advantageous in 1941 compared to that in 1914. We should recall that in 1914 to 1917 the Germans successfully defeated and dismembered Russia, and so hopes of a repeat victory were reasonable rather than delusional.

Many have made the case that Hitler should have left the USSR alone and focused on other military options available to Germany in 1941. However, this book will attempt to show that these other options were fraught with risk and unlikely to succeed. In addition, if pursued, their failure could place the Third Reich in a position of great disadvantage if the USSR subsequently chose to attack. Hitler knew Stalin had engaged in discussions to ally his nation militarily with Germany's enemies before and after the war began. The ideologies of the Nazis and the Bolsheviks were diametrically opposed, and the two nations coveted many of the same territories. War between Germany and the USSR in the 1940s was all but inevitable.

In 1914, Kaiser Wilhelm's government enumerated its war aims in the *Septemberprogramm*. One of these goals, the conquest of western Russia, was achieved in 1917. Hitler made clear that he planned to refight and win World War I. He wrote in *Mein Kampf* that Germany should conquer the western half of the USSR in its quest to achieve Great Power status. Since 1919 the Soviet government had been supporting the Comintern, which fomented violent Bolshevik revolts across Western Europe. Certainly, a reading of the Moscow newspapers and communist theory would lead a rational German strategist to expect the Soviets to march West and conquer as much of Europe as possible at the first opportunity. An attempt had already been made to do this in 1920, but the Poles turned back the Red Army on the outskirts of Warsaw.

Perhaps a German-Russian war could have been delayed past 1941. Peace could have been maintained for a time with Soviet acceptance of German preeminence in Europe. But Stalin engaged in his own aggressive territorial and diplomatic moves that brought the two totalitarian powers that much closer to war. The partition of Poland created a common frontier between the two Great Powers along which a clash of arms became possible. Stalin then ordered an invasion of the Baltics, which stationed Red Army troops on the German border for the first time. A slice of Romania was annexed, which advanced Soviet forces that much closer to Germany's primary source of petroleum. Finland was to be absorbed as yet another Soviet Republic, and the flow of critical German imports from Scandinavia would then continue only on the whim of Stalin's caprice. War was coming. To Hitler, the question was only if it was to be fought on German or Russian soil.

Part II will examine why the USSR triumphed over the German invaders. Not only the Nazi leadership, but most senior British, Japanese, and American military observers expected the Red Army to be defeated quickly. If nothing else, the almost universal international expectation of German success belies the argument that the Russian invasion was a foolhardy mistake. If Hitler was delusional that his army would conquer the USSR in the second half of 1941, then so too was the US Secretary of War and the British Imperial General Staff. That is not how history played out, but the failure of Operation Barbarossa, the German invasion of the USSR, was not preordained.

Scholars have offered various arguments to explain the Nazi regime's defeat in the East: it was due to a failure of its military capabilities, or its logistics train, or Hitler's leadership, or the fury of the Russian people and their winter. Despite these criticisms, the Wehrmacht advanced with remarkable speed, destroyed army after army arrayed against it, and fought its way more than nine hundred miles into the USSR—to Leningrad, to Moscow, to Stalingrad. This volume will advance an explanation that has not been sufficiently explored. While the most famous image of World War II may be a diplomatic one of Roosevelt, Churchill, and Stalin sitting together, little discussion has taken place arguing that the Soviet victory can be tied directly to a failure of German diplomacy and coordination with its allies. Had Hitler been able to cajole the Finns to advance further after their initial victories in 1941, and had Japan been persuaded to attack the USSR in the Far East, a Russian military collapse would have been all but assured.

Even after the Wehrmacht was driven back from Moscow, a German victory over the USSR could still have been achieved in 1942 when the two sides were so evenly matched. The Finns and the Japanese fielded fresh legions massed close to Murmansk and Vladivostok as well as the two railways leading from those ports. Critical shipments of US aid to the Red Army moved along these rails, yet Germany's allies failed to attack. The USSR stripped these quiet fronts of hundreds of thousands of troops to fight and defeat the Germans from the Baltic to the Volga, and then in the long campaign to Berlin.

A note on the tone and viewpoint of this book: it attempts to analyze the military strategies of Germany, and within that context, the decisions of its dictator in the initial years of World War II. It is not a polemic against the evil of Hitler, nor an attempt to rank his homicidal policies against those of Stalin. Other books have done that in great detail and in a more compelling manner than I could ever hope to achieve.

GOALS

Part I of this book will attempt to persuade that the German attack on the USSR, generally viewed as a monumental blunder, was in fact a calculated, rational choice. In the context of achieving his nation's war aims, Hitler weighed the odds in 1941, concluded they were in his favor, and rolled the dice. He knew he was taking a great gamble in Russia, and his voiced fears, sleepless nights, and rapid increase in drug use belied the boastful promises of an easy victory he issued to larger audiences.

Part II will attempt to show that while Hitler came tantalizingly close to victory in the USSR, it was primarily a failure of diplomacy rather than a deficiency in German military acumen or generalship that led to defeat. The cold of the winter, the fighting spirit of the Russian soldier, and the inability to take Moscow will always loom large in the German failure. Nevertheless, I hope to show that the choices made by Finland and Japan in 1941 to 1943 reveal the true proximate cause for Soviet victory.

Part I

THE GERMAN QUEST FOR GREAT POWER STATUS AND THE LOGIC OF BARBAROSSA

• *1* •

The German Strategic
Predicament and Hitler's Rise

$\mathscr{A}$s with all nations, geography has defined Germany's existence.
The country sits on the western side of the European Plain, a generally
flat area broken up by forest and the rivers that flow primarily to the
North, Baltic, and Black seas. With no defining geographic barrier to
stop armies, this region has repeatedly been one of the great battlefields
of history. In the centuries before the creation of modern Germany, the
Plain provided an easy avenue for invasion and counterattack by the
powers of the day. The Romans invaded from the west, and waves of
tribal invaders flowed in from the steppe to the east. The Goths, Huns,
Franks, Swedes, French, Prussians, and Russians all sent army after army
back and forth across these lands.

This geographic position was both Germany's greatest asset and its
greatest weakness. As northern Europe became the richest and most powerful part of the world after 1600, Germany's central position on the continent placed it strategically to prosper from the region's growth. An array
of navigable rivers—the Rhine, the Danube, the Elbe, the Oder, and their
tributaries—allowed for the economical and rapid movement of goods from
the interior of the nation to the coast, facilitating the accumulation of capital at population centers along their banks. This process was accelerated by
the Industrial Revolution, mechanization of production, and the expansion
of railroads that were most useful in flat areas such as the European Plain.
In the late nineteenth century, Germany emerged as a major continental
power, defeating its primary rival France in 1870, and embarking on a drive
toward economic and military hegemony. To the east, Germany had to
contend with the massive but backward Russian Empire. In the west, it was
confronted not only by a wary France but also by Britain.

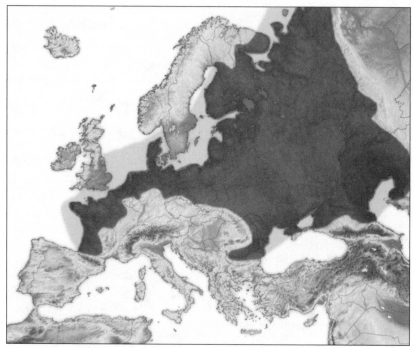

The European Plain (shaded region)[1]

By the start of the twentieth century, France remained a Great Power, but even with its overseas territories it could not keep pace with a rising Germany. Britain was most interested in maintaining its vast empire and ensuring that no hegemonic power arose in Europe that could threaten its command of the seas or penetrate its channel moat. Britain had been happy to side with German states in the 1700s and 1800s to maintain a balance of power against the French. With Teutonic ascendency and the building of the High Seas Fleet, the British backed France to manage the equilibrium. Russia was late to industrialize but was catching up, and its huge population, vast raw materials, and territorial reach offered significant potential. The Russians were also an imperialist power looking to secure greater control of the littorals of the Baltic and Black seas. Such aims were bound to conflict with an equally expansionist Germany no matter who were the leaders in Moscow and Berlin or the ideologies that drove them.

A peaceful continuation of the status quo was made increasingly unstable by Germany's alliance with the Austrian-Hungarian Empire and its kaleidoscope of ethnic nationalities straining for self-determination. A

spark was all that was needed to end the peace. That spark was of course ig-
nited in Sarajevo in 1914 with the assassination of the Austrian archduke.
So began a thirty-year conflict in which Germany fought to vanquish its
continental foes and become a preeminent world power. This struggle only
concluded with the final defeat of the last fanatical Nazi soldiers around
Hitler's Berlin bunker in 1945.

At the start of the conflict in 1914, the geography the European Plain
determined the scope of plans for German conquest just as it would in
World War II. As the German armies advanced into France in the opening act of the "War to End All Wars," the government of Kaiser Wilhelm
under its chancellor, Theobald von Bethmann-Hollweg, established goals
for the conflict in what became known as the *Septemberprogramm*. Despite
later protestations that the Allies were just as complicit in the violence of
1914 to 1918, Germany's explicit war aims were aggressive and extreme
in scope: in the west, France was to be permanently relieved of its territory along the English Channel, many of its colonies, and its Great Power
status. In addition, French trade with the British Empire would be forbid-
den, and crippling long-term war reparations would be paid to preclude
a potential Gallic rearmament program. Luxembourg was to be annexed,
Belgium was to become a dismantled vassal state, and the Netherlands
would only survive as an economic dependency.[2]

Looking eastward, the German government and its industrial elite
concluded that Russia could be defeated first: "A separate peace in the east
is certain, if Italy does not enter the war. But even if Italy does become
involved, the moment may arise in certain circumstances when Russia
is no longer willing to continue the war, and we can as a result conclude
a separate agreement with Russia."[3] When this capitulation took place,
Germany planned to annex much of western Russia. "In the interest of
striking a balance between industry and agriculture, it is also necessary to
demand that we obtain new territory in the east—land for settlement—in
which new farms could be created for German settlers and land could be
provided as well to German workers who might arrive from Russia."[4] This
was a plan to implement what we would now refer to as the war crime of
"ethnic cleansing." German farmers could only safely move east into newly
annexed territories if the established Slavic occupants were forced off their
land and into the shrunken remaining domains of the Russian State. The
German government realized that such actions would trigger a retaliation
by whoever ruled Russia after the war. Thus, much of the German-ethnic
minority that had been living in the tsars' domains for centuries would be
expelled and could be resettled in the newly conquered eastern lands of the

expanded Reich. While the German goals of World War I should in no way exonerate Hitler and his henchmen of the crimes committed in the USSR in 1941 to 1944, it is quite clear that the Nazis were following a path blazed by their predecessors.

The greatly expanded German Empire resulting from a successful implementation of the *Septemberprogramm* would dominate the continent through a *Mitteleuropa* economic union that would "provide for ostensible equality among its members, although it will in fact be under German leadership; it must stabilize Germany's economic predominance in central Europe."[6]

The kaiser's government also envisioned that its European continental empire would secure shipments of natural resources from newly created *Mittelafrika*, stretching from the Atlantic to the Indian oceans and made up of then-current German holdings combined with ceded colonial possessions of France, England, and Belgium.

What is striking is how neatly the goals of the *Septemberprogramm* match up with the geography of the European Plain. By 1943 the Third Reich achieved these aims for a short period. Hitler's armies conquered most of the Plain after they seized the littoral along the English Channel and the Bay of Biscay in the west, and then pushed to the Volga River in the east. In both world wars, the Germans were motivated by a perceived need to expand to defendable geographic boundaries.

From 1914 to 1918, Germany maximized its three great advantages: interior lines of communications, better artillery, and its Army General Staff, which institutionalized military excellence in planning and battle. These factors allowed the Germans to handily outfight and outkill their opponents.[7] The British, French, and Americans suffered more war dead on the Western Front than the Germans did in all theaters of the conflict. In addition, despite the common view of World War I as static trench warfare, historian John Mosier points out, "With each year of war, the Central Powers eliminated a major adversary, destroying its army completely and occupying enormous amounts of its territory: Belgium in 1914, Serbia in 1915, Romania in 1916, Italy in 1917, and at the end of 1917, Russia as well."[8] Front lines were pushed back away from the German borders, and the Allies were stretched to the breaking point.

With the signing of the Treaty of Brest-Litovsk, Germany secured its territorial goals in Russia and appeared poised to push on to total victory as it redeployed upward of fifty divisions from the Eastern to the Western Front in early 1918. In the Spring Offensive that followed, the Allied armies were driven back toward Paris, and the Germans seemed on the cusp of victory. However, US troops had begun to arrive in France in late 1917. With them came the first cases of the "Spanish flu," which quickly swept across the continent. By the following August, the American Expeditionary Force, with more than one million men, went on the offensive against a German army ravaged by disease. In the end, weight of numbers, a starving German population, and an outsized impact of the global influenza pandemic on the Central Powers won out, leading to an armistice.[9] Instead of shearing off territory from its foes, Germany's borders shrank as it lost 13 percent of its national territory and ceded its overseas colonies. Rather than receiving massive war reparations, Berlin had to make economically debilitating payments to the Allies. The empires of the Central Powers were shattered. In light of the goals of the *Septemberprogramm* and the terms of the Brest-Litovsk settlement, the Treaty of Versailles was lenient in comparison. Of course, "fair" is not how most historians have viewed the agreement that ended the "War to End All Wars."

The deadliest conflict to date in the history of the world was over and, for a time, Germany was defeated in its quest to dominate Europe. It lost all its overseas colonies as well as a significant chunk of what it considered its home territory to France and Poland. The High Seas Fleet was scuttled, its army reduced in size, and its economy ravaged by hyperinflation. The nation reached a nadir in early 1923. Germany defaulted on its reparations payments, and in response, France militarily occupied the industrial Ruhr region. Few would have believed that twenty years later Germany would rise to militarily dominate Europe and conquer even more territory than envisioned in the *Septemberprogramm*. The year 1923 is also the year Adolf Hitler found himself confined to a comfortable jail cell in Bavaria. Once there he began to write *Mein Kampf*, which envisioned a dramatic recovery for his adopted nation.

THE GEOPOLITICAL IMPERATIVES OF GERMANY'S ADVERSARIES

To conquer the European Plain and assume the role of a Great Power, Germany would first have to reconstitute itself and rearm. Then it would have to defeat several enemies who each had their own core interests that were antithetical to Hitler's plans. Let us consider these antagonists in turn.

Smallest, but of consequence, was Poland, which divided East Prussia from the bulk of Germany and would have to be conquered or subjugated to allow for a Teutonic revival. The Poles had proven their willingness to fight for their independence against long odds as recently as in the victory over the USSR in 1920. Poland's geographic position was terrible, sandwiched as it was between two larger and more powerful states who desired its territory. With a population and GDP much smaller than that of Germany's, Poland would fight, but its best chance to survive was through securing allies.

Next was the old nemesis, France. It could be counted upon to resist Hitler's goals though it also needed allies to achieve victory against a resurgent Germany. Even with its overseas possessions, France had a smaller GDP than Germany and a smaller local population base. For centuries, the lands west of the Rhine had been attacked by scores of invaders from the east flooding through the European Plain. The modern Germans were only the most recent attackers. The French knew they could not win on their own—they had been beaten by Prussia in 1870 and bled white in 1914 to 1918 before the timely arrival of the American Expeditionary Force. Thus, France had a keen interest in maintaining Germany in a prostrate condition. To the imprisoned Hitler, the recent invasion of the Ruhr and confiscation of its coal output to fuel an adversary's steel industry was the most concrete example of postwar German national weakness versus the Gallic rival to the west.

Britain opposed the occupation of the Ruhr and favored allowing Germany to pay a lower level of reparations. Nonetheless, that was not to assume that Britain would support a resurgent and rearmed Germany. Britain could be counted upon to continue its strategy of maintaining a balance of power on the European continent. Over the centuries, the British had undermined the Spanish, the French, and then the Germans in turn. It lent support to whichever lesser continental allies it could find that would occupy the main power of the day. This minimized the possibility of both a loss of control of the seas and the possibility of an invasion of England. British opposition to German continental hegemony could be taken as a given. While Britain maintained the world's largest navy with a tradition of excellence and victory, the same level of success had rarely been achieved by the Empire's smaller army. Britain's military strategy against European rivals had historically been to (1) use its navy to protect the homeland, (2) blockade and raid coastal areas to weaken an opponent, and (3) add its army to those of continental allies so as to eventually form an armed coalition strong enough to resist any hegemonic aspirant. Germany could not hope to control the European Plain unless it secured Britain's acquiescence. To achieve this, the Germans would have to defeat Britain militarily and end all hopes of the island nation securing continental allies.

East of Poland lay the Soviet Union, which had reconquered almost all of the lands of the tsars and adopted many of the same expansionist urges. Like the Russian Empire before it, the USSR showed an interest in expanding its borders to the west and southwest. Russia's historic goals included territorial conquest along the Baltic coast of the European Plain, controlling the Turkish Straits as well as establishing hegemony over the Balkans. But of course, Bolshevik ideology demanded more—much more. Through the Comintern, the Soviet Union endeavored to export its Bolshevik revolution to every corner of the world. Germany was a prime target. Moscow had supported the recent March Action workers' revolt of the Communist Party of Germany in 1921, which had been violently suppressed by the police and army of the Weimar Republic. While devastated by almost a decade of war (1914–1922), the USSR's huge population and abundant natural resources represented a great industrial potential that, if achieved, threatened any hopes of German continental hegemony.

Finally, across the Atlantic waited the United States. Early in its history, the United States had enunciated the Monroe Doctrine and a desire to limit European expansion in the Western Hemisphere. As American power grew, this doctrine morphed into an active policy to push the old powers entirely out of the New World. The French, Russians, and Spanish were ushered out, leaving only the British as a possible hemispheric rival. After the emergence of the United States as a world power in the Spanish-American War, the United States expanded its geopolitical goals to ensure that no hegemonic power arose in Eurasia that could possibly project its power across the oceans. A shared language, legal system, and intertwined financial structures made the United States a natural ally of Britain in supporting the British goal of maintaining a balance of power on the European continent. This explained the US intervention in World War I to halt the rise of Germany. Despite retreating into isolationism after 1918, Hitler would have to assume that American foreign policy would oppose any attempt by Germany to dominate northern Europe.

HITLER'S STATED GOALS

Hitler understood that a German rise to European preeminence could only take place after the acquiescence or conquest of several foes. His writings are a scary and jumbled mess—the musings of a racist lunatic. One needs to push through hundreds of pages of vitriol and ramblings to get to the clear strategic goals in the latter parts of *Mein Kampf.* It is only in Volume II, Chapter 14, that Hitler finally laid out the core of his goals for German hegemony on the North European Plain. Consider the following five quotations (italics from the original text):

(1) *"Only an adequately large space on this earth assures a nation of freedom of existence....* Hence the German nation can defend its future only as a World Power.... The German people entered this struggle as a *supposed* world power. I say here "supposed" for in reality it was none. If the German nation in 1914 had had a different relation between area and population, Germany really would have been a world power and the War, aside from all other factors, could have been terminated favorably."[10]

(2) *"If the National Socialist movement really wants to be consecrated by history with a great mission for our nation, it must be permeated by knowledge and filled with pain at our true situation in this world; boldly and conscious of its goal, it must take up the struggle against the aimlessness and incompetence which have hitherto guided our German nation in the line of foreign affairs. Then, without consideration of 'traditions' and prejudices, it must find the courage to gather our people and their strength for an advance along the road that will lead this people from its present restricted living space to new land and soil, and hence also free it from the danger of vanishing from the earth or serving others as a slave nation."*[11]

(3) *"The demand for restoration of the frontiers of 1914 is a political absurdity of such proportions and consequences as to make it seem a crime. Quite aside from the fact that the Reich's frontiers in 1914 were anything but logical. For in reality they were neither complete in the sense of embracing the people of German nationality, nor sensible with regard to geo-military expediency."*[12]

(4) "For it should scarcely seem questionable to anyone that even the restoration of the frontiers of 1914 could be achieved only by blood. Only childish and naïve minds can lull themselves in the idea that they can bring about a correction of Versailles by wheedling and begging."[13]

(5) *"Germany will either be a world power or there will be no Germany.* And for world power she needs that magnitude which will give her the position she needs in the present period, and life to her citizens. *And so we National Socialists consciously draw a line beneath the foreign policy tendency of our pre-War period. We take up where we broke off six hundred years ago. We stop the endless German movement to the south and west, and turn our gaze toward the land in the east. At long last we break off the colonial and commercial*

policy of the pre-War period and shift to the soil policy of the future. If we speak of soil in Europe today, we can primarily have in mind only *Russia* and her vassal border states."[14]

Hitler stated his objectives for his nation quite clearly: (1) Germany needed to become a world power if it wanted to control its own destiny, and it could only do so by expanding its sovereign territory; (2) this expansion would not stop solely at the reclamation of the 1914 borders; (3) Germany would fight to gain the land it required or be destroyed in the attempt; (4) the prime areas of conquest were to the east with a focus on the territory of the USSR.

Hitler promoted the goal of greater *Lebensraum*, or "living space" for Germany, but he did not invent the concept. The Pan-German League popularized the term by 1901, and it remained a goal of German nationalists in the decades that followed.[15] Long before he rose to power, Hitler acknowledged that his policies would lead to war and the German people needed preparation for a long period of armed conflict. This was quite clear when he wrote, "The task which therefore falls to all really great legislators and statesmen is not so much to prepare for war in a narrow sense, but rather to educate and train thoroughly a people so that to all intents and purposes its future appears inherently assured. In this way even wars lose their character as isolated, more or less violent surprises, instead becoming part of a natural, indeed self-evident pattern of thorough, well secured sustained national development."[16]

THE MARCH TO APPEASEMENT

There are many factors that led to the rise of militarism, fascism, and dictatorship in Europe in the 1920s and 1930s. Foremost was the economic contraction of the Great Depression, resentment in the shattered pieces of the Central Powers regarding the terms of the Treaty of Versailles, economic elites' reaction to the threat of communist revolution, and the lack of will exhibited by France and England to stand up to the totalitarian regimes that arose across Europe.[17]

Hitler came to power in early 1933 assuming the office of chancellor. He then created the title Führer after also assuming the powers of the presidency in 1934. Hitler engaged in a multifaceted program to implement the strategy laid out in his previous writings:

1. Engage in diplomacy to gain back some of the losses of 1918.
2. Rearm and expand the military.
3. Encourage other dictatorial states and movements across the world and form a united front against the power of the British/French alliance.
4. Agitate among Germanic populations in other nations and encourage them to clamor to join the Reich.
5. Violently suppress all domestic groups likely to offer resistance to the program.
6. Prepare the German people for war.

Hitler received significant support from a military wishing to regain its former glory. Driven back on the battlefield in 1918, and then stripped of its equipment, size, and stature after Versailles, the German officer corps was eager for a rematch. Prior to the Nazi's assumption of power, the military had already begun to rebuild and expand its forces. In 1932, Chancellor Franz von Papen approved a secret plan of accelerated rearmament, which continued once Hitler took power.[18] From 1935 onward, the German military or *Wehrmacht* (composed of the army, *Heer*; the navy, *Kriegsmarine*; and the air force, *Luftwaffe*) expanded openly.

Of great consequence was the creation in the interwar period of a military doctrine that became known to the world as *Blitzkrieg*, or "lightning war." These new practices very much grew out of the older doctrine of the Prussian army of *Bewegungskrieg* or "maneuver warfare," as well as *Kampfgruppen* or "combined arms." Simply put, this line of military thinking married the older concepts of rapid movement, breaching of enemy lines, and encirclement of opposing armies with the modern weapons of war. The new German military doctrine led to complementary interactions between the large units of tanks, squadrons of dive bombers, batteries of artillery, and traditional infantry that dominated the battlefield in World War II.

Diplomacy and propaganda were Germany's greatest weapons in the 1930s as it expanded and undermined the nontotalitarian nations of Europe. Of course, Hitler's goal as he had published and repeated in public speeches was a Germany with borders that were significantly larger than those in 1914. Thus, appeasement was always doomed to fail. Hitler did not want only what he gained through diplomacy: the Rhineland, Austria, the Sudetenland, the rump of Czechoslovakia, and the city of Memel. No, he believed that Germany needed to be much larger and have the economic output, workforce, and industrial might to militarily defeat its rivals and achieve its goal of dominating the European Plain.

Much has been written regarding the folly of the policy of appeasement and that a more robust British and French response to German aggression between 1933 to 1939 could have halted Hitler's geographic aggrandizement. Certainly, the remilitarization of the Rhineland could have been blocked with only a small amount of military force, and the Czechoslovakians were willing to fight if supported by allies. Many British were of differing opinions regarding Hitler's true goals. As General Sir Maurice Hankey put it in 1933, "Are we still dealing with the Hitler of *Mein Kampf*, lulling his opponents to sleep with fair words to gain time to arm his people, and looking always to the day when he can throw off the mask and attack Poland? Or is it a new Hitler, who discovered the burden of responsible office, and wants to extricate himself, like many an earlier tyrant from the commitments of his irresponsible days? That is the riddle that has to be solved."[19]

In general, France was willing to follow the British lead, and the Little Entente (Czechoslovakia, Romania, and Yugoslavia) was willing to follow the French. Sadly, British leaders solved the Nazi "riddle" by believing that Hitler could be appeased with only small tweaks to the borders drawn at Versailles in 1919. Thus, Germany gained the Rhineland, Austria, and Czechoslovakia in turn without firing a shot and then turned its focus east toward Poland.

One factor behind the appeasement policy was the great fear in the ruling circles of Britain and France of Soviet communism. Many in London and Paris thought that Nazi Germany could be directed against the USSR and its export of revolutionary communism. Former prime minister Lloyd George gave a speech in the British House of Commons in late 1934 in which he stated, "In a very short time, perhaps in a year or two, the Conservative elements of this country will be looking to Germany as the bulwark against Communism in Europe . . . do not let us be in a hurry to condemn Germany. We shall be welcoming Germany as our friend."[20]

As late as 1937, Nevile Henderson, the British ambassador to Germany, wrote, "On the other hand, though Germany must be regarded as the most formidable menace of all at the present moment, there is no reason provided she does not ruthlessly disregard the vital principles of the League of Nations or revert to a policy of naval and overseas rivalry or a renewed push to the West, or deliberately threatens us by air, why—restless and troublesome though she is bound to be—she should perpetually constitute a danger of war for us. To put it quite bluntly, Eastern Europe emphatically is neither definitely settled for all time nor is it a vital British interest and the German is certainly more civilized than the Slav, and in the end, if properly handled, also less potentially dangerous to British interests."[21]

The historical focus on the British in general, and Prime Minister Chamberlain in particular, as deserving of the lion's share of blame for appeasement is not truly fair. The French withdrawal from the Rhineland, failure to oppose its militarization, and construction of the Maginot Line in the 1930s signaled to its allies in Eastern Europe that France was only willing to fight a defensive struggle against Germany. It is difficult to view the 1934 German-Polish Non-Aggression Pact today as something other than a factor contributing to Poland's fate. Democratic nation support for the Republican side in the Spanish Civil War was nothing short of pathetic when contrasted with the focused efforts of Fascist Italy and Nazi Germany. Even across the Atlantic, FDR was known to escape Washington and the American press corps by taking long fishing excursions when German troops were on the march.[22]

Let us also remember that Germany was not alone in fascism's rise. Hitler found significant allies across Europe. Well before the signing of the 1939 Pact of Steel, Mussolini's Italy had become a partner of the Third Reich. Similarly, Admiral Horthy's Hungary was willing to ally itself with Germany in its own quest to wrest territory from its neighbors. Nazi Germany also found amenable governments in Spain, Portugal, and Romania and active fascist movements in Austria, Czechoslovakia, Norway, Croatia, the Netherlands, and even Britain.

To summarize the results of Hitler's policies from his ascension to power in 1933 through the summer of 1939:

- German troops returned to the Rhineland and militarized the region.
- A union, or *Anschluss*, with Austria took place.
- The German economy surged as it rearmed and experienced a dramatic decline in unemployment.
- Dissidents, Communists, Jews, the infirm, the disabled, and all others viewed as possible threats to the Nazi regime were harassed, driven from the country, or killed.
- Hitler's National Socialist government banned all other political parties.
- The German armed forces expanded rapidly and prepared to execute on their vision of modern combat.

- Italy and Germany provided decisive military aid to the Nationalists in Spain to overthrow the democratically elected Republican government.
- The nation of Czechoslovakia was dismembered, with the bulk being absorbed by Germany.
- A robust military and political alliance was signed with Italy. Germany also became diplomatically closer with other militaristic regimes such as those of Japan, Hungary, Spain, and Romania.
- The strategy of appeasement was finally viewed as flawed, and the Western democracies promised to fight to protect the borders of its Polish ally.

Germany gained a great deal in a short number of years through diplomacy. By 1939, the period of bluster and threat had ended and war was in sight. The military conflict Hitler had foreseen in *Mein Kampf* fifteen years earlier was at hand.

• 2 •

German Relative Economic
Weakness and the Fall of France

$\mathcal{O}$n the cusp of World War II in Europe, let us evaluate the relative economic strengths of the parties involved and how these measures would impact German plans for a war of territorial expansion.

A German leader considering fighting a European war in 1939 against the Allies could draw several conclusions from the economic data of the time. Clearly, a short war, or *Blitzkrieg*, would be advantageous to Germany. Its GDP, with that of annexed Austria and Czechoslovakia, as well as an allied Italy, was roughly equivalent to the combined output of France, Britain, and Poland. Population levels were also similar. Chances of victory were favorable if it could be achieved in short order: the Third Reich would be operating on interior lines of communication, and it did not have to allocate forces to garrison duty in far-off colonies as required by France and Britain. In addition, the *Wehrmacht* had primarily built its military for a land conflict compared to its opponents with their relatively larger naval forces. The odds against Germany would lengthen if a conflict were to drag on and the economic weight of the French and British colonies were brought to bear. Things would get even worse if the British Dominions joined the conflict to aid the mother country. Canada, Australia, and New Zealand would add thirty-four million in population and a combined GDP a third the size of Britain's, to the scale's weight against Germany.[1]

At least those additional potential foes were far away across the oceans. Of greater concern would be if the USSR joined the alliance to oppose a Germanic drive for continental European dominance. The Soviet Union had been industrializing rapidly, had a massive population, and its GDP had surged past that of Germany's. It was imperative that the USSR

Table 1. GDP by Nation 1929–1939 in Millions of 1990 Geary-Khamis Dollars[2]

	France	Britain	Italy	Germany	USSR	US	Poland	Austria
1929	194,193	251,348	125,180	262,284	238,392	843,334	58,980	24,647
1930	188,558	249,551	119,014	258,602	252,333	768,314	56,247	23,967
1931	177,288	236,747	118,323	238,893	257,213	709,332	52,177	22,044
1932	165,729	238,544	122,140	220,916	254,424	615,686	48,107	19,769
1933	177,577	245,507	121,317	234,778	264,880	602,751	46,771	19,113
1934	175,843	261,680	121,826	256,220	290,903	649,316	47,439	19,277
1935	171,364	271,788	133,559	275,496	334,818	698,984	48,107	19,652
1936	177,866	284,142	133,792	299,753	361,306	798,322	49,504	20,238
1937	188,125	294,025	142,954	317,783	398,017	832,469	58,980	21,317
1938	187,402	297,619	143,981	342,351	405,220	799,357	67,788	24,037
1939	200,840	300,539	154,470	374,577	430,314	862,995		27,250

be excluded from a war at least until after Poland, France, and Britain had been dealt with on the battlefield.

As if the odds were not already stacked against Germany, the United States was yet another Great Power ready to oppose the creation of a hegemonic state on the European mainland. How could Germany hope to oppose the industrial might of the United States? By the late 1930s, the economic output of much of Europe had recovered from the shock of the Great Depression and then surged ahead. In contrast, the economy of the United States suffered another recession in 1938 and had only recovered to the level of GDP recorded in 1929. Despite this, America's economic output was double that of Germany's even with a wealth of underutilized American plant, equipment, and labor. If the United States mobilized its potential, its GDP would swell further past that of Germany's, allowing the Americans to intervene in a European conflict as they had in 1918.

In contrast, if Hitler was able to first consolidate the bulk of European economic output under Axis control, then the Third Reich would approach the United States on more or less even terms. Such a consolidation of European power might be sufficient to force a grudging American acceptance of Germany's new status as a Great Power. Economic considerations made it of paramount importance to Hitler that America not enter a European war until the Third Reich's continental conquests were complete.

GERMANY'S LACK OF THE "RIGHT" NATURAL RESOURCES: OIL, IRON, AND NICKEL

Germany certainly had an advantageous location with few geographic barriers, productive agricultural regions, and a large number of navigable

Table 2. 1939 Population of Selected Nations in Millions

Austria	6.8
Czechoslovakia	10.5
UK Dominions	30.0
Poland	35.1
France	42.0
Italy	43.4
UK	47.5
Germany	68.6
Japan	71.9
USA	130.5
USSR	192.4

rivers emptying into the Baltic, Black, and the North seas so as to facilitate trade and the rise of industry. Unfortunately for Germany, the technology of warfare had evolved in ways not advantageous to that nation's natural resources. The great inputs of World War I: infantrymen, draft horses, machine gun bullets, barbed wire, and artillery shells all arrived at the front lines by rail. These required great amounts of food, fodder, iron, and coal. The Central Powers were able to supply these, and only years of naval blockade by the Allies finally led to critical shortages, particularly of food. However, by 1939, the tank, the truck, and the airplane had come of age. This is not to say that petroleum, aluminum, and steel were unimportant in World War I, or that horses and railroads were no longer used in World War II. Rather, there had been a massive shift in the importance of, and quantities required of, several industrial commodities to the functioning of armies and economies by the outbreak of World War II.

While Germany possessed large supplies of coal, it had effectively no oil, insufficient reserves of iron ore, and little in the way of essential metals such as chromium, nickel, manganese, and tungsten required by the steel industry.[3] In addition to this crucial deficiency in petroleum, Hitler's Third Reich of 1939 was not self-sufficient in iron. The loss of territory in the Treaty of Versailles deprived Germany of much of its iron ore mines as well. France and Britain had the continent's largest iron output, but these nations were certainly not reliable sources for a Germany bent on territorial expansion. On the eve of World War II, a US government study on European industry argued, "The more one thinks about the status of iron as a power among metals, greater than that of all other metals combined, the more he realizes why nations must secure control of iron ore resources. No war can be waged without considerable stocks of iron, and countries that have achieved dominion over the principal sources of supply have the best chance to win the conflict, provided that they have the furnaces and fuel to melt the iron into steel for munitions."[4] Neutral Sweden ranked third in European reserves of iron, and by the end of the 1930s, it was Germany's largest source of that import that arrived by ship in Hamburg via Norwegian or Swedish ports.[5] Also from Scandinavia came nickel, as the closest mines to Germany were located in northern Finland.

The only significant source of petroleum close to Germany in 1939 came from the Balkans, which also supplied several other critical natural resources: "South-eastern Europe provided half of Germany's cereal and livestock requirements. Greece, with Yugoslavia, was the source of 45 percent of the bauxite (aluminum ore) used by German industry, while Yugoslavia supplied 90 percent of its tin, 40 percent of its lead and 10 percent of its copper. Romania and, to a marginal extent, Hungary provided the only supply of oil which lay within the radius of German strategic control."[6] Even with the output of the Balkans, petroleum supplies for the Nazis in wartime would be tight. In addition, by the end of 1940, Germany and its allies only controlled 4 percent of the world's oil refining capacity. Its declared enemies had 22 percent, and neutral nations (including the USSR and the United States) had the rest.[7] Maintaining and protecting a sufficient supply of petroleum to power its tanks, trucks, and aircraft was critical for Germany's war plans. Perhaps Hitler did not have to conquer Scandinavia and the Balkans, but he could not allow those regions to fall into the hands of any other power.

Geographically the USSR was the best positioned nation to threaten Germany's trade links. From the Kronstadt naval base near Leningrad, Soviet forces could interdict Baltic shipping with the world's largest fleet of submarines.[8] From the Ukraine, the Red Army could push into Romania and utilize its Black Sea Fleet to land forces on the Bulgarian coast. Of lesser concern would be a potential British effort to threaten Scandinavian and Balkan trade flows. It would be extremely hazardous for the British navy to sail past Denmark into the Baltic Sea in the face of German naval and aviation opposition. Thus, the British would have to land forces in Norway and advance into Sweden and Finland to impact German ore imports. In the south, the Royal Navy could place an expeditionary force ashore in Greece as it had done in World War I and push up into the Balkans to threaten the Ploesti oil fields in Romania.

Incorporating geographic, economic, and demographic factors of 1939 versus 1914, a Germany looking to achieve Great Power status and expanded territorial borders would have to defeat Poland, France, and Britain. This victory would need to be achieved quickly before the resources of the overseas French and British empires could be brought to bear, and a naval embargo damaged the German economy. In addition, Hitler required a clear plan as to how to deal with the USSR. In the short term, he needed to forge an understanding with the Soviets to keep them out of the Baltic, the Balkans, and the conflict. If such an understanding could not be maintained until the end of a war, or if the war was not a short one, then Germany would have to conquer much of western USSR to protect its economic base. This would also complete the territorial goals as laid out in the *Septemberprogramm* a generation before.

THE FAILURE OF THE ALLIES, THE FOOLISHNESS OF STALIN, AND HITLER'S DIPLOMATIC TRIUMPH

After the bloodless conquest of Czechoslovakia, the focus of the coming conflict shifted to German demands on Polish territory. Hitler threatened war unless the Free City of Danzig reverted to German sovereignty along with an extraterritorial corridor through Poland to that port. These "limited" demands were intended to be intolerable to Poland and provide a pretext for a German invasion.

The Western powers reopened discussions with the USSR in hopes of forming an alliance that would dissuade Germany from further aggression. Despite the threat posed by the fascist nations, France and Britain were hesitant to come to an agreement with the communist state that they had viewed as a threat for so long. This ambivalence led to the dispatch of what was only a low-level delegation to Moscow bereft of plenipotentiary power. The Soviets offered to send a massive army to western Poland to help face down the Germans.[9] Not surprisingly, the Poles were unwilling to grant permission for the Red Army to move into their territory, and the negotiations were, in the end, unsuccessful. Nikita Khrushchev, at the time a newly elected member of the Politburo, summed up the Soviet point of view: "The English and French representatives who came to Moscow to talk with Voroshilov [Defense Minister Marshal Kliment Voroshilov] didn't really want to join forces with us against Germany at all. Our discussions with them were fruitless. We knew that they weren't serious about an alliance with us and that their real goal was to incite Hitler against us. We were just as glad to see them leave."[10]

French and British vacillation led to a diplomatic opening for Hitler. On August 11, 1939, he announced to Carl Burckhardt, the League of Nations' High Commissioner in Danzig, "Everything I undertake is directed against the Russians. If the West is too stupid and blind to grasp this, then I shall be compelled to come to an agreement with the Russians, beat the West and then after their defeat turn against the Soviet Union with all my forces. I need the Ukraine so that they can't starve us out, as happened in the last war."[11]

Discreet diplomatic messages were sent to the Soviets in an attempt to improve relations, and an offer was made for German foreign minister Joachim von Ribbentrop to travel to Moscow for high-level talks. The Soviet foreign commissar Vyacheslav Molotov responded positively and expressed interest in discussing both commercial treaties and a nonaggression pact between the two nations.[12] Ribbentrop arrived on August 23, 1939, and met with both Molotov and Stalin in a marathon set of meetings over the next thirteen hours. This led to the signing of a nonaggression treaty (usually referred to as the Molotov-Ribbentrop Pact), which contained several secret protocols that divided the states of Eastern Europe between the two totalitarian powers.

Stalin believed he received the better deal: "Of course it's all a game to see who can fool whom. I know what Hitler's up to. He thinks he's outsmarted me, but actually it's I who have outsmarted him!"[13] The USSR gained time to build up its military and an opportunity to seize significant territory in the Baltics, eastern Poland, and along the Black Sea. Stalin hoped that Germany would engage in a long, drawn-out war with France and Britain, which would exhaust the combatants and allow the USSR to become the master of Europe. This strategy was extremely risky. Germany and its weak partner, Austria-Hungary, had only been defeated in World War I by the combined efforts of France, Britain, Russia, Italy, and the United States along with several smaller allied states. If Hitler's armies were quickly able to defeat a coalition composed of only the French and British, the USSR would be in a dire position. Had Stalin joined France and Britain in staunchly opposing German expansion, Hitler would likely have refrained from attacking Poland in 1939. In retrospect, Stalin's gambit granted him territorial gains in the short term, but it led directly to the invasion and devastation of his country and the early deaths of more than twenty-five million Soviet citizens.

With the Molotov-Ribbentrop Pact in place, Germany launched its invasion of Poland on September 1, 1939. Two weeks later the Red Army attacked from the east. While the Poles fought back valiantly, the two much larger invading forces crushed the defenders. By early October, the fighting was over and Poland was occupied and partitioned. In the West,

**TERRITORIES OF POLAND ANNEXED
BY THE THIRD REICH AND THE SOVIET UNION
(Lines of partition from 10/21/1939 to 6/22/1941)**

The 1939 German/Soviet Partition of Poland[14]

the French launched an offensive into the industrial German Saarland. Luckily for Hitler, the attack was weak and timid. After a short period, all French troops withdrew back to their positions along the Maginot Line.

So began the six-month "Phony War," in which Britain and France did little to attack German territory, allowing the strategic initiative to remain in Hitler's hands. The *Wehrmacht* took great advantage of the situation, seizing Denmark and Norway despite the much larger combined Allied naval and air forces. Germany then launched a major invasion of France in May 1940 through the neutral nations of Belgium, Luxembourg, and the Netherlands. The French army and the British Expeditionary Force (BEF) were thoroughly outmaneuvered and outfought. The BEF evacuated via the port of Dunkirk while Italy entered the war and invaded across the Alps. France capitulated after only six weeks of fighting and surrendered the northern half of the country to German occupation. The French navy was interned in port, and the French army was dismantled, with many thousands of its soldiers shipped east to serve as forced laborers.

• 3 •

Seelöwe

The Planned Invasion of England

$\mathcal{F}$rance had been defeated, Italy was in the war as a full ally, Poland had been dismembered, and the Low Countries—Denmark and Norway—were overrun and occupied. Had Hitler achieved his goals? For the Führer, the answer was "no." Certainly, Germany had rapidly improved its position. Compared to early 1918, Germany had vanquished France rather than Russia, Italy was an ally rather than an enemy state, and the United States was not yet in the conflict. What had been Imperial Russia, now the USSR, was stronger than ever in the east; Britain remained defiant, and the United States was inching toward active armed involvement. In many ways, Germany's position was similar to that of France under Napoleon at the peak of his power: Western continental Europe was conquered, but the British would undoubtedly fight on as long as Russia remained a potential mainland ally.

So what was Hitler to do? He held the strategic and tactical initiative and had many potential paths to consolidate his victories. His public overtures of a negotiated peace were spurned, and so war with the British would continue. His primary options were as follows:

1. Invade England to impose a victor's peace.
2. Utilize sea and airpower to starve Britain into capitulation.
3. Combine forces with the Italians to attack the British Empire in the Mediterranean: seize Gibraltar, the Suez Canal, and perhaps even the oil fields of Persia and Iraq so as to force Britain to the negotiating table.
4. Invade the USSR to remove Britain's remaining potential continental ally, seize the critical natural resources that Germany needed, and complete the war aims of the *Septemberprogramm*.

Of course, we know that in the end the final option was chosen, and the destruction of the Third Reich followed. Hitler explored the other paths listed above before they were discarded. Many historians have argued that Hitler chose poorly and the attack on the USSR was a great mistake that doomed Germany to destruction. The next three chapters will argue that other potential options were fraught with risk, unlikely to succeed, and that the invasion of the Soviet Union gave Germany its best chance of victory. To prove this point, we will first have to investigate paths #1–3 above in detail so as to logically conclude their weaknesses.

Many historians state that England was ripe for invasion after the defeat of the British army in France in the summer of 1940. That this conquest never happened is supposedly due to Hitler's "racial soft spot" for the "Germanic" Anglo-Saxons, or the small number of brave fighter pilots of the RAF who defeated the *Luftwaffe*. The Germans believed the most obvious way to knock Britain out of the war was through an invasion of England and occupation of London. Thus, to show the logic of Germany attacking the USSR, we must first delve into some detail as to why such an amphibious invasion of England would have failed.

Even before the German invasion of France and the evacuation of the BEF from Dunkirk, the German High Command had begun preparations for an amphibious attack on England. In November 1939, Admiral Erich Raeder, commander-in-chief of the *Kriegsmarine*, ordered planning to begin for an assault staged from seized Channel ports.[1] Planning took on more urgency after the fall of France in June 1940. On July 16, Hitler signed Führer Directive No. 16, which ordered preparations for an invasion under the code name Operation Seelöwe (Sea Lion).

The Directive imagined a landing on a wide front across the south English coast. Prior to the sailing of the invasion fleet, the RAF was to be driven from the skies. The Royal Navy would be kept away through the use of minefields, as well as diversionary actions by the *Kriegsmarine* and the Italian navy. British coastal guns were to be neutralized while German ones were to be installed along the French coast. Then a large army would be transported across the Channel with the unopposed *Luftwaffe* acting as flying artillery to support the landings.

The consensus view today is that in the second half of 1940 the British army was disorganized, beaten, and disarmed, leaving southern England protected only by the Spitfires and Hurricanes of the RAF. If not for that small force of plucky pilots, the German army would have landed and rolled into London. This conclusion is far from the truth. A review of British and German military resources available to repel or support the invasion respectively reveals the weakness of Operation Seelöwe. The operation's problems from the German point of view can be broken into the following categories:

a) relative strength of the opposing naval forces
b) relative strength of the German invasion force versus British land defenses
c) relative strength of the opposing air forces

a) *The Sea*. An invasion of England required not only landing fighting men but also tanks, artillery, and trucks. This meant the Germans needed to amass a large concentration of specialized landing craft and merchant shipping to ferry vehicles, guns, and supplies to southern England. These vessels would have to be defended from naval attack prior to, during, and after they brought the troops across the Channel. The German beachhead would need to be continually sustained by massive shipments of ammunition, petrol, and spare parts. Even in the event of a successful initial landing, if British air and naval forces were able to cut the supply lines across the Channel, the invasion force would grind to a halt and be quickly starved into submission.

While the *Wehrmacht* had achieved great victories since the start of the war, the invasion of Norway was a pyrrhic victory for Germany. On the plus side, Scandinavian ore supplies were protected from any potential British interference. The *Kriegsmarine* and *Luftwaffe* also gained strategic bases from which to attack Britain and its maritime supply lines. On the negative side, Hitler felt compelled to garrison 250,000 soldiers in Norway for the duration of the war. More importantly, in relation to Operation Seelöwe, were the severe naval casualties suffered in the operation.

> The Kriegsmarine lost 3 cruisers, 10 destroyers and 4 U-boats while the [battleships] *Scharnhorst* and *Gneisenau* sustained serious damage. By the end of the campaign, only one heavy and two light cruisers and four destroyers remained fit for action. British losses were on a similar scale, but could be easily absorbed by the Royal Navy. For the far smaller German Navy, Norway was a campaign from which its surface fleet never fully recovered. It was certainly in no position to contest control of the English Channel with the Royal Navy once France was defeated.[2]

Table 3. British Naval Forces in Home Waters, July 1, 1940[3]

Port	Capital Ships	Cruisers	Destroyers
Scapa Flow	5	3	9
Rosyth		2	
Tyne			2
Humber		3	7
Harwich			9
Sheerness		1	3
Dover			5
Portsmouth			5
Escort Duties			38
Totals	5	9	78

Against the small number of remaining ships of the *Kriegsmarine*, the Royal Navy could field a dramatically larger fleet to oppose a seaborne invasion.

In addition to this overwhelming force, a large number of smaller British ships assembled at southern English ports. By the start of September, there were more than eight hundred vessels of the Royal Navy in the area ready to detect and oppose any invasion force.[4] In addition to the larger ships listed in table 3, these included thirty-five submarines, twenty-five fast minesweepers, 140 minesweeping trawlers, thirty-four sloops and corvettes, and many smaller gunboats. More than two hundred of these ships were at sea at all times patrolling the English coast.[5] If that was not enough, there was also a significant British fleet, "Force H," stationed at Gibraltar to counter the Italian navy in the western Mediterranean. While the Germans hoped that the Italian navy would keep these British ships occupied, it is likely that they would have been recalled at full speed to home waters if German troops began to land on English soil.

The *Kriegsmarine* simply did not have the ships to protect a landing force against the much larger Royal Navy in late 1940. The new "superbattleships" *Bismarck* and *Tirpitz*, with their massive main guns, might have made a difference, but they were not ready for action until 1941. Similarly, production was only just starting to ramp up of the Type VII U-boat that was to cause such havoc in the Battle of the Atlantic. Even if more German submarines had been available, the constrained and relatively shallow waters of the English Channel would have been a poor environment for their deployment. In final analysis, Admiral Raeder knew that his *Kriegsmarine* could not survive a major fleet action against the Royal Navy. Even before the grievous losses of naval strength off the coast of Norway, the admiral had stated, "The surface forces are so inferior in numbers and strength that they can do no more than show that they know how to die gallantly."[6]

To appreciate the challenges facing the German invasion plan, the Allied D-Day landings in Normandy in 1944 utilized more than 1,200 warships, 3,800 purpose-built landing craft, and 1,200 merchant vessels to support an invasion force of ten divisions (of which three were airborne). Compared to this, the *Kriegsmarine* planned to land thirteen divisions (two airborne) utilizing a sealift flotilla composed of a handful of warships, 168 merchant ships, 386 tugs, 1,600 motor boats, and 1,900 barges.[7]

The first landing detachments of around two thousand Germans per beach were to cross the Channel in minelayers or minesweepers and then make their final approach in small motor boats or in *sturmboots*, which were army vessels designed to carry eight men each for river crossings. Then the main body of men and supplies would come ashore via barges. These flat-bottomed, wooden vessels represented an important part of the economic infrastructure of northern Europe and were not designed for a military operation. Assembled from across the expanse of the territories under German control, they were manned by conscripted sailors used to operating on rivers and canals rather than the open sea. "Most of the canal barges had carrying capacities ranging from 500 to 800 tons, and river barges up to twice that, but very few were self-propelled, so over 400 tugs would be needed. Furthermore, when loaded, the average barge would be low in the water, which might not have been of particular concern on the inland waterways and rivers of Europe, but most certainly would be in the choppy waters of the English Channel."[8]

The *Kriegsmarine* plan called for groups of around three hundred barges to be pulled across to England by tugs while protected by a screen of small naval vessels. One can only imagine the carnage that would have ensued had a squadron of British destroyers moving at upwards of thirty knots been able to penetrate such a slow-moving convoy heavily laden with mixed cargos of petrol, munitions, and humans. Another risk was that even a small storm could have sent many of the best units of the *Wehrmacht*, weighted down in full combat gear, to the bottom of the sea. To make matters worse, the barges needed to survive several trips back and forth across the Channel over a period of more than a week. The *Kriegsmarine* was quite aware of the significant chances of a major storm descending upon the area in late summer. If a major gale were to hit (as occurred soon after the D-Day landings in June 1944), the results on such flimsy craft would have been catastrophic to the operation.

Each tug in the invasion fleet would pull a couple of barges in a large, ungainly flotilla. Moving at not much more than a brisk walking pace, the vessels would cross the Channel and head for the intended landing beach. Then, at just the right moment, the tugs would release their lines and momentum would carry the barges onto the sand. After landing, it would be the responsibility of the unloaded German soldiers to push the barges back out to sea. The tugs would then regain the towlines to pull the now empty vessels to France for reloading. How this was to take place in the face of even moderate surf or active armed resistance is not entirely clear.

b) *The Land.* Certainly the British army had been dramatically weakened by the debacle suffered in France. Nevertheless, it was significantly stronger in July 1940 than the popular vision held today. Not only did Operation Dynamo rescue more than three hundred thousand troops from Dunkirk, but the lesser-known Operations Cycle and Aerial evacuated more than 190,000 additional soldiers along with 310 artillery guns, 2,300 military vehicles, and 1,800 tons of supplies from Brest, Cherbourg, and other western French ports.[9] Combined with arriving Commonwealth formations and a few British units that had not been deployed to France, the evacuees constituted a large, trained force well in excess of half a million men. There were also more than a million members of the Home Guard. While poorly trained and even more poorly equipped, the Guard still represented a massive pool of manpower highly motivated to fight a German invasion. Guardsmen dug tank traps, barricaded roads, removed road signs, and prepared to act as a guerilla force behind enemy lines and oppose any airborne landing.

Arming the British land force was the primary problem. Much heavy equipment was sorely lacking through the end of 1940. However, by September the British certainly had the means to oppose an invading force that (as we will see) would be primarily composed of light infantry. In June, across all of England there were only fifty-four antitank guns, 537 tanks and armored cars, and 583 artillery tubes.[10] These small numbers rapidly increased as British factory workers labored around the clock and more than a hundred thousand civilians went to work building fortifications. Churchill tells us that within a few months

> all the beaches now bristled with defenses of various kinds. During this same month of July American weapons in considerable quantities were safely brought across the Atlantic. . . . The arrival of the first installment of the half-million .300 rifles for the Home Guard . . . enabled us to transfer three hundred thousand .303 British-type rifles to the rapidly expanding formations of the Regular Army. . . . The

factories poured out their weapons. By the end of August we had over two hundred new tanks![11]

The first consignment of arms arriving from the United States aboard the SS *Eastern Prince* not only contained some of these previously mentioned rifles, but also forty-eight crated 75mm field guns, twenty-eight million rounds of ammunition, fifteen thousand machine guns, and a large number of .45 caliber Thompson submachine guns. An additional fifteen ships with similar cargos arrived from America over the next month.[12]

As of June 12, the Royal Navy had also installed upward of one hundred six-inch naval guns in camouflaged batteries along likely landing beaches with crews ordered to hold their fire until enemy landing craft were well within range. Eventually the British installed 650 shore-based artillery tubes of all calibers at likely invasion points. Explosive charges were set and blockships prepared at more than fifty harbors to deny the invader the use of any captured port. Thus, all German supplies, equipment, and vehicles would have to land across open beaches. Demolition charges were also set along rail lines and roads leading away from the coast, and minefields were laid offshore.[13]

Another threat to German troops earmarked for the initial landing was the British government's plan to utilize poison gas. General (later Field Marshal) Alanbrooke, in charge of English land defenses, wrote in his war diaries that he had "every intention of using sprayed mustard gas on the beaches."[14] Churchill was very much in favor as well, writing on June 30, "supposing lodgements were effected on our coast, there could be no better points for application of mustard than these beaches and lodgements."[15] In addition to mustard, the British also prepared chlorine and phosgene gas for use. The primary means of delivery was to be through the air from bombers and crop dusters. Gas artillery shells and truck-mounted delivery systems were also readied.

The potential effects of mustard gas on men wading through the surf from grounded barges could have been the difference between a successful landing and wholesale slaughter. Consider the horrific effects of an accidental release of this weapon in the Italian harbor of Bari in 1943: a major air raid by more than one hundred bombers of the *Luftwaffe* hit several docked vessels in the port, including the US Liberty ship, *John Harvey*, which carried a secret load of two thousand mustard gas bombs. Thousands of soldiers and sailors rescued from the contaminated harbor's waters and quays soon went into shock, developed massive blisters, and were blinded. Many died for lack of rapid treatment. The best course of medical action for such men wearing damp uniforms contaminated with mustard gas was removal of all clothing and bathing in clean water.[16] Such treatment would have been inherently difficult for German soldiers fighting their way up onto a beach while under fire from British defenders.

Hitler knew and feared mustard gas and had been temporarily blinded by it at the front in World War I. His trademark clipped mustache was a battlefield affectation allowing for the proper seal of a gas mask to the face. While the Nazis had no compunction regarding using poison gas on civilians in their concentration camps, Hitler never authorized the use of gas weapons on the battlefield. The Germans knew that British deployment of gas in a battle for their home island was a distinct possibility and one that would weigh heavily against an invader.

How was the *Wehrmacht* to deter the British from using gas during Seelöwe? Threats could be made that the *Luftwaffe* would drop gas bombs on British cities. That would not necessarily deter the British from using gas on their own beaches and could also result in the RAF retaliating in their ongoing bombing of population centers in Germany. The Germans could also announce that they had invented, manufactured, and were willing to use large stocks of nerve agents such as Sarin. These new weapons were dramatically more deadly than mustard and the other gases that had been used in World War I.[17] Possession of these weapons was one of the most closely guarded German secrets of the conflict, and voluntary disclosure would have been highly unlikely in 1940. Thus, if *Seelöwe* were to proceed, it would have to do so in the hope that the British would not deploy gas weapons, or if they did, the effect on the invasion force would be minimal.

The German army and navy had a difficult time agreeing on a specific plan for the size of Seelöwe. The generals initially proposed a landing of forty-one divisions (of which six would be panzers, three motorized and two airborne) over a few days on a broad front across the breadth of Southern England from Weymouth to Dover.[18] The admirals of the *Kriegsmarine* argued that it did not have the warships to screen such a large area and the proposed effort was dramatically greater than the available sealift capacity. A major problem was that the German generals had no experience with amphibious operations across salt water and throughout the period viewed Seelöwe as simply an "extended river crossing." Arguments between the two forces became quite heated.[19]

Eventually a compromise was reached with "only" eleven infantry divisions, a special forces regiment, a few hundred waterproofed or amphibious tanks, and three airborne regiments to be landed across a narrower front (though one that was still almost twice the length used for the D-Day landings in 1944). However, the assembled shipping would allow only a portion of the invasion force to land in the first wave, equaling about three divisions. It would take an additional week and a half until the rest of the assigned invasion force could be brought across the channel. After that, an additional two divisions of reinforcements could ferry across every four days.[20] Due to a lack of landing craft, the *Kriegsmarine* convinced the generals to leave most of their large guns behind in France until a significant usable English port had been captured. Until then, the invaders would depend upon the *Luftwaffe* to act as its artillery support for the operation. Without large numbers of tanks and artillery, Seelöwe would commence as a landing force of light infantry. Such an invading army would have been at risk of being overwhelmed by the significantly larger mass of more heavily equipped defenders.

By September 1940, the British army (excluding the Home Guard) totaled twenty-nine divisions and six armored brigades. Of these, sixteen divisions deployed across the south coast to oppose the expected invasion, and the armored units were stationed inland with plans to counterattack enemy landings.[21] In all major categories—artillery, tanks, trucks, not to mention soldiers on the ground—the British would have outnumbered and been better equipped than the German invaders by significant margins.

c) *The Air.* The Germans realized it was of paramount importance that the *Luftwaffe* gain air supremacy over the Channel and the planned landing zones of Southern England for Seelöwe to succeed. Victory would not be easy for the attackers in the Battle of Britain as both sides began with a similar number of fighter planes of comparable quality. Destruction of German aircraft was the RAF's sole and clear objective. In contrast, the *Luftwaffe* had multiple missions: degrade the RAF and its infrastructure, sink naval units in England's southern ports, and as the battle went on, bomb British cities.

The *Luftwaffe* fought not only the RAF but in many ways the entire population of Britain. An early warning network of human spotters as well as the newly invented technology of radar had been deployed across the English coast. This provided the RAF with a critical real-time informational advantage. Fighting over its homeland was also invaluable to the defenders. The limiting factor in the battle was often not flying machines but trained crew. British aviators who safely bailed out over the battlefield could fly again. Germans who did the same were captured and incarcerated for the rest of the war. The British public knew that the battle was for their homes: privately donated funds purchased many Spitfire fighters that were named after the benefactor towns, clubs, and organizations. Assisting the RAF were large ground units operating antiaircraft batteries and thickets of barrage balloons that destroyed many *Luftwaffe* aircraft.

To clear the air for Seelöwe, the *Luftwaffe* had the task of winning the dogfights and putting British airfields and aircraft factories out of commission. The RAF could call upon hundreds of thousands of Home Guard members and other civilian volunteers to repair damage and build new facilities. This part of the *Luftwaffe*'s mission was complicated by a lack of heavy bombers in the German inventory in 1940. Unlike today's precision munitions guided by GPS, radar, and lasers, in an era of "dumb" bombs dropped by eyesight from aircraft, there was no substitution for delivering the maximum weight of ordnance over a target. The main *Luftwaffe* bombers, the Heinkel He-111, Dornier Do 17, Junkers Ju 88, and Ju 87 (*Stuka*) generally carried between one thousand to five thousand pounds worth of bombs each. This compared unfavorably to the contemporary British Whitley, which could be armed with eight thousand pounds of ordinance and later (1942 onward) aircraft such as the British Lancaster, which could carry twenty-two thousand pounds. As we know, the Germans lost the Battle of Britain: while the *Luftwaffe* did great damage to the RAF, British cities, and industrial sites, they were unable to gain command of the air over southern England.

Many historians claim that Hitler lost the Battle of Britain because he directed his air force to bomb British cities rather than concentrating its efforts on degrading the infrastructure of the RAF. Even if the *Luftwaffe* had remained focused on air superiority missions, it is not clear that there was enough time to drive the RAF out of the sky between July and October 1940 during the period that Seelöwe was initially contemplated. An invasion during the stormy winter weather at the end of 1940 or early 1941 would have been exceedingly risky in the unsettled waters of the Channel. With each month, British land forces in England expanded and became better equipped by the output of local factories, arriving reinforcements from the Empire, and the largesse of the United States. Perhaps with more time, preparation, and focus the Germans could have achieved tactical air superiority in the spring of 1941 to launch Seelöwe. Nevertheless, by then the strength of the British army in southern England would have grown significantly, and the Royal Navy would still have outclassed the much smaller *Kriegsmarine*.

Had the Germans won the Battle of Britain in the air in 1940, would it have resulted in a success for Seelöwe? The answer is likely not a positive one. Most importantly, local air superiority would not have eliminated the threat of the Royal Navy to the Seelöwe invasion force. The *Luftwaffe* was designed to gain control of the air over a battlefield and provide close air support to advancing ground forces. The *Luftwaffe* had no dedicated torpedo bomber aircraft in 1940, few pilots trained in the use of the weapon, and a stock of torpedoes that often failed in the field (see the next chapter on the Battle of the Atlantic).

The concept of "skip bombing" against naval targets was still in its infancy, strafing was not going to sink a major ship of the Royal Navy, and level-flight bombing attacks from altitude were never particularly effective throughout the entire course of World War II. Thus, dive bombing was the only way Germany could hope to successfully attack shipping from the air. While this tactic was effective against stationary targets, it was difficult to execute against a fast ship taking evasive action and putting up a screen of antiaircraft fire. Even then, the *Luftwaffe* was not equipped with armor-piercing munitions and had to make do with high explosive bombs.

German bombers had a very mixed record in the two months of the campaign in Norway. Despite several opportunities, the *Luftwaffe* was only able to sink two ships of the Royal Navy. The evacuation at Dunkirk showed that German pilots were often unable to hit destroyers even when they had docked or had anchored to embark evacuating infantry. Chances of inflicting hits on such ships when they were maneuvering at more than thirty knots would have been significantly lower. Over the course of the nine days of Operation Dynamo off Dunkirk, the *Luftwaffe* and *Kriegsmarine* made continual attacks on the constrained mass of Allied shipping engaged in the evacuation. Of 933 naval ships involved, 236 were sunk and a further 61 were damaged.[22] In other words, more than two-thirds were unharmed. Attacks on the *Luftwaffe*'s primary target, British destroyers, were more successful: of thirty-nine engaged in the evacuation, six were sunk and nineteen damaged.[23] Again, these results were achieved against warships that were often stationary and taking on troops. Even if the *Luftwaffe* could replicate this statistical success against fast-moving vessels in open water, had the Royal Navy been able to sail one-third of a flotilla of destroyers through air attacks and get into the mass of a slow-moving German armada, the losses to the invasion forces would have been disastrous.

Things would get even worse for Operation Seelöwe when the sun set. The *Luftwaffe* did not have the ability to accurately attack discrete, small naval targets after dark and so would have only been able to provide effective air cover to the invasion fleet during the day. The Royal Navy was trained in night fighting and would have been able to sortie into the Channel at will, intercepting German shipping and bombarding landing beaches as well as French ports. Proof of this can be seen in the British efforts to disrupt the invasion fleet at anchor in what became known as the "Battle of the Barges." Throughout the nights of August and September 1940, British cruisers and destroyers shelled the masses of shipping assembled in French harbors while RAF bombers flew sorties against port areas. While not sufficient to sink enough transports and barges to make Seelöwe untenable on their own, these raids show that the invasion fleet and its logistics train would certainly not have been able to operate unmolested even in the event of German daylight air superiority.

The Germans also planned to lay minefields on either side of the Channel to keep the Royal Navy out of the area. However, the British had already learned to degauss their warships to protect them from the magnetic mines the Germans planned to deploy. The British also had a dramatically larger fleet of both mine-laying and mine-sweeping vessels that could work at night without interference from the *Luftwaffe*. The German invasion flotilla was likely to be at a much higher risk of mines than the Royal Navy in an attempted invasion operation.

Admiral Raeder recognized the overwhelming strength of the Royal Navy and believed that

> so far it had not been used to the full, but a German landing in Britain would be a matter of life and death to the enemy and they would not hesitate to throw in all their available naval strength ruthlessly and decisively. It could not be assumed that the *Luftwaffe* would be in a position to prevent all enemy warships from getting at our transport ships, particularly if the weather, on which the whole operation was very dependent, went against us. Our Navy would support the operation by conveying the transport ships, and also by laying mine barriers and by diversionary actions to draw off enemy naval forces, but it was essential to remember that mine barriers did not offer absolute security against a determined enemy. The possibility must therefore be reckoned with that, even if the first invasion wave was successfully landed, enemy naval forces would succeed in penetrating between the troops on shore and the transports following in the second wave.[24]

Let us also consider the *Luftwaffe*'s planned ground support role for the invasion force. In June 1940 the two *Luftflotten* (air fleets) based on the Channel coast had more than seven hundred medium bombers and 250 additional Junkers Ju 87 *Stukas*.[25] These numbers declined due to battle losses over the course of the Battle of Britain, and replacements did not make up for all the attrition suffered. Medium bombers would have softened up British defenses along the landing beaches with level-flight bombing, and *Stukas* could have been used for more targeted bombing attacks. Yet many of the dive bombers would have been held in reserve for use against the expected sorties of the Royal Navy. Thus, while the *Luftwaffe* could have supported the invasion force once it landed, chances are slim that it would have been able to make up for the shortage of dedicated artillery. The British army, as underequipped as it was, would have had a significant advantage in artillery "throw weight" in any battles in southern England. Finally, even if the *Luftwaffe* had been able to gain air superiority in the skies above Seelöwe, it would have been difficult to keep the RAF from getting a few bombers or crop dusters through to deploy mustard gas on the beaches.

In 1942, the British launched a large raid on the French port of Dieppe. An amphibious force of tanks, artillery, and infantrymen put ashore with support from destroyers and the RAF. The operation was a fiasco, with well over half the landed troops lost. Historian Robert Jackson concluded that "without doubt, the most important lesson learned at Dieppe was the absolute need for massive fire support, from both sea and air, in amphibious operations. Another lesson was the need to devise special equipment to overcome defensive obstacles, the realization of which resulted in a formidable array of specially equipped tanks being available to the forces that went ashore in Normandy two years later. But the overall lesson of Dieppe was how not to do it, and it was better learned in 1942 than in 1944."[26] The Germans did not have the advantage of such "training exercises" and would have had to learn such lessons the hard way had they attempted to land in England in 1940.

Consider for a moment a counterfactual scenario where Seelöwe took place and was successful despite the strength of the Royal Navy, the qualitative and quantitative edge of the British army, the efforts of the Home Guard, and the use of mustard gas on the beaches. Would the capture of London have led to the surrender of Britain? We know that King George VI planned to flee and rule from exile in Canada in the event of an invasion. At the very end of Churchill's most famous speech, he proclaimed, "We shall never surrender, and even if, which I do not for a moment believe, this Island or a large part of it were subjugated and starving, then our Empire beyond the seas, armed and guarded by the British Fleet, would carry on the struggle, until, in God's good time, the New World, with all its power and might, steps forth to the rescue and liberation of the old."[27]

In retrospect, Seelöwe was an operation with a dramatically high chance of ending in critical failure for the *Wehrmacht* and a low chance of achieving German war aims. When Hitler suspended the plan in late 1940, it was not solely due to the failure of the *Luftwaffe* to win the Battle of Britain. Those who argue that the Germans should have taken the chance to end the war via an invasion of England in 1940 despite the risks are deluding themselves to the facts on the ground, sea, and air. To summarize, the major problems with Seelöwe were as follows:

- The Royal Navy enjoyed an enormous quantitative superiority over the *Kriegsmarine*.
- The German military had no experience in executing a major amphibious attack against a determined foe. In contrast, the Allies engaged in a great deal of experimentation and learning from a large number of amphibious operations in the Mediterranean and the Pacific before the successful execution of the landings on D-Day.
- Even had the *Luftwaffe* been able to gain daylight air superiority, by night the RAF and Royal Navy would have been able to attack the invasion force at sea, on the beaches, and in its supply ports in France.
- The Germans had won the earlier major land battles of the war by engaging in fast-paced armored thrusts backed by artillery and close air support. This strategy would not have been possible after a landing in southern England.
- The British army had suffered severe losses, but it still fielded forces significantly larger and better equipped than what the Germans could land and supply to defeat them. Mustard gas would have been deployed against the invaders as they landed, with likely devastating effect. Finally, the response of the citizenry of England to the bombing of the "Blitz" indicated that Home Guard units would stand and fight alongside their better-trained professional comrades.

Admiral Raeder concluded, "The lack of a German fleet of a size sufficient to deal with the enemy was never at any time so painfully felt as in connection with Operation Sea-Lion. The *Luftwaffe* could not be expected to make up entirely for Britain's command of the sea. I therefore regarded it as a piece of good fortune for us that the invasion plan was finally abandoned. In my opinion it could have ended only in a severe set-back. The difficulties experienced by the Allies in carrying out their Normandy landings in 1944 showed clearly that landing operations on a big scale cannot be improvised."[28]

We will give the last word on the subject to General Gerd von Rundstedt, who commanded the armies earmarked for the Seelöwe landings. After the war, when interviewed by British Intelligence, he stated the following: "The proposed invasion of England was nonsense, because adequate ships were not available. . . . We looked upon the whole thing as a sort of game because it was obvious that no invasion was possible when our Navy was not in a position to cover a crossing of the Channel or carry reinforcements. Nor was the German Air Force capable of taking on these functions if the Navy failed. . . . I was always very skeptical about the whole affair."[29]

· 4 ·

Two Maritime Strategies

$\mathcal{W}$ith the postponement of Seelöwe and the failure of the Battle of Britain, Hitler remained in the same position as before. He had achieved much of his territorial goals, but Britain refused to make peace. The British were rearming behind the twin shields of the RAF and the Royal Navy while casting about for allies to assist in the land war to come. Unless Britain could be knocked out of the war, it would rebuild its forces and eventually return to the Continent to contest a hegemonic aspirant. The *Luftwaffe's* bombing "Blitz" on London and other British cities in 1940 made clear that while serious damage could be inflicted on the population of Britain, it was unlikely that it could be terrorized into surrender. So, if bombing of cities would not force the British to make peace and a direct invasion could not succeed, perhaps Germany could starve the British into submission through interdiction of its maritime supply lines. Many historians have asked why this would not have been a better option to achieve victory than the 1941 invasion of the USSR.

While *Luftwaffe* operations could shift to target port facilities where merchant ships unloaded, the large number of harbors in Britain and the workforce available to repair damage made this strategy problematic. Thus, attacks on the actual ships bringing supplies to Britain were more likely to succeed. Britain had a population in excess of forty-five million dependent upon seaborne deliveries in 1940. Without the constant arrival of ships containing petroleum, food, rubber, and many other bulk items, the nation would grind to a halt and eventually starve. Certainly, a maritime interdiction campaign, or a "Battle of the Atlantic," had been tried before in World War I and had failed. This time the Germans appeared to have a significantly better chance to strangle Britain compared to twenty-five years earlier. Most importantly, the *Wehrmacht* was in an improved geographic position. It could now launch its navy and air force out to sea from a great arc of bases running from northern Norway to the west coast of France. The French fleet, rather than escorting merchant convoys, had been sunk or was interned in port. Also, the U-boats and bomber aircraft of the 1940s were more technologically advanced than the ones of 1914 to 1918 in terms of speed and range of operation, while the basic design of the large merchant ship had changed little.

Despite these advantages, there were several problems with a German strategy of fighting another Battle of the Atlantic:

1. Germany's military had been built to fight and win continental land wars and did not have the right weapon systems to conduct a long-range maritime effort in 1940 to 1941 against the strength of the Royal Navy.
2. Success would take a significant period of time, possibly to be measured in years. This went against the clear German need to knock Britain out of the war before it could mobilize the resources of its empire and its dominions. These years would also allow the British to adapt and develop countermeasures to contest German interdiction efforts.
3. A lengthy sea-lane campaign in the Atlantic threatened to bring the United States into a European war as a similar German strategy had in 1917.
4. The British could be counted upon to engage in a reciprocal blockade of Axis-controlled Europe. The longer this continued, the more Germany would become dependent upon the USSR for supplies of raw materials. In addition, as we will see, a long-term diversion of German military resources to the development of a large fleet of U-boats and maritime aircraft was potentially dangerous in the face of the rapid expansion of the Soviet armed forces.

(1) *Wrong tools for the job.* While Germany possessed the world's greatest army in 1940, it did not have the air and surface naval forces required to successfully wage a Battle of the Atlantic against the much larger Royal Navy. Certainly, the *Kriegsmarine* was woefully short of large warships that could sortie into the Atlantic to raid British shipping. When the "unsinkable" *Bismarck* finally sailed into the open ocean in May 1941 in search of merchant convoys, the Royal Navy sank it. The small number

of remaining German capital ships such as the *Scharnhorst*, *Gneisenau*, and the *Tirpitz* found themselves under constant RAF attack.

The *Luftwaffe* also was not equipped to wage a significant maritime interdiction campaign against Britain. The German air force excelled in achieving local air superiority over a battlefield and providing close air support to advancing armored formations. In 1939 to 1941, it proved itself repeatedly in these roles. However, as discussed earlier, the *Luftwaffe's* primary bombers were classified as "medium" in ordinance-carrying ability and were not designed for long-distance missions with lengthy loitering times over patrol areas. These planes could only reach inbound Atlantic convoys when the ships were close to their destination ports along the British coast on the Irish Sea. Such range constraints forced the German bombers to fly directly over much of England through radar-directed RAF fighter patrols to reach their targets.

The Germans did have a small number of long-range aircraft in 1940. The *Kampfgeschwader 40* (heavy bomber wing) began to fly the Fw200 Condor on anti–ship bombing patrols. The planes took off from Bordeaux and flew around the western approaches of the British Isles before landing in Norway, refueling, and continuing back to France. These planes were converted long-distance civilian passenger craft not specifically designed for their new role. Initially the Condors had success bombing slow-moving merchantmen. However, it was only a matter of months before an increase in the number of fighters flying from RAF bases and Royal Navy escort carriers forced the German planes into a reconnaissance role of shadowing British convoys and reporting their positions via radio. Even in these missions, poor training often led to *Luftwaffe* crews transmitting incorrect location data. At the same time, the RAF successfully increased the range of their escort aircraft, and as the Battle of the Atlantic wore on, these German hunters increasingly became the hunted.

This left the U-boat. Its use had failed to win the Battle of the Atlantic in World War I, but the Germans hoped it would succeed in the second. A significant problem for the *Kriegsmarine* was that their torpedoes often failed in the opening months of the conflict. As Admiral Karl Doenitz, commander of the U-boat fleet, wrote,

> On September 17, 1939, *U-39* (Lieutenant-Commander Glattes) sighted the aircraft carrier *Ark Royal* cruising in his area and attacked her. He fired three torpedoes with magnetic pistols, all of which exploded prematurely under water, close to the ship but before they had reached a position below her, thus robbing us the chance of an outstanding success. Nor was that all. As a result of the columns of water thrown

up by the exploding torpedoes, the destroyers escorting the aircraft carrier were able to discover the U-boat and destroy it. . . . On October 30, 1939, U-boat Command received the following signal from *U-56* (Lieutenant-Commander Zahn): "1000 *Rodney, Nelson, Hood* and ten destroyers, Square 3492, 240°. Three torpedoes fired. None exploded." The crew of the *U-56*, which, of course, was submerged at the time clearly heard the noise of the impact as the three torpedoes struck the *Nelson*. They all three failed to explode.[1]

Admiral Raeder's memoirs contain a chapter titled "The Torpedo Crisis," which includes the following: "Our submarine operations during the Norwegian campaign were bitterly disappointing, because their torpedo attacks met with no success at all. Complaints made by submarine commanders in the past about the behavior of their torpedoes, and in particular concerning their running at depth, were now confirmed. It could now be safely assumed that most of the torpedoes discharged with contact pistols had run harmlessly under their targets without exploding . . . overcoming the defects themselves required long and protracted tests on a large scale . . . by 1942 the crisis was finally overcome . . . the new torpedoes were reliable and they were produced in sufficient quantities."[2]

In 1939, Raeder's U-boat fleet was much smaller than it grew to be later in the conflict: "At the beginning of the war we had, as stated before, 57 U-boats. To this total were added 28 new boats commissioned during the first year of hostilities. In the same period 28 boats were lost, with the result that our total U-boat strength on September 1, 1940, stood once more at 57, the same figure as that with which we had started."[3] Combat losses and operational rotations reduced this number to only eighteen by early 1941, and at times there were only three U-boats out on station hunting convoys at a time.[4] Even with a great increase in ship building and crew training, by the middle of 1941, the *Kriegsmarine* could only maintain thirty-five U-boats in the Atlantic, and these with a stripped-down complement of trained personnel.[5]

Italian submarines also joined the fight. Many of these boats successfully sortied past Gibraltar to new bases in Bordeaux. That proved to be the easy part. When operating in the North Atlantic, the Italian vessels' level of success was poor: the thirty-two boats engaged in the effort from 1940 to 1943 only sank 3 percent of the gross tonnage of merchant shipping lost by the Allies during that period. However, half of the Italian submarines were destroyed.[6] The Italians were also ineffective in supplying accurate reconnaissance intelligence to the *Kriegsmarine*.[7]

Admiral Doenitz estimated he would need one hundred U-boats operating simultaneously in the Atlantic and the sinking of 750,000 tons of merchant shipping per month (nine million tons a year) to starve out the British.[8] In the end, his submarines, and other German naval and aviation attacks, were unable to attain such desired results. The best chance for the German interdiction effort to cripple Britain was when the Seelöwe invasion fleet of barges and tugs assembled in French harbors in 1940. This "armada" forced the Royal Navy to redirect much of its fleet from convoy duty to English ports to repel a potential German landing. This robbed the convoys of much of their protection and resulted in a temporary surge in merchant ship losses. Germany could not maintain its invasion fleet in harbor indefinitely as the civilian ships requisitioned for the effort were suffering from British attacks and were a critical component of the northern European economy. As winter approached, Hitler postponed Seelöwe, and the invasion armada of barges and tugs dispersed. This released many British destroyers, corvettes, and cruisers to resume escort duty, and there was a commensurate decline in merchant ship losses.

Table 4.   Loss of Merchant Ships from All Causes in 1940 by Month[9]

Month	Number	Thousand Gross Tons
March	15	47
April	6	31
May	10	48
June	58	284
July	38	196
August	56	268
September	59	295
October	63	352
November	32	147
December	37	213

While convoy losses were heavy in 1940 and 1941 and caused real hardship in Britain, it was only in early 1942 that the Germans were able to approach levels of supply interdiction that Admiral Doenitz had forecast would result in a decisive war-winning victory in the Battle of the Atlantic. This increase in sinkings was due primarily to the entry of the United States into the war and the *Kriegsmarine* finally targeting American shipping. During this "Happy Time" of early 1942, U-boats sunk many unescorted ships moving between US ports along the eastern seaboard.

Table 5.   Loss of Merchant Ships from All Causes 1939–1943 by Year[10]

	British		Allied		Neutral		Total	
	Number	Thousand Gross Tons	Number	Thousand Gross Tons	Number	Thousand Gross Tons	Number	Thousand Gross Tons
1939	158	498	17	90	148	347	323	935
1940	728	2,725	201	822	416	1,002	1,345	4,549
1941	892	3,047	344	1,299	183	347	1,419	4,693
1942	782	3,695	987	4,394	90	249	1,859	8,338
1943	361	1,678	388	1,886	63	82	812	3,646
Total	**2,921**	**11,643**	**1,937**	**8,491**	**900**	**2,027**	**5,758**	**22,161**

Despite this German success, once the United States entered the conflict it became unlikely that Britain would negotiate a separate peace with the Axis unless its people were experiencing outright starvation.

(2) *Time was Britain's ally.* A naval interdiction strategy was the opposite of *Blitzkrieg* and allowed the British significant time to adapt and devise countermeasures. These included forcing the besieged population to change their consumption and production habits. A people famous for their personal flower gardens became committed growers of cabbage and potatoes on their small home plots. The government-imposed food rationing, and thousands of acres of grassland were cultivated.[11] This converted land was sown primarily with potatoes and wheat, which produced multiples of the calories generated by the same acreage being used for animal grazing. "At the time, it was calculated that while ten acres of grassland for stock-raising could feed twelve people, the same area under wheat could feed 200 while ten acres planted with potatoes could feed as many as 400."[12] This program was so successful that bread never had to be rationed in Britain during the war, and there was often a surplus of potatoes.[13] Food imports were shifted away from bulky starches to calorie-dense protein such as beef, mutton, condensed milk, dried eggs, and cheese from the United States, Argentina, and the Dominions. Cargo loading also become more precise, and the holds of refrigerated vessels soon carried much higher amounts of calories per shipment as hanging cattle or sheep carcasses were replaced with boxes of deboned, lean cuts of meat.

Similar rationing measures were taken with nonfood imports such as clothing and fuel. Harbor operations were rationalized as well, and "Britain reduced its need for imports from 60 million to 26 million tons a year, paradoxically increasing the average health of its citizens in the process. . . . Improved port management alone is reckoned by some to have saved the Allies three million tons by the end of 1941."[14] Using less meant that many residents of Britain had to suffer through cold nights throughout the winters of 1939 to 1945, but they did not freeze to death. Consumer items disappeared from store shelves and life was harder, but it was not nearly as difficult as the privations endured by the citizens of Russia or Japan. The history of World War II showed the near impossibility of forcing a nation to surrender solely due to an interdiction of its supply routes.

To contest the Battle of the Atlantic, not only did Britain start the war with the world's largest fleet and huge capital resources, she also received a windfall from Germany's rapid series of victories in 1939 to 1940 as merchant vessels from Poland, France, Denmark, Belgium, Norway, and the Netherlands took refuge in British ports. These ships acted as a welcome addition to Britain's total available shipping tonnage. British geographic positioning was advantageous as well with its control of ports and airfields in Nova Scotia, Newfoundland, Iceland, and Ulster to provide naval and aerial escorts to convoys moving across the North Atlantic.

(3 and 4) *The US, the USSR, and the defeat of the U-boats.* The Battle of the Atlantic played into the hands of a US president needing time to rearm the military and cajole an isolationist population toward war. FDR made clear at the start of the conflict that his administration was going to be strongly pro-British. Even without the United States entering the conflict as a combatant, there were many measures short of war taken against Germany in the Battle of the Atlantic. The "Cash and Carry" policy of late 1939 allowed Britain to buy as much armament output as the massive US economy could produce. The president even had a reluctant American military sell off all its "surplus" artillery, rifles, and ammunition, which were rushed by sea to Britain. In return for the US taking control of British bases in the Western Hemisphere, the Royal Navy also took control of fifty older US destroyers to perform convoy escort duty to assist in the safe passage of supplies across the Atlantic.

The Battle of the Atlantic presented a nearly impossible conundrum for Hitler. How could the British be starved into submission without causing significant US casualties and an early entrance of the United States into the war? While Hitler often spoke of the United States in dismissive terms, he repeatedly ordered his armed forces to scrupulously avoid attacking American shipping:

> From the beginning Naval Operations Command and the German Government realized which way the situation was developing, and the strictest possible orders were issued to all German units operating at sea to avoid any incident with United States shipping. We did not officially recognize the Pan-American Safety Zone, but in practice all our surface

and submarine forces were given strict instructions not to operate in it. All our commanders realized that any incident, even though no fault on their part, might lead to political complications with the United States. They all knew that, even if it should prove impossible to prevent the entry of the United States into the war against us, then at least everything possible must be done to delay it as long as possible.[15]

A German maritime strategy against Britain would inevitably cause US casualties. Nonetheless, the Germans worked hard to avoid *Lusitania* events similar to the 1915 sinking of the British cruiseliner of that name by U-boat attack in the Atlantic while on its way from New York to Liverpool. Despite the German embassy in Washington running a large number of advertisements in US newspapers warning against booking passage on the doomed ship, of the 1,200 casualties of its sinking, more than 125 were American. That Germany claimed the *Lusitania* a legitimate target as it was carrying many tons of munitions (denied falsely by the British at the time) made little impression on Americans outraged by the attack. The casualties represented a major catalyst leading to the later US declaration of war and eventual landing of a massive American army in France. Restraining the U-boats from firing on vessels clearly flying the stars and stripes from 1939 to 1941 may have helped keep the US public from becoming enraged, but these rules of engagement reduced the number of targets that were sunk and increased the supplies landing in Britain.

Those who argue that Germany should have focused its military and industry on starving out the British and remaining at peace with the USSR need to consider the dramatic amounts of aid the United States could have shipped to the British via the Lend-Lease program.[16] As will be explored in greater depth later in this book, the United States supplied the USSR with more than 3.5 billion pounds of food, seven thousand tanks, and eleven thousand aircraft, among many other supplies by the end of 1945 (see tables 13 and 14). In the absence of Operation Barbarossa, it is logical to assume that much of this aid would have gone to Britain instead. The trading of fifty US destroyers in September 1940 was also a significant assist to British convoy protection to bring supplies across the Atlantic. Additionally, Lend-Lease allowed damaged British ships to refit in US ports when they were able to limp back after a U-boat attack. Finally, the new US policy did not require immediate payment for military supplies, so British industry could forgo production of exportable goods to generate the capital required to buy US aid. Ships could now sail back west across the Atlantic as soon as they had unloaded their cargo, which sped up the resupply process and freed critical British port and railway space.

A naval interdiction strategy could also be turned against the Axis. While to a lesser extent than the British, Germany also depended upon seaborne imports of food and raw materials before the outbreak of the war. This flow of trade across the oceans to European ports was relatively easy for the Royal Navy to sever. The German situation was better than in 1914 to 1918 as large amounts of required supplies could now be expropriated from occupied territories or purchased from neutral nations, most significantly the USSR. However, an ever-increasing dependence upon the whims and good graces of Comrade Stalin was not something Hitler would want to bet on over an extended period of time. At some point, Germany needed assured supplies of the natural resources its economy required to function. These inputs could be sourced by seizing what it needed from east and south of its borders, or it could come from global sea lanes. One way or another, a "Thousand Year Reich" could not maintain its status as a world power if it were beholden to the dictates of the Soviet Union or the United Kingdom.

The Axis lost the Battle of the Atlantic in the first half of 1943. Antisubmarine warfare in the North Atlantic improved as the number, experience, and technology of aerial and naval escorts rose during the course of the war. Despite a dramatic increase in U-boat strength, which peaked in May with 240 operational vessels, the Allies gained the upper hand, and merchant ship sinkings dropped precipitously while U-boats were destroyed in ever-higher numbers. A major reason for the Allied victory was that the U-boat during the Battle of the Atlantic was primarily a fragile and relatively slow surface ship. As explained by Admiral Raeder in his memoirs:

> The landsman's idea of a submarine as he knew it in the two world wars is that it is a vessel which sails mostly under the water and comes up only now and then to the surface. That is to say, therefore, that he thinks of it as an *under*-water vessel. In this he is wrong. The submarines of the types which both we and the other nations possessed up to 1944 submerged only when it was necessary to do so for their own protection or in order to attack in daylight. Most of their time was spent on the surface. In reality they were *diving*-vessels, that is to say surface vessels capable of disappearing from view by diving. A submarine would always remain on the surface as long as it could because it was anxious to have as wide a radius of vision as possible, and because, above all, it wished to retain its maximum mobility so that it could move at speed into the position most favourable to the attack it was contemplating. These things it could not do with the same efficiency when submerged. The under-water speed of the boats of those days was low—at the most seven knots and that only for short periods at a

time. At that speed they had no hope of being able to close with the surface vessels which were normally much faster and thus they could not gain a position from which to launch their attack. Under water the submarine was more or less stationary, and its effectiveness was reduced, more or less, to that of a mine.[17]

Increased aircraft patrols equipped with new radar sets that could detect a surfaced submarine's conning tower was the primary reason for the defeat of the German effort. Again and again a U-boat on the surface was surprised and attacked by aircraft before it could dive to safety. Of the 785 recorded U-boat sinkings during the war, more were caused by aircraft attack at sea than any other category.[18] Even when an aircraft attack was not successful, it forced the U-boat to submerge, reducing its mobility and range of target detection. This prevented many attacks on merchant convoys. The combination of increased success in antisubmarine warfare and accelerated allied merchant shipbuilding meant that the Axis fell ever further behind in the effort to reduce deliveries to Britain. In just one month, "Black May," the Germans lost forty-one U-boats. Admiral Doenitz effectively announced defeat the next month in a speech to senior commanders of the *Kriegsmarine*: "From November 1942, the U-boats encountered strong A/S defenses which, after a slow start in the last half of the year, became gradually more effective towards May 1943. High aircraft superiority with a ratio of 7:1 and the use of aircraft carriers in convoys closed the air gap in the North Atlantic. . . . According to the German saying, if you beat my Jew I will beat your Jew. That is why you cannot hit the Englishman by using the air force for air raids on cities. His 'Jew' is and remains tonnage. Even if the U-boat war does not sink more than the enemy is building, we have to go on with it."[19]

The Battle of the Atlantic was never likely to result in a German victory. The British would tighten their belts, the US ability to build new ships was prodigious, and the U-boat of the era was too vulnerable. While useful as a cost-effective strategy to force the Allies to direct significant resources to organizing and protecting convoys, rather than to the buildup of an invasion army, a different approach was required to force Britain to sue for peace.

A MEDITERRANEAN STRATEGY

Admiral Raeder proposed to Hitler on multiple occasions that he choke off the British Empire by cutting its supply line through the Mediterranean with a seizure of Gibraltar in the west and the Suez Canal in the east.[20] Many historians, including the extremely well-regarded John Keegan, have expanded on this course of action and argue that Germany could have won the war with a drive across the eastern Mediterranean and then the deserts of Syria and Arabia to capture the oil fields at the head of the Persian Gulf.[21]

That the British would surrender if the Axis seized control of the Mediterranean, while argued by Admiral Raeder, was questioned even among the higher ranks of the *Kriegsmarine*. Doenitz's opinion was that, "although the loss of the Mediterranean and her positions in the Near East would be a grievous blow to Britain, it would still be only an indirect blow, as had been the loss of France as an ally. It would constitute no real and direct threat to her island base and its vital lines of communication. Then again, conquest of the Mediterranean could not be accomplished by our Italian allies single-handed. German help, both on land and at sea, would be required, and the only way in which we could make the requisite naval contribution would be to draw on our already wholly inadequate forces fighting against the greatest sea power in the world in the decisive theatre of operations, the Atlantic."[22]

Raeder began agitating for a shift to the Mediterranean as early as September 1940, with a focus on capturing Gibraltar and the Suez Canal. The major problem with this course of action is that it required the cooperation of Spain and France. The closest target at hand was the natural fortress of Gibraltar. Safely transporting the necessary *Wehrmacht* men and equipment by sea from Italy to land on 'The Rock' was unlikely in the face of the Royal Navy. Thus, the Germans would have to obtain permission for overland passage from Pétain's Vichy France and Franco's Spain. Hitler pursued this strategy and set out by train to meet with the Spanish "Caudillo" at Hendaye in late October 1940. Unfortunately for the Führer, Franco wanted too much in return for joining the war. Not only did he ask for supplies of oil that Germany could not spare, but he also demanded that Vichy France cede the colonies of Morocco, Algeria, and Cameroon to Spain.

Hitler then traveled on to meet with Marshal Pétain. There was hope that the Vichy government would join the war effort on the side of the Axis after the British attack and sinking in June of much of the French fleet at Mers-el-Kebir. Pétain demurred on entering into an alliance and insisted on maintaining Vichy's neutrality. The Germans accepted the ongoing status quo as it kept de Gaulle's Free French Forces and the British from taking control of the overseas French empire along with its resources and military units.

Hitler returned to Germany discouraged. Gibraltar remained an attractive target, but Spain never joined the war, so "The Rock" survived as a British base. Potentially more viable was the capture of British-controlled Egypt and the Suez Canal due to the large Italian army already pushing eastward from Libya. The flaw in this strategy was its dependence upon the effectiveness of Mussolini's military. While Italy's military appeared strong on paper, its success on the battlefield was quite limited.

Italy easily overran tiny Albania in 1939, but the subsequent invasion of Greece in October 1940 ground to a halt and was then thrown back by the poorly equipped Greek army. The Italian forces that invaded western Egypt in September 1940 suffered an even worse calamity. Forward progress soon bogged down, and a counterattack by a weak British force resulted in a full-scale Italian rout. An army of fewer than twenty-five thousand British soldiers soon captured more than 130,000 Italian troops along with a vast supply of tanks, guns, and aircraft. This setback led to the dispatch of German General Rommel and his famous Afrika Korps to Libya to regain the initiative.

Keegan and others who promote the merits of a "Mediterranean Strategy" claim that had Hitler ordered a few more divisions to Africa, he could have driven the British out of Egypt, and from there all the way to the Persian Gulf. Possibly this could have happened, but it would have required a great number of "ifs" going the Axis's way. First, the British crown colony of Malta, between Italy and Libya, needed to be neutralized or conquered. British attacks on Italian shipping from this island strained the supply lines of the Axis armies as they marched east toward Suez. Malta's bases remained operational despite incessant air attacks. Thus, an amphibious and/or airborne invasion would have been required. The presence of two fleets of the Royal Navy in the region, and the bloody experience of the German seizure of Crete in 1941, meant that such a landing on Malta would have been no sure thing.

Second, even with control of Malta, supplying the German legions would have represented the greatest challenge in an attempt to take Suez. There were few miles of railway across North Africa at the time, and the roads that existed along the coast were poor, subject to flooding, air attack, and interdiction by naval gunfire. Port facilities along the one thousand miles of coast between Tripoli and Alexandria were insufficient to supply a modern army of size. Prominent historian Martin van Creveld has delved into the logistical issues of the Axis advance in North Africa and concluded that capture of Egypt was not feasible: "Given that the *Wehrmacht* was only partly motorized and unsupported by a really strong motor industry, that the political situation necessitated the carrying of much useless Italian ballast, that the capacity of the Libyan ports was so small, the distances to be mastered so vast; it seems clear that, for all Rommel's tactical brilliance, the problem of supplying an Axis force for an advance into the Middle East was insoluble."[23] Van Creveld concludes that with the logistical flow available, even if successful on the desert battlefields, Rommel would have arrived in Alexandria with only two battalions of soldiers and thirty tanks to defeat the mass of British army and naval forces in the city.[24] Even if this estimate is too conservative, the Germans would still have arrived in eastern Egypt with a relatively small force.

If Rommel had been able to drive the British out of Alexandria, Cairo, and the Suez Canal, what then? One can imagine that major port facilities along the Egyptian coast would have been sabotaged precluding sufficient seaborne supply of Axis land forces as they pushed east. By this point, the Germans would be operating along a supply line that extended from Germany, over the Alps, through Italy, and across a great stretch of the coast of North Africa. Some have argued that the British would have sued for peace with the loss of the Suez and its fastest route to India. Yet Churchill's government did not fall with the far more painful defeats suffered in the Far East in early 1942. As long as the British could hold out hope for an alliance with the United States and/or the USSR, surrender was unlikely.

So if Rommel got to Suez Canal, what could he do next to "win the war"? Keegan imagines the Afrika Korps striking east across the Sinai, the Negev, and then into the fierce deserts of the Transjordan and northern Saudi Arabia to arrive among the oil fields of southern Iraq.[25] Anything is possible in counterfactual history, but supplying a mechanized army across such an expanse of roadless wasteland would have stretched the Germans to the breaking point. The difficulties the Afrika Korps experienced maintaining its tanks in the heat and the sand along the Mediterranean coast would have been dwarfed by the conditions prevailing in the western deserts of Iraq. What mechanized forces Rommel might still have had with him after such a brutal advance would have confronted rested and prepared British army units based in Baghdad and Basra. This strategy had an additional challenge: the Germans would have had to deal with the residents of Palestine. The Jewish army of the time, the Haganah, was not well equipped by World War II standards, but it fielded more than fifty thousand soldiers who could be counted upon to fight with extreme intensity against an invading Nazi army.

Today's Mediterranean Strategy proponents also suggest Hitler could have sent his forces into Iraq through either Syria or Turkey. As John Keegan tells us:

> The inducement was strong. Had he been able to solve the logistical difficulty of transferring an army from Greece to Vichy French Syria he would have then have been well placed to strike at northern Iraq, a major center of oil production, and thence at Iran, with even ampler oil reserves. The establishment of a strong military presence in northern Iran would have positioned his forces close to the Soviet Union's own oil production centers on the Caspian Sea, while a drive into southern Iran would have given him possession of the Anglo-Iranian Oil Company's wells and vast refinery at Abadan. From eastern Iran, moreover, the route lay open toward Baluchistan, the westernmost province of British India, and thence to the Punjab and Delhi. The occupation of the Levant—Syria and Lebanon—would, in short, have placed him astride a network of strategic highways leading not only to the main centers of Middle Eastern oil supply but also to entry points giving onto the most important imperial possession of his last remaining European enemy, Britain, and also the southern provinces of his chosen ideological opponent, Stalin's Russia.[26]

Such an invasion via Syria would have required not only the conquest of British Cyprus, but also a large supply of maritime shipping, which simply was not available. Even Keegan, when writing about this gambit, admits, "This scenario depends for its success on the assembly of sufficient shipping in the eastern Mediterranean to transport the force required. . . . The reality was that the British had already acquired most available vessels, forcing the Germans during the assault on Crete, for example, to depend on a fleet of wholly inadequate coastal craft to transport its ground forces. The probability is, therefore, that a strategy that depended on using island 'stepping-stones' toward the Levant, attractive as it looks, would have foundered for want of shipping capacity."[27]

This leaves the option of the Germans invading overland through Turkey to get to Iraq. Keegan claims it would have been possible, and the Turkish army would not have been able to put up much resistance. However, the Turks had proven themselves to be stout fighters when on the defensive during World War I. In addition, British troops from Iraq would have likely moved west to join the Turks in the interior of Anatolia. As they advanced east, the Germans would have been fighting uphill to dislodge the defenders from positions in the mountains. There were few major roads and rail lines across Turkey in the 1940s, and a glance at a topographic map shows that moving west to east would have required advancing through terrain poorly suited to the mechanized warfare that characterized the preferred tactics of the German army.

For such a strategy to succeed presupposes that Stalin would fail to react as the Germans took control of the Balkans, the Bosporus, and then marched ever closer to the Russian oil fields along the Caspian Sea. Such an adventure by Hitler could have led to many preemptive Soviet countermeasures. Among other options, Stalin could have sent "volunteers" and war matériel to Turkey. Alternatively, Stalin could have taken advantage of the extended German supply lines, allied himself with the British, and attacked, interdicting Baltic shipping, sending his Black Sea Fleet to attack Istanbul, and surging his armies into Romania to capture the Ploesti oil fields. The Nazi war economy would have been effectively crippled with many of its panzers trapped on the wrong side of the Bosporus.

If the Germans had conquered Iraq and its oil fields, what then? Would Britain have surrendered if it could receive alternative supplies of petroleum from North America?[28] The British would have blown up much of the sole pipeline from Iraq to the Mediterranean (running from Mosul to Haifa) as they retreated. Even if the Germans could quickly get a measure of production up and running at the captured oil fields, they did not have the tankers to transport the petroleum to Europe from the Persian Gulf. In the event the Axis procured such ships, the Royal Navy would have interdicted their passage.

In retrospect, a Mediterranean Strategy was unlikely to lead to German victory in its war with Britain. As Franco did not join the conflict, Gibraltar was not going to fall to the Germans. Vichy France remained neutral, and the Italian armed forces performed poorly in the field. The loss of Malta and Suez would have been great blows to Britain but would not have necessarily led to its surrender. Capture of the oil fields of the Middle East would not have supplied the Reich for years, nor would it have cut off oil imports to Britain.

We have considered and discarded the major German alternatives to an invasion of the USSR that were put forward during (and after) the war: an invasion of southern England, a maritime siege of Britain, and variants of a Mediterranean Strategy. They were not pursued because they were not likely to result in German victory. Not only did these options have a low chance of success, but they would have been time-consuming, expensive, and in the case of an invasion of England or Iraq, could very well have trapped a large German army on the wrong side of a body of water with severed supply lines. If we accept that the German goal was to achieve hegemonic control of northern Europe, then such maritime adventures would have represented a distraction from a potential confrontation with the USSR whose military was most likely to threaten German goals. We will now move on to what Hitler saw across his borders to the east and why the invasion of the USSR represented a logical decision for achievement of Nazi war aims.

• 5 •

The Rising Soviet Threat to German European Hegemony

*W*hile Germany was conquering all, or large parts of six western European nations in the first full year of the war, the USSR was doing the same to five other countries in the continent's eastern half. As Hitler battered Britain, the Red Army moved more than one hundred divisions and thousands of tanks and airplanes ever closer to both the German border and the Reich's critical sources of raw materials in Scandinavia and the Balkans.

First to fall to the USSR was Finland. In the autumn of 1939, the Soviets demanded the following: (1) an annexation of southern Finnish territory to provide Leningrad with greater security; (2) cession of several islands in the Gulf of Finland; and (3) a long-term lease for a military base on the Hanko Peninsula that would allow the Soviets to interdict shipping to Helsinki. Stalin told a Finnish delegation in Moscow that his demands were due to fear of German aggression, even though, "The Soviet Union at present enjoyed good neighbourly relations with Germany—'But,' said Stalin, 'everything can change in this world.' When, the head of the delegation, Juho Kusti Paasikivi, stated, 'We wish to remain at peace and outside all conflicts,' Stalin replied, 'I understand that, but I assure you that it is impossible. The Great Powers will not permit it.' Thus the objective side of the discussions left much to be desired."[1]

Finland refused to concede its territory, and the Soviets invaded in the Winter War of 1939 to 1940. While the Red Army fought poorly, its huge size eventually wore down the defenders, and the Finns were forced to cede 11 percent of its overall territory and an even greater share of its most productive agricultural and industrial regions. Then in June 1940, while German forces surged into France, the USSR occupied the three Baltic States of Estonia, Latvia, and Lithuania as well as the Romanian provinces of Bessarabia and North Bukovina. The invaded territories were all formally annexed and incorporated into the USSR. The scope of these conquests exceeded the agreements of assigned spheres of influence of the 1939 Molotov-Ribbentrop Pact, which did not include any of Bukovina or the part of Lithuania closest to Germany.

With the buffer states removed, Nazi Germany and the USSR now shared a common military border that stretched from the Baltic shore to the Carpathian Mountains. The Red Army dismantled its "Stalin Line" fortifications along the old frontiers and advanced the majority of its forces west to the new Soviet borders. With naval and air bases in Latvia, Estonia, and Finland, the Soviets were positioned to interdict German trade with Sweden and Finland. In the south, the Red Army was now on the Danube River, and the oil fields of Ploesti lay only one hundred miles away across the flat, agricultural heartland of Romania.

There were several issues driving Soviet/German enmity in addition to competing geographic desires. The fighting of World War I in the east from 1914 to 1917 had been particularly brutal. Now, the two hereditary Caesars were gone. Moscow's new rulers were revolutionary Bolsheviks, who had supported violent communist uprisings in Germany. In Berlin the fascist Nazi government coveted the land and resources of the Ukraine while espousing a racial ideology that considered the Slavs subhuman. Clearly, conflict was highly likely.

Stalin had gambled that offering Hitler peace in the East would give the USSR large new territorial buffers and result in a lengthy war in the West, which would exhaust Germany, France, and Britain. When the time was right, the USSR could surge west across the continent and impose the Marxist revolution to the Atlantic. This strategy collapsed with the rapid German victory. "Stalin's nerves cracked when he learned about the fall of France. He cursed the governments of England and France: 'Couldn't they put up any resistance at all?' he asked despairingly. . . . He let fly with some choice Russian curses and said that now Hitler was sure to beat our brains in."[3]

The Soviet dictator was right to be afraid. The German strategic quandry had always been how to achieve victory in the East and the West in succession. Soon after the Molotov-Ribbentrop Pact was signed, Hitler's lack of faith in Stalin was clearly expressed: "Treaties are kept only as long as they are useful. Russia will keep this one only so long as Russia itself considers it to be to its benefit. . . . Russia still has far-reaching goals, above all the strengthening of its position in the Baltic. We can only oppose Russia when we are free in the west."[4] With the French now knocked out of the war and the British driven off the continent, Hitler was in a much stronger position either to negotiate with Stalin or take what he wanted by force. The Soviets were unlikely to accede to German demands to hegemony over Europe. The risk of war was obvious in both Moscow and Berlin.

After the evacuation at Dunkirk, and even before the final capitulation of France, Hitler ordered his generals to begin planning for an attack on the USSR. However, Britain was still in the war, and Hitler had warned in *Mein Kampf* against repeating the 1914 German error of having to fight on two fronts. With his forces facing west, he worried about a Russian attack in the east. German intelligence agencies were aware of ongoing diplomatic communications between Moscow and London, and Hitler believed that the British refused to make peace only due to hopes that the USSR would join them in the war against Germany. General Franz Halder, the *Heer*'s Chief of Staff, related the following in his diary on July 13, 1940: "The Fuehrer is greatly puzzled by Britain's persisting unwillingness to make peace. He sees the answer (as we do) in Britain's hope on Russia, and therefore counts on having to compel her by main force to agree to peace. Actually that is much against his grain. The reason is that a military defeat of Britain will bring about the disintegration of the British Empire. This would not be of any benefit to Germany. German blood would be shed to accomplish something that would benefit only Japan, the United States, and others."[5]

The territorial gains of the USSR from 1939 to 1940 caused immediate friction with the Nazis from the Arctic to the Balkans. With his victories in the West and strengthened strategic position, Hitler took measures viewed as provocative by the Soviets. In 1939, Hitler had agreed to allow Finland to fall into the Soviet sphere, but for both economic and strategic reasons he now wished to see the Nordic nation remain an independent state. The future of that independence was in question. Moscow incited communist-led riots in Helsinki, the Red Army demanded passage rights on the Finnish rail network, and the Soviet military rapidly built up its forces in the newly leased base at Hanko, only eighty miles from the Finnish capital city. Molotov also declared that the Petsamo nickel mines must be sold in the near future to a company controlled by the USSR.[6] These Soviet demands were resisted, and the Finns looked to Berlin for assistance.

Germany's response was significant: "On August 18, one of Göring's agents obtained Finnish permission to ship *Luftwaffe* supplies and personnel across Finland to northern Norway and at the same time the Reich was granted an option on the Finnish nickel mines desired by the Soviet Union. In return the Finns were to receive war materiel from Germany."[7]

More than one thousand *Wehrmacht* members were soon established in Finland along this transportation corridor in the far north, and the Finnish military duly received "300 artillery guns, 500 anti-tank guns, 650,000 grenades and 50 modern fighter aircraft."[8]

A similar situation played out in the south. According to Ribbentrop, "The strong Russian troop concentrations in Bessarabia also caused the Führer serious anxiety because of the further conduct of the war against England, for the Rumanian oil was vital to us. If Russia struck there we would have to depend on Stalin's good will to carry on the war. It was only natural that such considerations made Hitler suspicious of Russia's intentions, and he told me during that meeting in Munich that he, too, would have to consider military dispositions, since he did not intend to allow the East to spring a surprise on him."[9]

After the USSR had seized a significant portion of Romanian territory, General Antonescu rose to head a dictatorial government and quickly moved to ally himself with the Nazis. The Axis powers oversaw a negotiated settlement to the conflicting Hungarian/Romanian claims on Transylvania and Germany, then issued a security guarantee for Romania's new borders. Soon a large German military force was crossing the frontiers. On September 20, the German military high command (*Oberkommando der Wehrmacht* or OKW) issued the following order:

The Army and Air Force will send Military Missions to Rumania. To the world their tasks will be to guide friendly Rumania in organizing and instructing her forces.

The real tasks—which must not become apparent either to the Rumanians or to our own troops—will be:

    (a) To protect the oil district against seizure by third Powers or destruction.

    (b) To enable the Rumanian forces to fulfil certain tasks according to a systemic plan worked out with special regard to German interests.

    (c) To prepare for deployment, from Rumanian bases, of German and Rumanian forces in case a war with Soviet Russia is forced on us.[10]

This was clearly provocative to the Soviets. A significant German military force based on the Black Sea between the Turkish Straits and the Soviet ports of the Ukraine was a strategic threat. Next, on September 27, Germany, Italy, and Japan signed the Tripartite Pact, which promised a military alliance if any of the signatories were attacked by an outside power. Japan was "given" a free hand to impose a "new order" in Asia, and Germany and Italy received the same in Europe. While the signatories told Moscow that the treaty was aimed at the United States, the Soviets must have questioned the validity of such statements.

Relations between Berlin and Moscow were deteriorating rapidly, but there was still room for diplomacy rather than conflict in the east. If Stalin could be convinced to join the war against Britain and accept Germany's new standing as a world power, then perhaps an invasion of the USSR would not be necessary.

MOLOTOV'S FATEFUL VISIT TO BERLIN

It was against this backdrop that Molotov traveled to Berlin in November 1940. Hitler stated his hope that it would be possible to continue the peace with the USSR. When he met with Mussolini in Florence in October, the Führer expressed his wish to construct "a world front against England, stretching from Japan across Russia to Europe."[11] If the two great totalitarian powers hammered out an accommodation, Germany could consolidate its conquests to date and direct its attentions to opposing the budding Anglo-American alliance. If not, a clash of massive proportions loomed. This set of meetings was one of the most consequential in the history of the twentieth century. Those who argue that Germany made a rash decision to attack the Soviet Union would be advised to reconsider Molotov's visit and what it portended.

As Ribbentrop tells us, "There can be little doubt that until Molotov's visit to Berlin Hitler still entertained the hope of an enduring settlement with Russia but he presumably gave up this hope when Molotov presented his demands. From that moment Hitler watched Russia's military dispositions even more keenly. . . . I was later told that the following Russian measures were discovered: fortifications of the new Western frontier, the building of airfields close to the frontier, enormous troop concentrations, and the stepping up of armament production and co-ordination of the munitions industry."[12]

The Berlin meetings were contentious from the start, with Molotov arguing for German acceptance of his nation's sphere of influence as agreed to in 1939. Hitler and Ribbentrop pushed instead for a carving up of the British Empire and argued that the Soviets redirect their expansionist urges from the Baltic and the Balkans, to the south toward Iraq, India, and Iran. Such a shift would not only reduce friction with German territorial and economic designs but would also aid in the defeat of Britain. When Molotov sat down with Hitler on November 13, the conversation quickly moved to the status of Finland. The Führer accepted that the Nordic nation was in the Russian sphere of influence, but insisted the status quo remain for the duration of the war with Britain due to German dependence on Finnish shipments of nickel and lumber. Molotov would not accept this point and insisted on removal of *Wehrmacht* troops from Finland. The German dictator refused and insisted on Finland's continued independence: "With a reference to the changes made in the agreement at Russia's request, the *Führer* stated that there must not be any war in the Baltic. A Baltic war would be a heavy strain on German-Russian relations and the great collaboration of the future."[13]

When Hitler asked what Russia wanted regarding Finland, Molotov replied that "he imagined a settlement on the same scale as in Bessarabia and in the adjacent countries and he requested the *Führer* give his opinion on that."[14] In other words, the USSR planned to completely conquer Finland and incorporate its territory. "When the *Führer* replied that he could only repeat that there must be no war with Finland, because such a conflict might have far-reaching repercussion. Molotov stated that a new factor has been introduced into the discussion by this position, which was not expressed in the treaty of last year."[15]

The two soon moved on to disagree on the Balkans. Molotov protested that regarding the recent security guarantee issued by Germany to Romania, the Soviet Union "was of the opinion that the guarantee was aimed against the interests of Soviet Russia, 'if one might express oneself so bluntly.' Therefore, the question had arisen of revoking this guarantee. To this the *Führer* had declared that for a certain time it was necessary and its removal therefore impossible."[16] Molotov then asked if Germany would accept a USSR guarantee to Bulgaria and a greater Soviet presence in the Turkish Straits. A frustrated Hitler demurred to give an answer to these questions and soon excused himself from the meeting, never to speak to Molotov again. In this final exchange, the German dictator had made clear that he was not willing to accept Soviet control of Finland or the Balkans.

Ribbentrop and Molotov continued their meeting until midnight in an air raid shelter as British bombs fell on Berlin. The German minister offered his Soviet counterpart a draft proposal to settle their differences by having the USSR move south instead of west and become a signatory to the Tripartite Pact. The agreement was outlined as follows:

The Governments of the states of the Three Power Pact Germany, Italy, and Japan on the one side, and the Government of the U.S.S.R. on the other side, motivated by the desire to establish in their natural boundaries an order serving the welfare of all peoples concerned and to create a firm and enduring foundation for their common labors toward this goal, have agreed upon the following:

ARTICLE 1

In the Three Power Pact of September 27, 1940, Germany, Italy, and Japan agreed to oppose the extension of the war into a world conflict with all possible means and to collaborate toward an early restoration of world peace. They expressed their willingness to extend their collaboration to nations in other parts of the world which are inclined to direct their efforts along the same course as theirs. The Soviet Union declares that it concurs in these aims and is on its part determined to cooperate politically in this course with the Three Powers.

ARTICLE II

Germany, Italy, Japan, and the Soviet Union undertake to respect each other's natural spheres of influence. In so far as these spheres of influence come into contact with each other, they will constantly consult each other in an amicable way with regard to the problems arising therefrom.

ARTICLE III

Germany, Italy, Japan, and the Soviet Union undertake to join no combination of powers and to support no combination of powers which is directed against one of the Four Powers.

The Four Powers will assist each other in economic matters in every way and will supplement and extend the agreements existing among themselves.

The agreement itself would be announced to the public. Beyond that, with reference to the above-mentioned agreement, a confidential (secret) agreement could be concluded—in a form still to be determined—establishing the focal points in the territorial aspirations of the Four Countries.

As to Germany, apart from the territorial revisions to be made in Europe at the conclusion of the peace, her territorial aspirations centered in the Central African region.

The territorial aspirations of Italy, apart from the European territorial revisions to be made at the conclusion of the peace, centered in North and Northeast Africa.

The aspirations of Japan would still have to be clarified through diplomatic channels. Here too, a delimitation could easily be found, possibly by fixing a line which would run south of the Japanese home islands and Manchukuo.

The focal points in the territorial aspirations of the Soviet Union would presumably be centered south of the territory of the Soviet Union in the direction of the Indian Ocean.

Such a confidential agreement could be supplemented by the statement that the Four Powers concerned, except for the settlement of individual issues, would respect each other's territorial aspirations and would not oppose their realization.[17]

Soviet reaction to this proposal represented one of the most important turning points of the war, yet it is rarely discussed. Germany was effectively offering peace if the USSR was willing to trade conquest of Finland and the Balkans for that of Iran and Iraq with their oil fields and warm-water ports. If Molotov and Stalin had been able to accept such an agreement, the USSR would have joined the Tripartite Pact with the Red Army attacking the British in Iraq and Iran. Barbarossa would not have taken place or at least been delayed. In such a scenario the Churchill government would have been under extreme pressure by late 1941. It's oil fields lost, India under threat, and the Germans focused on bombing England, sinking merchant shipping in the Atlantic, and pushing the Afrika Korps east toward the Suez Canal.

Molotov duly returned to Moscow to discuss the proposal with Stalin. Germany once again signaled diplomatically that it was not going to cede eastern Europe to the USSR as the Tripartite Pact was signed by Hungary (November 20), Romania (November 23), and Slovakia (November 24). Thankfully for the world's democracies, the Soviet reply on November 25 was one that Hitler would not accept. The USSR offered to join the Tripartite Pact and accept the proposed plan for carving up the Eastern Hemisphere, if:

1. German troops were withdrawn from Finland,
2. the USSR was given a free hand to attack Turkey so as to gain control of the Bosporus and Dardanelles,
3. Bulgaria was to sign a mutual-assistance pact with the USSR and provide the Soviet military with bases along the Black Sea coast.

Such new Soviet outposts in Bulgaria could direct military force north as well as south, and allow the Red Army to attack Romania from multiple directions. "Hitler said that once Soviet military influence was established in Bulgaria, the whole of the Balkans, especially Rumania with her oil fields would automatically become a Soviet domain."[18] Adding in the demand for the removal of *Wehrmacht* troops from Finland meant that Stalin was demanding military dominance over the source of German supplies of nickel, oil, and other critical military-industrial inputs. The Soviet counterproposal clearly influenced Hitler's decision. General Franz Halder noted the following in his diary regarding Hitler's address to his military commanders in early January 1941: "Stalin: Intelligent and shrewd; his demands will become bigger and bigger. German victory incompatible with Russian ideology. Decision: Russia must be smashed as soon as possible. The British might easily have 40 Divisions within two years. This might induce Russia to side with Britain and U.S."[19] Germany never formally replied to the Soviet proposal of November 25, and relations between the two totalitarian powers continued to deteriorate.

Was this offer for the USSR to join the Tripartite Pact just a ploy by Hitler? Would Germany still have attacked in June 1941 if the Russians had agreed to "go south" and leave Finland, Romania, and Bulgaria alone? Perhaps, but clearly if the USSR had accepted the Nazi offer, it would have been in Germany's interest to abide by the new agreement, if only for a time. Were a large mass of the Red Army driving south into the British domains of what is now Iran, Iraq, and Pakistan, then certainly:

1. Concerns of a Soviet attack on Germany in the near term would have been alleviated.
2. Stalin would have been assisting Hitler's goal of defeating Britain and codifying German control of northern Europe. Had this led to a British capitulation, the global sea lanes would reopen to Germany, allowing it to reduce its dependence on supplies of natural resources from Eastern Europe.
3. Launching Barbarossa while the Red Army was killing British soldiers and forcing Britain toward the negotiating table would make little sense. It would also have undermined (as we will see) a primary military goal of Hitler's invasion plan, which was to encircle and destroy the bulk of the Red Army west of the Dnieper River. Such destruction could not take place if Germany attacked while much of Stalin's forces were engaged south of the Caucasus.

Imagine the impact on history if Stalin had accepted the German offer. Moving south and seizing Iran and Iraq would have made the USSR the world's predominant oil producer. It would have also bought him the time he desired to build up the Red Army, which was undergoing rapid expansion, refit, and retraining. A Soviet move to the south would have forced the British to shift much of their forces in the Pacific and send them to the Middle East in what would likely have been a futile defensive effort. Such a military redeployment would have accelerated the 1942 Japanese victories in Malaya, Singapore, and Burma and allowed Tokyo to direct more of its forces to holding off the United States.

Had the USSR joined the Tripartite Pact, the Axis powers could have carved up the bulk of the Eastern Hemisphere before the United States entered the war. Chances for victory would have been much bleaker for Churchill and Roosevelt in such a scenario. We must be thankful that Stalin did not accept the offer presented by Ribbentrop to Molotov in that air raid shelter in Berlin. If he had, the war may very well have ended differently and in a way much less advantageous to the democracies of the world. Instead, Stalin chose to antagonize Germany and turn up the heat. Hitler was more than willing to reply in kind.

· 6 ·

Hitler's Decision, Marita, and the Countdown to Invasion

$\mathscr{H}$itler's writing and words indicated that he always expected to fight the USSR at some point. As noted previously, in *Mein Kampf*, he wrote that Russian lands would become the focus of German expansionist efforts. In 1939 he promised to attack the USSR after he was victorious in the west. By the start of 1941, Hitler commanded the world's best army, flush with victory and with little to occupy them. He had attempted to subdue the British with his weaker military arms (the *Kriegsmarine* and *Luftwaffe*), but to date he had failed. Options for a quick victory were dim, and he was confronting Britian's strength in its navy and air force, which was increasingly being aided by the economic power of the United States. Hitler knew that the British had attempted to negotiate an alliance with the USSR in 1939 and believed correctly that Churchill held out hope that the Russians would join the war against Germany.

Recent attempts at diplomacy highlighted the irreconcilable differences between German sources of raw materials in Eastern Europe and Soviet territorial desires. Both Hitler, bent on German hegemonic control of northern Europe, and Stalin, desiring conquests in Scandinavia and the Balkans, believed that the start of a war between the two totalitarian powers was only a matter of time. German reliance on Romanian oil made a possible Soviet surprise attack in the Balkans a significant risk to the Reich's overall economy. As Hitler stated to his generals, "Now, in the era of air power, Russia can turn the Rumanian oil fields into an expanse of smoking debris . . . and the life of the Axis depends on those oil fields."[1]

With Britain still in the war but safe from amphibious attack, and the USSR becoming increasingly antagonistic toward German interests, Hitler decided to move forward with what he believed to be a preventive war in the east. Ribbentrop argued this point repeatedly in his memoirs written in a jail cell as he awaited the hangman's noose:

> From what Hitler told me then and on later occasions the political considerations which made him decide on an attack on Russia can be summarized thus. Since about 1938, Hitler was, of course, convinced that Britain and America would go to war against us, once they were sufficiently armed. His fear was an alliance of these two Powers and Russia so that Germany would again be exposed to simultaneous attacks from East and West, as had happened in 1914. . . . I repeat: the *Führer* thought that the only way of escape from the threat of an attack on two fronts was to eliminate the Soviet Union first. The main reason for his attack was to prevent a blow from being struck simultaneously from east and west, but later this happened nevertheless. Hitler foresaw that a joint assault by the three world Powers would mean defeat.[2]

Soon after Stalin's rejection of the German offer to join the Tripartite Pact, Hitler assembled his senior military commanders on December 18, 1940, and issued "*Führer* Directive 21." This document laid out the basic plan for Operation Barbarossa, which called for a rapid conquest of all of the USSR up to the Urals:

The preparations of the High Commands are to be made on the following basis:

I.   General Purpose:

The mass of the Russian Army in western Russia is to be destroyed in daring operations, by driving forward deep armored wedges, and the retreat of units capable of combat into the vastness of Russian territory is to be prevented.

In quick pursuit a line is then to be reached from which the Russian Air Force will no longer be able to attack the territory of the German Reich. The ultimate objective of the operation is to establish a cover against Asiatic Russia from the general line Volga-Arkhangel. Then, in case of necessity, the last industrial area left to Russia in the Urals can be eliminated by the *Luftwaffe*.

In the course of these operations the Russian Baltic Sea Fleet will quickly lose its bases and thus will no longer be able to fight.

Effective intervention by the Russian Air Force is to be prevented by powerful blows at the very beginning of the operation.

II. Probable Allies and their Tasks:
   1. On the wings of our operation the active participation of Romania and Finland in the war against Soviet Russia is to be expected.

      The High Command will in due time arrange and determine in what form the armed forces of the two countries will be placed under German command at the time of their intervention.
   2. It will be the task of Romania to support with selected forces the attack of the German southern wing, at least in its beginnings; to pin the enemy down where German forces are not committed; and otherwise to render auxiliary service in the rear area.
   3. Finland will cover the concentration of the German North Group (parts of the XXI Group) withdrawn from Norway and will operate jointly with it. Besides, Finland will be assigned the task of eliminating Hanko.[3]

Hitler also made clear in the Barbarossa directive that the final decision had not yet been made for the panzers to roll east across the border. There was still time to avert an armed conflict, but only if Stalin was prepared to acquiesce to German demands and give up his claims in the Baltic and the Balkans: "All orders to be issued by the Commanders in Chief on the basis of this directive must clearly indicate that they are *precautionary measures* for the possibility that Russia should change her present attitude toward us. The number of officers to be assigned to the preparatory work at an early date is to be kept as small as possible; additional personnel should be briefed as late as possible and only to the extent required for the activity of each individual. Otherwise, through the discovery of our preparations— the date of their execution has not even been fixed—there is danger that most serious political and military disadvantages may arise."[4]

OPERATION MARITA

Many historians depict Stalin's strategy in the first half of 1941 as aimed at appeasing Hitler so as to gain time for the Red Army to expand, upgrade its equipment, and retrain after the Great Purge.[5] This conclusion ignores the provocative diplomatic policies pursued by the USSR in both Finland and the Balkans, which solidified Hitler's decision to attack.

With the start of 1941 came the announcement of an economic embargo on Finland by the USSR. Marshal Carl Mannerheim, commander in chief of the Finnish military from 1939 to 1944, relates, "The cutting off of supplies from the Soviet Union was in these circumstances calculated to produce a serious crisis, especially where grain and fuel were concerned. In consequence, we became dependent on Germany's resources which of course in time enabled Germany to apply political pressure. The extent to which Finland became dependent on importation from Germany is illustrated by the fact that soon ninety per cent of our whole imports came from Germany. This was the result of a Soviet trade policy which cannot be described as other than short-sighted."[6]

It was indeed short-sighted if Stalin truly wished to avoid an armed conflict in 1941. After all, the wheat and petroleum Finland received from Germany was simply redirected from fungible shipments arriving from the USSR itself. At the same time that Finland was becoming utterly reliant on Germany, developments in the Balkans led to a further deterioration in Nazi-Soviet relations. The invasion of Greece, which had started poorly for the Italians in the autumn of 1940, became a disaster with a Greek counteroffensive from November to January, which pushed Italian troops well back into Albania. Hitler worried that these events might allow Britain to establish a new front in Southern Europe from which it could threaten German economic interests, particularly through air attack on the oil wells of Romania. Initial planning of Operation Marita, an invasion of Greece through Bulgaria, began in December.

To aid the Greeks against the Italians, Britain deployed bombers to the Peloponnese and troops to Crete. On January 13, the Greek government requested nine British divisions and additional airpower. Churchill's diplomats worked to cobble together a "Balkan Front" of Yugoslavia, Turkey, and Greece to oppose the Axis. London's ambassador to the USSR, Sir Stafford Cripps, had developed a good relationship with Molotov and attempted to involve the USSR in the formation of this "Balkan Front." Cripps related these discussions to the Yugoslav ambassador in Moscow, Milovan Gavrilović, whose telegrams back to Belgrade were intercepted by Axis intelligence agencies. In Berlin, the impression was solidified that the Soviets were actively working with the British to form an alliance to oppose Germany.[7]

In response, Germany pressured Bulgaria to join the Tripartite Pact. In return for signing and allowing the *Wehrmacht* transit rights through its territory, Bulgaria was promised the lands it had lost to Greece along the Aegean in the 1919 Treaty of Neuilly-sur-Seine. The authoritarian Tsar Boris III of Bulgaria was amenable to this offer, as he had come to power in the wake of his nation's defeat and partial dismemberment by the Allies in World War I in what was remembered locally as a national catastrophe. Moscow closely monitored these moves with increasing alarm. On January 17, the Soviet ambassador in Berlin, Vladimir Dekanozov, handed over a diplomatic note that included the following: "The Soviet Government has stated repeatedly to the German Government that it considers the territory of Bulgaria and of the Straits as the security zone of the U.S.S.R. and that it cannot be indifferent to events which threaten the security interests of the U.S.S.R. In view of all this the Soviet Government regards it as its duty to give warning that it will consider the appearance of any foreign armed forces on the territory of Bulgaria and of the Straits as a violation of the security interests of the U.S.S.R."[8] The German reply on the 22nd was that its troops might transit Bulgaria to force British forces out of Greece, but it would not occupy Turkish territory, and German forces would be withdrawn at the conclusion of a successful campaign.[9]

Events in the Balkans then moved quickly toward a crisis. At the end of February, German formations crossed into Bulgaria and took up positions along the Greek border. The USSR was subsequently notified that Bulgaria was joining the Tripartite Pact. Molotov immediately responded with a strongly worded complaint. The British began transporting large numbers of troops and equipment to Greece from Egypt in early March, and within six weeks this force totaled more than sixty thousand men. When the Italian navy tried to interdict the British effort, it was soundly defeated in the Battle of Cape Matapan.

With German forces deployed on the Greek-Bulgarian frontier, Yugoslavia was pressured to join the Tripartite Pact, which its government reluctantly did on March 25. Germany received military transit rights across the country, and Yugoslavia was promised the great Greek port of Thessalonica and its surrounding territory. Two days later a coup took place in Belgrade that brought to power a junta of Serbian military officers headed by General Dušan Simović. The Serbs had been traditional allies of Russia, and the change in government was welcomed by the USSR. The Soviet ambassador in Belgrade proposed a military alliance, and the new Yugoslav government promptly sent representatives to Moscow to hammer out an agreement. In the end, Stalin hesitated to take such an antagonistic step toward Germany. On April 4, Yugoslavia and Moscow entered into a weaker treaty of "friendship and nonaggression," but the Serbs received the impression that this was an interim step toward a more thorough military pact with subsequent deliveries of Soviet armaments, munitions, and aircraft.[10]

Molotov summoned the German ambassador, Friedrich von der Schulenburg, to the Kremlin and explained that the pact with the new

Yugoslavian government was solely an effort to maintain peace in the Balkans, and the USSR was extremely interested in Germany doing all it could to refrain from fighting in the region as well. Schulenburg replied that "the moment chosen by the Soviet Union for the negotiation of such a treaty had been very unfortunate, and the very signing would create an undesirable impression in the world. The policy of the Yugoslav Government was entirely unclear, and its attitude, as well as the behavior of the Yugoslav public toward Germany, was challenging."[11] A potential Yugoslavian-Russian alliance was a clear strategic threat to Germany since it could place the critical Romanian oil fields at risk of attack from multiple directions. The perceived change of sides in Belgrade infuriated Hitler, who decreed that Marita start immediately and now include the conquest of Yugoslavia as well as Greece. In a decision that many argue led to Germany's eventual defeat, Hitler ordered a month-long postponement of Barbarossa so as to first complete the conquest of the Balkans.

The *Luftwaffe's* ruthless bombing of Belgrade began on April 6 and killed fifteen thousand of the city's inhabitants. German, Italian, and Hungarian armies invaded Yugoslavia on multiple fronts. Soon after the start of the fighting, Stalin reportedly told Gavrilović, "I hope that your army can stop the Germans for a long time. You have mountains and forests, where tanks are ineffective."[12] Such lengthy resistance was not to be, as many of the Yugoslav army's ethnic Croat divisions mutinied and the nation's Serb-dominated government capitulated within days. Croatia proclaimed itself a separate state, welcomed the invaders, and its new government soon signed the Tripartite Pact.

The collapse of Yugoslavia left the Greeks and British outnumbered and outflanked. By the end of April, the British were in retreat and the Royal Navy was once again engaged in a demoralizing evacuation. The conquest of Greece was completed in late May with a bloody airborne assault on Crete. British troops were ejected from the European mainland for a second time in less than a year. Bulgarian and Italian troops occupied most of Greece, and the panzer divisions returned north where they waited for the order to invade the USSR.

If preparations for Barbarossa had begun as a "precautionary measure," the perceived Soviet interference in Finland, Bulgaria, and then Yugoslavia was a final catalyst for war: "Göring testified at Nuremberg that Hitler and the Germans were convinced the Simović coup had been a conspiracy organized by the Soviet Union and financed by Britain. For the Nazi leader it was a final, crucial reason for attacking the Soviet Union in June 1941."[12] While Marita may have delayed the launch of

fensive operations. In addition, its enormous forces of aircraft and tanks (both four times that of the *Wehrmacht*) pointed to a deep strike capability that must have been of concern to the German military.

While evidence of a planned Soviet military offensieve in 1941 is solely circumstantial, one cannot discount the indications that such an event was increasingly likely at a later date. Hitler told his generals that the invasion of the USSR was a preemptive attack to stave off one by the Red Army on Germany and its allies. It was reasonable to conclude that a war between Nazi Germany and Soviet Russia was inevitable in the 1940s. The question was not so much when it would occur, but if it was to take place on Russian or German soil.

We will now consider the reasons that Hitler believed an attack on the USSR had significant odds of success despite the size of the Soviet military. The invasion was clearly evil and genocidal in its execution, but in military terms it was not a march of folly, hubris, or madness, as many have since declared. Barbarossa was a calculated gamble taken when Germany's chances of victory were maximized.

THE ALIGNMENT OF NATIONS IN EUROPE

In 1914 to 1917, the Central Powers (effectively the German and Austro-Hungarian empires) had been able to defeat the Russian Empire while at the same time pushing back the combined armies of Britain, France, and Italy. By 1941, compared to 1914, Germany was in a dramatically more advantageous position in Europe to defeat its great foe to the east. It had regained its pre–World War I territories and had brought the lands of the former Austro-Hungarian Empire under its control as Austria, Hungary, Czechoslovakia, and Croatia had either been annexed or had signed the Tripartite Pact.

Across the rest of Europe, the situation was much more to Germany's advantage than in World War I. Rather than being armed foes of Germany, Italy and Romania were now Axis allies and Portugal and Ireland were neutrals. Previously part of the Russian Empire, Finland was now an independent state eager to fight its former master. In the west and south, things were also better for Germany as the entirety of Denmark, Norway, Greece, Belgium, Serbia, Albania, and the Netherlands had been conquered and could now be managed by occupation authorities to supply the Axis war effort. Of even greater importance, France was defeated, its great armies dissolved, and its northern lands occupied by the *Wehrmacht*. Finally, Britain's expeditionary forces had retreated from the continental mainland, leaving most of its heavy equipment behind in France or Greece. British forces were in no state to mount a major offensive that could challenge German dominance.

A significant relative economic improvement of the Axis and its allies had also taken place by 1941. Germany had occupied the entirety of six nations with a combined GDP roughly half the size of the Reich's prewar economy. The Nazis had also seized large parts of France and Poland and incorporated the economic output of these regions as well. In total, Germany had roughly doubled the GDP directly under its control since the start of the war. Its military allies in Europe (Italy, Hungary, Romania, Finland, Slovakia, Bulgaria, and Croatia) generated GDP close to 50 percent of the newly enlarged Third Reich. The occupied territories of Yugoslavia and Greece added a bit more to the Axis's economic output.

Neutral European nations geographically dominated by the Axis military also offered economic advantages. The banking capital of Switzerland, the agricultural bounty and deported laborers of Vichy France, the tungsten of Spain, and the industry of Sweden (iron ore, ball bearings, etc.) would be of great assistance to the German war effort. The USSR could not count on any such support.

By 1941, Germany, its conquests, and its allies generated a GDP larger than that of the Soviet and British empires combined. With Britain held at arm's length in peripheral battles, the Axis's ecomomic preponderance could be brought to bear against the Soviets. The Axis's economic advantage could be improved further as the vast majority of the USSR's productive output was located in the western part of its territory and vulnerable to seizure in the opening phase of a German offensive.

Hitler knew that a lack of natural barriers had traditionally allowed invading armies to penetrate deeply into Russia. In modern history, such attacks had taken place in the seventeenth century by the Poles, in the eighteenth by the Swedes, in the nineteenth by the French, and already once in the twentieth by the Germans. Peter Zeihan, one of today's most incisive geopolitical strategists, explains:

> Russia's geography, in a word, sucks. Russian lands are barely temperate, with all but one Russian city lying at a higher latitude than Minneapolis. Moscow itself gets under 20 hours of sunlight for the entire *month* of December. Russia only has one commercially navigable river, the Volga, which is frozen one-third of the year and empties to the landlocked

Caspian Sea rather than the ocean. Short growing seasons make full tables something the Russians will never take for granted, while lack of easy movement condemns the country to being capital poor. But the real difference is the shape of the land itself. Russian lands are wide open. Roughly 80 percent of the Russian population lives in European Russia, a region some 1,500 miles north-to-south but at most points only 1,000 miles east to west that is the flattest on earth.[7]

Table 6.   1939 GDP in Millions of 1990 Geary-Khamis Dollars[6]

Germany	374,577			
German Conquests				
Belgium	43,216			
Denmark	22,803		**Totals**	
Czechoslovakia	41,578	(1937) data		
Netherlands	48,687		**German Empire**	
Norway	13,339		571,450	
Austria	27,250			
German Allies			**German Allies**	
Italy	154,470		265,083	
Hungary	26,184			
Romania	19,375	(1938) data		
Bulgaria	10,599			
Finland	12,561			
Greece	18,875		**German Empire & Allies**	
Yugoslavia	23,019		836,533	
Britain	300,539		**Britain & USSR**	
USSR	430,577		731,116	
Poland	67,788	(1938) data		
France	200,840			

The kaiser's conquests of Russian territory in World War I were only reversed as a consequence of the later German military defeat in France. Hitler believed that this time he could engineer a more lasting victory in the east. As explained in the initial directive for Barbarossa, *Wehrmacht* mechanized forces would advance much more quickly than previous invaders, destroy Soviet armies in the west before they could retreat into the vastness of the Russian steppe, and capture the bulk of the nation's industry, population centers, and valuable agricultural regions. The combined economic and military potential of an Axis-controlled Europe should then be more than adequate to hold the territory west of Arkhangelsk and Astrakhan against any attacks emanating from a rump USSR based east of the Ural Mountains.

THE JAPANESE THREAT IN THE EAST

After the fall of France, Germany was safe for a time from having to contest a land war on two fronts. The same was not true for the Soviet Union as the Japanese Empire constituted a major threat to its territory in the Far East. The history of relations between the USSR and Japan explains why more than one and a half million men of the Soviet military were based in the Far East even after the launch of Barbarossa. Enmity between the Japanese and the Russian empires was longstanding and deep. They had fought a major war in 1904 to 1905, leading to more than two hundred thousand dead and the destruction of most of the Russian navy. In the peace talks that followed, a victorious Japan gained Korea, the southern half of Sakhalin Island, and the ice-free harbor of Port Arthur.

Japanese-Russian disputes were subsumed in World War I as the Allies offered Japan the German Empire's holdings in Asia. Relations deteriorated as the ideology of the new USSR government with its goal to expand communism internationally represented a dire threat to the Imperial regime in Tokyo. A Japanese expeditionary force of seventy thousand men with smaller American, British, and French contingents landed in the Russian port of Vladivostok in 1918 and pushed westward all the way to Lake Baikal. Supposedly, these troops were to assist the reactionary "Whites" in the civil war against the new Soviet government. However, after the other allied forces withdrew in 1920, the Japanese supported a new buffer state, the Priamurye government in Siberia, and appeared to have territorial designs on the entire region. Only intense diplomatic pressure from the Western powers resulted in the Japanese finally evacuating their troops in 1922 after suffering five thousand dead. Relations between Japan and the new Soviet government in the Far East were never amicable and further deteriorated after Japan invaded Manchuria in 1931 and set up the puppet state of Manchukuo there.

Clashes along the frontiers of the Japanese and Soviet empires were common. The Manchukuo-Soviet border was arguably the most violent in the world in the 1930s. More than 150 military skirmishes took place along its length from 1932 to 1934, with an additional 176 in 1935, 152 in 1936, 113 in 1937, and 166 in 1938.[8] The fighting in this final year included a full-scale battle around Lake Khasan in Siberia. It was there that a Japanese force, outnumbered three to one, inflicted five thousand casualties on the Red Army, destroyed close to one hundred tanks, and only retreated after the fighting had ended.[9] The Soviet commander in charge of the Far

Eastern Front, Marshal Vasily Blyukher, was subsequently accused of incompetence, arrested by the NKVD, and tortured to death.

In 1939, the fighting shifted to a contested area of the Mongolian borderlands where the Khalkhin Gol River flows past the town of Nomonhan. Tens of thousands of Japanese soldiers of the elite *Kwantung* army massed along the border in July and advanced contingents into Soviet-controlled territory, resulting in several sharp engagements. Local Japanese commanders had acted primarily on their own initiative to precipitate the fighting. This angered the emperor as well as many in the government in Tokyo, who did not seek war with the USSR at that time. Such disgruntlement in the capital led to reinforcements being limited while the Soviets prepared a major offensive to push back the Japanese.

General (later Marshal) Georgy Zhukov, who would later distinguish himself as one of the greatest military commanders of the twentieth century, flew in from Moscow to take command. He assembled a much stronger force than the opposing Japanese in the area, with 50 percent more infantry, twice as many aircraft and artillery guns, and four times as many trucks and tanks.[10] By the end of August, his forces rolled forward and wiped out several surrounded Japanese units before a cease-fire went into effect. As at Lake Khasan, the Red Army's losses were much higher than those sustained by the Japanese, and almost a third of the Soviet tank force was destroyed.

Many conclude that the Khalkhin Gol defeat compelled the Japanese to avoid future conflict with the USSR. While peace prevailed along the Soviet Far Eastern frontier for the next several years, factions in the Japanese government and military continued to agitate for a general attack. Concern for such a war was so high that massive Red Army forces remained in the region even during the darkest days of the USSR's fight against the German invaders.

To conclude an analysis of the alignment of nations in early 1941, the situation was extremely poor for the Soviet Union. It was ringed by enemies and had no allies of significance. In contrast, the balance was extremely favorable for Germany after it had conquered much of continental Europe in brief wars that left the bulk of its economic infrastructure and population intact. Except for the Soviet Empire, what Hitler did not directly control on the continent was composed of treaty allies or friendly neutrals. Finland, Romania, and Japan were now enemies of Russia rather than allies, as they had been in 1914. Germany had effectively isolated the USSR and assembled a European coalition significantly larger than that of the Central Powers, which had defeated Russia in World War I while concurrently fighting a massive land war in France and Italy.

STALIN'S TERROR AND HIS SURLY MASSES

When Hitler looked across the border at the USSR, he saw a nation of people he believed to be less evolved humans than his supposed Aryan super race of German Übermensch. While government programs had yielded great improvements in modernizing the Soviet economy and expanding the armed forces, there truly was much weakness to behold in Stalin's empire. The cruelty and murderous nature of the communist regime had weakened the state and left it susceptible to invasion from the west. Many citizens of the USSR hated their government and would welcome almost any alternative.

Stalin's treatment of the people of Ukraine is the most tragic and disturbing of all his actions throughout a long, malevolent rule. Many Ukrainians wished for an independent state and chafed under the Soviet government. Stalin set out to eliminate these separatist urges through a wholesale destruction of Ukrainian culture, religion, language, and to a great extent, its people. These goals meshed well with the dictator's desire to shift the weight of his nation's population to the cities, collectivize agriculture output, and industrialize the economy. Stalin's policies resulted in the great "Terror-Famine" that peaked in 1932 to 1933. Food confiscation by the armed forces of the Soviet state led to mass starvation among the people of one of the world's most agriculturally productive areas. Ukrainians call this tragedy the "Holodomor": "In this period, about the same length as that of the First World War, a struggle on the same scale took place in the Soviet countryside. Though confined to a single state, the number dying in Stalin's war against the peasants was higher than the total deaths for all countries in World War I. There were differences: in the Soviet case, for practical purposes, only one side was armed, and the casualties (as might be expected) were almost all on the other side. They included, moreover, women, children and the old."[11]

The Terror-Famine resulted in between ten to fifteen million deaths due to starvation, overwork, executions, suppression of peasant resistance, and those shipped to the Gulag never to return.[12] More than a quarter of the population died across a great swath of the Ukraine. It was a catastrophic killing on a scale that had not been seen in Europe since the Thirty Years' War of the seventeenth century or the Black Death of the fourteenth.

Among those who survived the Holodomor, there remained an understandable deep resentment toward the Soviet regime that simmered for the few short years remaining until the start of World War II. This antipathy was so intense that many Ukrainians welcomed the racially homicidal Nazis as liberators.

Disgruntlement in the nation's most important agricultural and industrial region was a worry for Moscow in 1941, but not 1934. For Stalin, the Terror-Famine was a great success as a larger share of southern Russia's agricultural output was diverted to urban factory workers, and the industrial resources of the region (iron, coal, manganese, nickel, etc.) became more intensely utilized.

After the conclusion of the Holodomor and collectivization of agriculture, Stalin moved to eliminate any possible opposition to his rule throughout the rest of the USSR. This effort from 1936 to 1938, known as the Great Purge or the Great Terror, led to the imprisonment, torture, and execution of millions of the most successful members of the Soviet population on false charges ranging from Trotskyite leanings to espionage and conspiring with the Axis powers. Communist Party politicians and their families were the first to go. Diplomats, scholars, engineers, and scientists followed. Many of those accused of crimes were successful inventors in fields such as aviation, rocketry, and engine design—critical professions to the defense industries of the USSR. Thousands of scientists and engineers were shot and others ended up in special Gulag camps called Sharashka, where they labored under guard to design newer, better weapons and aircraft. One can imagine that their efforts would have been more successful in circumstances where they remained free men.

Historian Robert Conquest relates, "My rough totals, arrived at through the examination of a number of separate trains of evidence, were

Arrests, 1937–1938	about 7 million
Executed	about 1 million
Died in camps	about 2 million
In prison, late 1938	about 1 million
In camps, late 1938 (assuming	
5 million in camps at the end of 1936)	about 8 million."[13]

While this purge may have insulated Stalin's rule against internal threats, it also removed many who would have organized, worked, and fought for the USSR in a war with Germany. Hitler's attacks on his own people were certainly murderous, but at least he directed his purges primarily against segments of the population likely to oppose Nazi rule. Many arrested by the barbarous Soviet NKVD were committed communists and patriots who had risen to positions of power through merit.

But Stalin was not done, as the Great Purge moved on to decimate the command structure of the Soviet military. In just a few years, the following officers were removed from their posts:

3 of the 5 Marshals
13 of the 15 Army Commanders
8 of the 9 Fleet Admirals and Admirals Grade I
50 of the 57 Corps Commanders
154 of the 186 Divisional Commanders
16 of the 16 Army Commissars
25 of the 28 Corps Commissars
58 of the 64 Divisional Commissars
11 out of 11 Vice Commissars of Defense
98 out of 108 members of the Supreme Military Soviet.[14]

More than four hundred thousand army and navy officers were relieved from active duty, and many were imprisoned, shipped to the Gulag, or executed. While Stalin allowed thirteen thousand to reenroll in the military after the German invasion, many were broken men by that point with significantly diminished capabilities.[15] The negative impact of the Purge on the Soviet armed forces was dramatic: "The Russian officer corps was not isolated, it was crushed. When the purges were over, the Red Army was obedient to the point of witlessness; dutiful but without experience; stripped of political weight or ambition, at the expense of initiative, experiment, or the desire to innovate."[16] The loss of so many senior officers "led to 'inexperienced commanders' being promoted. As early as 1937, 60 percent of the commanding cadres in rifle units, 45 percent in tank units, and 25 percent in air units were given as in this category."[17]

The diminished effectiveness of the Red Army became painfully clear at the end of 1939 when the USSR invaded Finland in the Winter War. The outside world noted the progress of the fighting with keen interest. While small in the context of the overall violence of World War II, this conflict had a great impact as it led Hitler to believe the Soviet armed forces were weak and could be defeated in a rapid campaign. The USSR, with a population more than forty times that of Finland, committed a dramatically larger military force against its smaller opponent and expected an easy victory. The Red Army initially deployed nineteen infantry divisions, five tank brigades, and eight hundred aircraft totaling 300,000 men to the battlefront against 120,000 Finns. The Russian forces were much better equipped than their opponents and had eight times as many planes and one hundred times as many tanks.[18]

Despite these massive matériel advantages, the Red Army suffered numerous humiliating defeats in the opening weeks of the war. Finland's Marshal Mannerheim recalls of the initial Soviet advance, "The enemy's attacks in December could be compared with a badly-conducted orchestra, in which the instruments were played out of time. Division after division was thrown against our positions, but the co-operation between the different arms remained bad. The artillery kept up heavy fire, but it was badly directed and badly co-ordinated with the movements of the infantry and armour. The collaboration of the latter occasionally took strange forms. Tanks might advance, open fire, and return to their starting-point before the infantry had even begun to move. Such elementary mistakes naturally cost the Red Army heavy losses."[19]

Soviet reinforcements eventually wore down the defenders. Their battle lines broken, the Finns sued for peace and signed a treaty that achieved Soviet war aims. While the Red Army may have won the war, its reputation suffered immensely:

> If one reviews only the statistics of Russian losses of men and material, it becomes clear why Hitler believed the Soviet Union was a bumbling giant incapable of resisting the German war machine. By the time the war ended the Red forces massed against Finland totaled forty-five divisions; if one includes the special units and rear echelons, the forces amounted to approximately a million men. Of these it is conservatively estimated, at least 200,000 were killed and an unknown number wounded. In contrast, Finnish casualties were 68,480, of which 24,923 were killed or missing and 43,557 wounded. The poor showing of Russian armored forces and severe losses suffered by these units would have convinced anyone of the incompetence of the Soviet military. Against the Finns, the Russians had ranged 3,200 tanks, light, medium and heavy, and of these the Finns had captured or destroyed 1,600 not to mention the 3,000 to 4,000 trained specialists who perished or were captured. The Red Air Force did no better, having lost over 900 planes in the war.[20]

The effect of the Purge on the Red Army's effectiveness was closely monitored by its potential opponents. At the end of 1939 the German

General Staff classified the Soviet military as follows: "In quantity a gigantic military instrument . . . Organization, equipment and means of leadership unsatisfactory . . . Fighting qualities of the troops in a *heavy* fight, dubious—The Russian 'mass' is *no* match for an army with modern equipment and superior leadership."[21] The Germans were not the only ones who drew the conclusion that the Red Army was terribly flawed and poised for further defeats. Churchill's radio broadcast of January 20, 1940, contained the following: "The service rendered by Finland to mankind is magnificent. They have exposed, for all the world to see, the military incapacity of the Red Army and of the Red Air Force. Many illusions about Soviet Russia have been dispelled in these few fierce weeks of fighting in the Arctic Circle."[22]

Few outside observers noted that Soviet soldiers performed well when defending from prepared positions, often refused to surrender in hopeless situations, and were quite effective in urban combat.[23] In addition, many of the best Russian divisions were not committed, and those of lesser effectiveness did the fighting. Still, a result of the abysmal Red Army performance was Stalin's approval of a dramatic reorganization of the military under Marshal Seymon Timoshenko. Training was improved, exercises became more realistic, and discipline became harsher. The power of political commissars was weakened, which reduced interference in the leadership of the troops by unit commanders. Moreover, the experiences gained in the bitter Finnish climate led the Soviets to develop new winter clothing as well as equipment and lubricants that could operate in sustained extreme cold.[24] While these reforms were not complete by June 1941, the Red Army was in better shape to fight than it had been at the end of the Winter War.

Finally, in addition to a purged military and a decimated population, the cruelty of the Soviet regime extended to its newly conquered territories in Eastern Europe. The peoples of the Baltic states of Lithuania, Estonia, and Latvia would welcome the ejection of the occupying Red Army. Similarly, a great number of the residents of what had until recently been southern Finland and eastern Romania had not wanted to become part of the USSR. Germany could even expect to find support in the former eastern third of Poland. The people in this area of Soviet control suffered terribly. More than fifty thousand Poles were deported to the Gulag, and unmarked mass graves in the Katyn Forest became the final resting place of much of the Polish army's officer corps after their massacre at the hands of the NKVD.

On June 7, 1941, US ambassador Laurence Steinhardt reported his thoughts from Moscow regarding a potential German attack on the USSR:

"1. Because of the high proportion of peasants among the total Soviet population . . . the morale of the peasantry would be an important, if not determining factor in the military strength of the Soviet Union should an invasion occur.

2. Due to the oppressive policy of the Kremlin toward the peasantry which began with the introduction of enforced collectivization and which has continued to express itself in numerous burdensome decrees during the past year, the peasant population is believed to be bitterly hostile to the central government. Reports from the Ukraine, as well as from Russia proper, indicate that a foreign army would be welcomed as liberators by a large proportion of the rural population.

3. Though the morale of the Red army may be satisfactory at the present time . . . the Red army's morale cannot be regarded as wholly reliable.

4. Though the inherent loyalty of the Russian peasant to his fatherland, as opposed to the Stalinist regime, might eventually result in serious and widespread uprising against a foreign invader, it is highly probable that the Stalinist regime could not survive any invasion."[25]

THE EVE OF BARBAROSSA

In retrospect, a rational analysis in early 1941 was that the USSR was in a much less advantageous position to defend itself against a German attack than the Russian Empire had been in 1914. Stalin's domain was now ringed by multiple enemies. Russia's continental European allies of World War I—France, Belgium, Greece, Britain, Serbia, Italy, and Romania—had all been defeated in battle, occupied, or willingly joined the German side. The Soviet military was large but undertrained and poorly led. Much of the empire was populated by citizens who despised Stalin's rule and would welcome liberation if not actively fight alongside invaders to achieve it. In contrast, Hitler could count all of continental Europe west of the Soviet borders as either Reich territory, Allied states, or friendly neutrals. The *Wehrmacht* had recently proven itself the best led and most effective military in the world. It excelled in rapid combined-arms advances over level terrain, which described most of European Russia.

The balance of power had tilted toward Germany, but Hitler's advantage would not last forever. Britain, safe behind its Channel moat, was rearming, mobilizing its empire, and doing all it could to pull the United States into the conflict. The *Wehrmacht* had little to fear from the

Anglo-Americans in 1941, but with each passing year the threat would grow. With the defeat of France, Hitler could effectively fight a one-front war in the east against a Red Army that was expanding quickly, retraining its officer ranks, and equipping itself with the prodigious output of Soviet industry. The relative strength of Germany versus the USSR was at its apogee in 1941 and would deteriorate as time passed. If war was to come, Hitler could hardly choose a better time to start it than after the spring thaw of 1941.

Today's historical consensus is that the German invasion of the USSR was a terrible blunder and perhaps the greatest self-inflicted mistake ever committed in human history. The facts argue against such a conclusion. It is true that eventually Germany lost the war in the east, but that does not mean the gamble's odds were not in Hitler's favor. Historians today often describe the invasion as doomed from the start and largely ignore several of the largest military victories ever recorded. Similarly, Stalin's foolish strategy of giving Germany a free hand to win in the west in 1939, antagonizing almost all of the USSR's neighbors, decimating his own military, and intentionally starving the population of the Ukraine is generally overshadowed by the later heroic resistance of the Red Army and the Soviet population.

Other options besides war with the USSR were proposed as better strategies for Hitler to pursue in 1941. Yet analysis yields conclusions that those choices were likely dead ends at best for a nation bent on European domination and Great Power status. A diplomatic solution was offered to Stalin to avoid war, but he insisted on control of eastern European lands that would have given him a stranglehold on the German economy. Hitler believed a war was inevitable and decided to fight it on Russian soil. The odds were in Germany's favor. Domination of Europe was in its grasp. But the Teutonic dream faded in a storm of steel and fire. The question to be answered next is why.

Part II

GERMANY'S FAILURE IN THE EAST AND THE USSR'S MIRACULOUS VICTORY

· 8 ·

Drang nach Osten

The Drive to the East

$\mathscr{P}$art II will argue that the primary reason for the Axis defeat in the invasion of the USSR was a diplomatic failure of Germany. Its most militarily potent allies, Finland and Japan, had both the historical animus and the ability to tip the balance against the USSR and lead to its defeat. That they did not do so was the proximate cause leading to the Soviet victory in Europe. This position will be controversial, and to make a case for it the following chapters will outline the following:

1. the basic history of the invasion and its failure;
2. the traditional explanations given for Germany's defeat, why these reasons are insufficient to explain Soviet victory; and
3. argue, hopefully convincingly, that Japanese and Finnish inaction in 1941 to 1943 allowed the Red Army to achieve its remarkable recovery and victorious drive to the heart of Berlin.

THE PLAN, HITLER'S FEARS, AND STALIN'S WILLFUL DISBELIEF

Planning for Barbarossa was contentious from the start, and there were differing opinions as to the best strategy for conquest of the USSR. The Pripet Marshes in the center of the border area also complicated decisions on how to attack. The generals of the high command of the German army, or OKH (*Oberkommando des Heeres*), focused on orthodox military strategy as defined by the Prussian military theorist Clausewitz. This called for an immediate strike at the enemy's center of military power in a battle to annihilate its main armed force. The leaders of OKH believed a thrust toward Moscow would attract the bulk of the Red Army to the capital's defense and offer the *Wehrmacht* the opportunity to annihilate its opponent in one massive battle. After the fall of the capital, remaining Red Army resistance would wither away.

Hitler's thinking took into account economic and political considerations as well as destruction of the Red Army in the field. He wished to focus on the capture of the great port city of Leningrad in the north, and the concentration of Soviet agriculture and industry of the Ukraine in the south. A successful conquest of Leningrad would allow the German armies to link up with their Finnish allies, eliminate the Soviet Baltic fleet, secure a deep-water harbor to supply the invading army, and damage the enemy's morale by seizing the cradle of the Soviet revolution. Control of the southwest of the USSR would give Germany the productive farmland it required to feed its people as well as an abundance of natural resources to fuel its economy.

Denial of these territories to the Soviets would starve the Red Army of the manpower, food, and munitions it would need to continue the fight. In addition, a successful drive in the south would open up the next step of advancing into the Caucasus to seize the oil fields around Baku. This north and south strategy also offered the advantage of attacking into the former Baltic States and the Ukraine—regions of the USSR with populations most likely to rise up against the Soviet authorities and support the invaders. After the fall of Leningrad and the Ukraine, the German armies could capture Moscow in an enormous pincer movement and drive the fatally weakened Red Army east of the Urals. The final goal was an advance to the "A-A Line" running from the city of Arkhangelsk on the White Sea in the north to Astrakhan in the south, where the Volga River empties into the Caspian Sea.

General Friedrich Paulus, deputy chief of the General Staff (*Oberquartiermeister*), held Barbarossa war games at the end of November 1940 that utilized a three-pronged attack in the north, center, and south. An initial three-week phase of rapid advance was followed by a logistical pause of the same length. The planning session emphasized the primacy of a drive on Moscow, but the commander of Army Group South, General Rundstedt, requested forces be detached to his sector from the central attack to envelop Soviet troops around Kiev. When briefed on the results of the war games, Hitler emphasized his opinion that Moscow was not the most important target of the invasion.[1]

In the end, Hitler and his generals settled on a compromise plan for the *Ostheer* (East Army): Army Group North would drive for Leningrad and a link up with the Finns. Army Group Center would encircle and destroy the main Red Army formations blocking its way. After a planned pause to resupply with the capture of Smolensk, the Germans would then march on Moscow. Army Group South was to advance into the Ukraine with the assistance of Romanian and Hungarian allies. The central invasion force would be the strongest, which allowed flexibility to transfer strength to Army Group North or Army Group South if necessary. Hitler still had in mind an early capture of the northern and southern prizes, while OKH focused on the central drive for Moscow. This disagreement had significant consequences and led to the writing of many thousands of pages of finger-pointing regarding Barbarossa's eventual failure.

The historical record is clear that Hitler, the members of OKH, and the ranking members of the Nazi government planned to treat the Soviet population with barbaric harshness. Orders were issued that stipulated the immediate shooting of captured Soviet politicians and political commissar

The Final Plan for Operation Barbarossa[2]

officers of the Red Army. Jews would be rounded up and herded into ghettos if not simply killed outright. POWs were not to be granted the protections of the Geneva Convention and would be sent back to Germany to work as slave laborers or penned into giant, open-air, barbed wire enclosures and starved to death. In fact, the whole of the agricultural area of Ukraine was to be depopulated and then settled by Germanic farmers growing a bounty for the Nazi empire. The German planners deemed at least fifty million of those living in the European portion of the USSR to be superfluous. These Slavic "useless eaters" would have to migrate east of the Urals if they wished to avoid death by starvation.

As the launch date for Barbarossa drew near, Hitler's stress level grew dramatically. To his generals he promised an easy victory, stating that in contrast to the fight with France, "a campaign against the USSR would be like a child's game in a sandbox in comparison."[3] He also famously boasted that the Soviet Union was fragile, and that "we have only to kick in the door and the whole rotten structure will come crashing down."[4] Despite this bluster in public, it is clear that Hitler knew he was taking an enormous gamble. The odds of success may have been in his favor and the timing was optimized, but failure could spell the end of his reign and possibly the very existence of the German state that he professed to love so dearly. "In the final days before the invasion, Hitler became increasingly nervous and troubled—pacing constantly and needing sedatives to be able to sleep."[5]

Laboring under these fears of failure, "when Göring sought to flatter him before Barbarossa, asserting that his greatest triumph was at hand, Hitler sharply rebuked his marshal: 'It will be our toughest struggle yet—by far the toughest. Why? Because for the first time we shall be fighting an ideological enemy, and an ideological enemy of fanatical persistence at that.' At the Wolf's Lair, Hitler's headquarters in East Prussia built expressly for the invasion, he voiced unease to one of his secretaries about what lay ahead: 'We know absolutely nothing about Russia. It might turn out to be a one big soap-bubble, or it might just as well turn out to be something quite different.'"[6] On June 20th he told his staff, "I feel as if I am pushing open the door to a dark room never seen before without knowing what lies behind the door."[7]

The stress of leadership and the decision to invade the USSR took its toll on Hitler's mental and physical health. This deterioration coincided with what soon became daily doses of an ever-changing cocktail of psychoactive, mood altering, and hormonal drugs, including cocaine, opiates, and methamphetamines. "Such a process was not a one-off event; it was the norm. The injections increasingly determined the course of the day; over time the *Führer's* medical mixture was enriched by over eighty different, and often unconventional, hormone preparations, steroids, quack remedies and balms. . . . His natural intuition, which had served him well so often until the beginning of Operation Barbarossa, left him when the injections began to throw his body into chaos."[8]

On the other side of the border, Stalin refused to listen to increasingly strident warnings regarding the danger his nation faced. The massive preparations for Barbarossa did not go undetected by the intelligence agencies of the Great Powers. Representatives of both Britain and the United States in Moscow provided Stalin with warnings of the invasion, including the actual date of its launch. He rationalized away these reports as simply propaganda designed by the capitalist nations to lure him into a war with Germany. Multiple sources within the Soviet Union's own intelligence community also delivered notice of the impending attack. Stalin simply refused to believe that Hitler would strike while still at war with Britain. He believed he needed at least another year to prepare the Red Army to fight Germany and convinced himself that he would have that time. This conviction remained in place despite the recent aggressive Soviet moves in the Baltic and the Balkans that were sure to have antagonized Hitler.

The commanders of the Red Army informed Stalin of the multiple daily incursions of *Luftwaffe* reconnaissance flights over USSR airspace. They begged for approval to order a full mobilization and asked to launch a preemptive spoiling attack into Nazi territory to disrupt the coming invasion. The Soviet leader refused such measures except for a partial mobilization of reserves. On the eve of battle, the majority of the Red Army remained positioned close to the western border in uncompleted defensive positions within easy range of the artillery and air force of the *Wehrmacht*.

THE BATTLE JOINED

Germany and its allies attacked the USSR in the largest invasion in history on June 22. The initial front stretched from the Baltic in the north to the Danube delta in the south. While the Soviets deployed a larger number of tanks, planes, and artillery in the Western districts of the USSR, the Germans' qualitative advantages were of greater significance.

Table 7.   Operation Barbarossa Balance of Forces: June 1941[9]

	German Forces Assigned to the Invasion	German Forces on All Fronts	Soviet Forces in Western USSR	Soviet Forces in All Districts
Men	3.3 million	5.2 million	3.3 million	5.5 million
Combat Aircraft	3,277	4,878	10,775	20,474
Artillery Pieces	19,676	25,150	29,675	48,247
Motor Vehicles	577,000	831,000	173,137	272,600
Tanks	4,445	5,432	15,470	23,295

The initial German assault was devastating. The *Luftwaffe* destroyed almost nine hundred aircraft of the Soviet Air Force (*Voyenno-Vozdushnye Sily*, known as the VVS) in the first few hours of the attack.[10] Within days, the Germans' had achieved air superiority. On the ground, fast-moving panzer advances surrounded entire army groups in what the *Wehrmacht* referred to as *kessels* (cauldrons). While the defenders fought tenaciously, the Red Army was clearly outclassed, and hundreds of thousands of its troops surrendered. The ineffectiveness, hesitancy, and overall poor performance of the Soviet military, purged of many of its best commanders by Stalin, was obvious and resulted in massive military defeats. Many generals were arrested on Stalin's orders and shot for their failures. Others committed suicide. Despite these initial victories, the Germans still found the fighting against the Red Army to be tougher than what they had encountered in Poland or France, and casualties mounted rapidly.

General Halder triumphantly wrote in his diary on July 3,

> On the whole, then, it may be said even now that the objective to shatter the bulk of the Russian Army this side of the Dvina and Dniepr, has been accomplished. I do not doubt the statement of the captured Russian Corps CG that, east of the Dvina and the Dniepr, we would encounter nothing more than partial forces, not strong enough to hinder realization of German operational plans. It is thus probably no overstatement to say that the Russian campaign has been won in the space of two weeks. Of course, this does not yet mean that it is closed. The sheer geographical vastness of the country and the stubbornness of the resistance, which is carried on with all means, will claim our efforts for many more weeks.[11]

The *Wehrmacht*'s biggest problem in carrying out its operational plans in the initial phase of Barbarossa was maintaining its supply lines. Both ammunition consumption and mechanical equipment failure were higher than expected, and the poor road system slowed deliveries, resulting in depleted stocks of everything required by the frontline troops. The Soviet rail gauge was of a different width, and converting captured tracks and rolling stock to German standards took time. As the invaders pushed east, supply trucks burned ever more fuel motoring to the front, which reduced the amount of cargo that could be delivered. Similar problems were encountered by the *Luftwaffe*. Combat losses and the use of poorly maintained captured runways led to a reduction of servicable aircraft. Slowly, the VVS began to recover to contest German control of the air.

Even as the *Wehrmacht* surged east, its generals began to worry. The USSR had not collapsed after the first set of defeats. Additional German victories did not seem to blunt Soviet soldiers' will to resist nor the ability of the Red Army to raise new fighting formations from the vast nation's populace. As Halder wrote in his journal on August 11th, "At the outset of the war we reckoned with about 200 enemy divisions. Now we have already counted 360. These divisions indeed are not armed and equipped according to our standards, and their tactical leadership is often poor. But there they are, and if we smash a dozen of them, the Russians simply put up another dozen. The time factor favors them, as they are near their own resources, while we are moving farther and farther away from ours."[12]

THE WORLD HOLDS ITS BREATH

If Barbarossa was driven by hubris and doomed to failure, such a view was certainly not held in foreign capitals where there was little hope for the long-term survival of the USSR. In Tokyo, the Japanese military believed that the Red Army was on the verge of disintegration:

> When Yamashita's inspection team got back to Tokyo on 7 July, having traveled from Berlin via the Trans-Siberian Railway, it reported that the German war machine outnumbered the Soviet forces by 2:1 in infantry divisions, by 2.5:1 in overall ground strength, and by 3:1 or 4:1 in aircraft. The *Blitzkrieg* would probably shatter the Red Army, drive the Stalin government to the east, and exert pressure on Soviet Far Eastern forces. On 15 July, AGS Intelligence Bureau chief Okamoto

Kiyotomi judged that the Russians had already lost 70 percent of their air strength, 50 percent of their armor, and 25 percent of their firepower from the division artillery level upward. In Okamoto's opinion, the Soviet government had fallen into disarray and its flight from Moscow was near.[13]

While these Japanese estimates certainly overestimated German strength and Soviet losses, the outlook for the survival of the USSR was just as bleak in Britain and the United States. When word of the attack first reached the British, Field Marshal Sir John Dill, chief of the Imperial General Staff, summed up his outlook for the Red Army, "I suppose they will be rounded up in hordes."[14] The prime minister addressed a secret session of Parliament on June 25 to warn that the Nazis could be done fighting the USSR soon and would then turn their attention back to Britain: "In a few months or even less, we may be exposed to the most frightful invasion the world has ever seen."[15]

Churchill himself concluded that the Soviets were getting what they deserved after their recent cooperation with the Nazis:

> We must now lay bare the error and vanity of cold-blooded calculation of the Soviet Government and of the enormous Communist machine, and their amazing ignorance about where they stood themselves. They had shown a total indifference to the fate of the Western Powers, although this meant the destruction of that "Second Front" for which they were soon to clamour. . . . They hated and despised the democracies of the West; but the four countries Turkey, Romania, Bulgaria, and Yugoslavia, which were of vital interest to them and their own safety, could all have been combined by the Soviet Government in January with active British aid to form a Balkan front against Hitler. . . . War is mainly a catalogue of blunders, but it may be doubted whether any mistake in history has equaled that of which Stalin and the Communist chiefs were guilty when they cast away all possibilities in the Balkans and supinely awaited, or were incapable of realizing, the fearful onslaught which impended upon Russia. We had hitherto rated them as selfish calculators. In this period they were proved simpletons as well. . . . But so far as strategy, policy, foresight, competence are arbiters Stalin and his commissars showed themselves at this moment the most completely outwitted bunglers of the Second World War.[16]

There was talk in Washington and London of intentionally wrecking the Soviet petroleum infrastructure in the Caucasus so it could not fall into the hands of the Germans. Sumner Welles, acting secretary of state, related the following on June 26:

Lord Halifax called to see me this morning. The Ambassador inquired whether there would be any objection on the part of this Government to a request by the British authorities in the Near East to certain [American] oil experts engaged in the oil industry in the Near East to join the British oil experts in order to advise the Russian authorities as to the best means of destroying Russian oil wells in the event of imminent German occupation of those portions of Russia which include the sources of Russian oil supplies. I replied that I saw no objection.[17]

Mr. Welles was not the only senior US official with a bleak view of the USSR's chances. US Secretary of War Henry Stimson wrote in a memorandum to FDR that he and senior US military officers believed that "Germany will be thoroughly occupied in beating Russia for a minimum of one month and a possible maximum of three months."[18] William Bullitt, the former US ambassador to the USSR from 1933 to 1936, stated, "I know no man in Washington who believes that the Soviet Army can defeat the German Army."[19]

Despite Anglo-American concerns about the Soviet dictatorial government and its ability to survive, the democracies rallied to aid Germany's new enemy. Churchill, a long-time strident anticommunist, famously quipped, "If Hitler invaded Hell, I would make at least a favorable reference to the Devil in the House of Commons."[20] He soon broadcast on the BBC, "We are resolved to destroy Hitler and every vestige of the Nazi regime. . . . It follows therefore that we shall give whatever help we can to Russia and the Russian people. We shall appeal to all our friends and Allies in every part of the world to take the same course and pursue it as we shall, faithfully and steadfastly to the end."[21] An Anglo-Soviet Agreement was signed on July 12, with the two nations entering into a military alliance and pledging not to enter into a separate peace with Germany. The United States extended its aid programs to the USSR, and FDR wrote, "I deem it of paramount importance for the safety and security of America that all reasonable munitions help be provided for Russia, not only immediately but as long as she continues to fight the Axis powers effectively."[22]

MOSCOW OR KIEV? THE FIRST GREAT DECISION

By the start of August, the Germans had come to a decision point. They had advanced quickly along the Baltic in the North while the Finnish army pushed south to retake the lands lost in the Winter War, and there was hope the Allies could link up around Leningrad. Army Group Center had advanced more than two-thirds of the way to Moscow and wiped out large Red Army formations in great encirclement battles around Bialystok, Minsk, and Smolensk. Army Group South, with its Romanian allies, had made good progress along the coast of the Black Sea. Stalin had stationed his largest concentration of troops in northwestern Ukraine, and here the Red Army fell back more slowly. This created a huge salient in the German line of advance, which was held by the Soviet Southwestern Front composed of several armies defending the city of Kiev. This force constituted the largest mass of the Red Army in the western USSR and threatened the flanks of the *Wehrmacht*'s Army Groups Center and South.

Hitler was in favor of wiping out the Kiev salient. This would destroy the large Soviet forces there, eliminate the threat to the flanks of Army Groups Center and South, and capture much of the industrial and agricultural heartland of Ukraine. He also wanted to aid the relatively weaker Army Group North so it could take Leningrad, and link up with the Finns. OKH commander-in-chief Field Marshal Walther von Brauchitsch and his chief of staff, General Halder, disagreed. So did the commanders of Army Group Center, such as Field Marshal Fedor von Bock, and Generals Herman Hoth and Heinz Guderian. They argued vehemently that the focus should be a continued drive east with a goal of taking Moscow at the earliest possible moment. Speed was of the essence: there was little time before the autumn rains would turn the Russian roads to mud, which would be closely followed by the harsh cold of winter. The *Wehrmacht* generals expected that capture of the capital would win the war, most of the Red Army would be wiped out in one enormous battle, and what remained of the defenders would capitulate or retreat to the far side of the Urals.

In the end, Hitler overruled his generals. The Second Panzer Group from Army Group Center wheeled south, while the First Panzer Group of Army Group South struck north, forming a giant pincer movement. Commanders of Red Army formations in the region begged Stalin for permission to retreat, but their pleas were denied. On September 16, the two German spearheads made contact at the town of Lokvista more than one hundred miles east of Kiev, and the trap was shut. Over the next two weeks a savage battle raged that systematically compressed the *kessel*. Kiev was taken and more than seven hundred thousand Red Army soliders were killed or captured along with great masses of equipment.

At the same time, mechanized reinforcements from Army Group Center added punch to the German advance in the north. By mid-September all land routes to Leningrad were occupied by the invaders. Then the defenses around Leningrad stiffened after it came under the command of General Zhukov on September 10th. Four hundred thousand residents of the city labored to build fortifications, trenches, and tank traps, while 150,000 others took up arms to join the defending forces. Army Group North penetrated to within seven miles of the city, but as it ground through Zhukov's belts of fortifications, German casualites mounted rapidly. The food supplies of the invaders were already stretched to the limit, and OKH planners had no idea how they would feed the millions of civilians in Leningrad if it were overrun.

Hitler's decision was a cruel one: mount a siege, bomb the city relentlessly from the air, and refuse to accept any surrender by its garrision. The Germans hoped that the three million residents of Leningrad would simply die due to starvation and winter exposure, after which the invaders could raze the ruins and wipe the birthplace of the Soviet Revolution off the map. Quartermaster-General Eduard Wagner joked that the plan was to "let Petersburg stew in its own juice."[23] Army Group North dug in along the front lines, and the borrowed tank formations returned to Army Group Center. In the first winter of the nine-hundred-day seige, upward of five hundred thousand residents of Leningrad starved to death, but the defenders never stopped resisting.[24]

By early September, the Germans and their allies had advanced deep into the USSR, conquered a vast amount of territory, and encircled and destroyed several Soviet army groups. The Red Army lost 2,800,000 men in less than three months of fighting.[25] The destruction of the *kessel* around Kiev by the end of the month brought that number to more than 3,500,000 and netted a massive haul of tanks, artillery, ammunition, and other military equipment. The *Wehrmacht* and its allies had captured, wounded, or killed almost the entire prewar strength of the Red Army in the Western USSR. The front line now stretched from the Leningrad siege lines in the north to Smolensk in the center, and the shores of the Sea of Azov in the south. Across the Baltics and Ukraine, many civilians welcomed the invaders with flowers and the traditional greeting of bread and salt.

MOSCOW, THE DON BASIN, LENINGRAD, OR HALT?
THE SECOND GREAT DECISION

Remaining good campaign weather was limited as the autumn rainy season (known in Russian as *Rasputitsa* or "time without roads") would soon turn the region's dirt tracks to mud. This would be quickly followed by the brutal cold of the Russian winter. Hitler was confronted with several options:

1. Follow the counsel of Field Marshal Rundstedt, who called for halting the advance, taking up defensive winter positions along the Dnieper, and resuming the offensive in the spring of 1942.
2. Capture Leningrad so as to link up with the Finns and free up much of Army Group North for operations in the central region.
3. Follow up on the victory around Kiev to seize the rich agricultural lands of Eastern Ukraine and the industrial Don Basin.
4. Take the advice of many senior officers at OKH and Army Group Center, who wanted to drive east to take Moscow before the onset of winter.

It seems that the first option was never seriously considered. After the war, Rundstedt claimed that he was not alone in wanting to halt the offensive until 1942: "We ought to have stopped on the Dnieper after taking Kiev. I argued this strongly, and Field Marshal von Brauchitsch agreed with me. But Hitler, elated by the victory at Kiev, now wanted to push on, and felt sure he could capture Moscow."[26] Digging in along the east bank of the Dnieper would have required the Germans to retreat in places and give up territory that had been won in hard fighting. The Red Army still resisted stoutly, but it was increasingly forced to throw untrained and underarmed units of conscripts into the fight against the seasoned German attackers. The weather had yet to turn, Operation Barbarossa called for an advance to the Volga not the Dnieper, and great victories still seemed possible.

Next, in the north there was the option of mounting a bloody frontal assault to take Leningrad. The advantages to the German war effort of taking the city were obvious:

1. Its port could be used to ship supplies in bulk across the Baltic to the German armies along the north and central portions of the front. This would greatly alleviate the difficulties of relying on the limited road and rail lines stretching back into Poland.
2. Much of Army Group North manning the front lines around the city, numbering ten or more German divisions, would have been able to turn east toward Moscow.

3. Linking up Army Group North with the Finnish army would allow the Finns the tactical flexibility to shift forces northeast to cut the railway that connected Murmansk to the rest of the USSR.

In retrospect, choosing a siege over a direct assault was reasonable in light of the lateness of the year and the other options open to Hitler. In addition, the Baltic approaches of Leningrad (now St. Petersburg) are not ice free all year. Even after being captured and cleared, the port would have been closed to merchant shipping by ice until the spring thaw of 1942. Hitler and his generals were also wary of suffering high levels of casualties that were likely in pacifying a large urban area where military intelligence indicated the defenders planned to booby trap an enormous number of buildings with explosives and engage in house-to-house fighting.[27] Finally, the Finns refused to assist in an assault (to be discussed in chapter 18), which would have extended the time required for German forces to take the city. It was reasonable to expect that an assault would not be needed and a seige would lead to a collapse of resistance by the spring. The Red Army no longer controlled a land route to Leningrad to bring in supplies, and Göring boasted that the *Luftwaffe* could flatten the city.

Before the launch of Barbarossa, Hitler had declared Ukraine to be the other primary geographic target of the invasion. After the option of an assault on Leningrad had been passed over, why did Hitler not send his tanks eastward into the Don Basin and strike for the Volga River? Certainly the strongest German tank force was now concentrated in the south with the successful conclusion of the Battle of Kiev. Both the First and Second Panzer Groups were poised to roll east through Ukraine. Red Army formations opposing such an advance were weak after the destruction of the Southwestern Front. While remaining good weather was short, every factory, mine, and farm captured by Germany would represent resources that could be denied to the military of the USSR.

Nevertheless, senior German generals at OKH urged that all be staked on the capture of Moscow, and the commander of Army Group Center (von Bock) argued strongly for such an effort. German intelligence pointed to Red Army reserves being positioned around Moscow in readiness for a final defense of the capital. The opportunity to destroy the last major concentration of organized mobile Soviet field armies west of the Urals was an attractive target. Also, there was no guarantee that these Soviet formations wouldn't be sent south to strike the flank of an Army Group South push into the eastern Ukraine.

The option of an attack on Moscow had several additional advantages: the capital was a major industrial center in its own right and was the transportation and communications hub of the nation. A German victory over Moscow's defenders and capture of the city could lead to a collapse of Soviet resistance in a way that was unlikely were Leningrad or the Don Basin to be overrun by the invaders. With the recent defeat of the major Red Army forces around Kiev and the surrounding of Leningrad, Army Group Center could advance without fear of being attacked in force on the flanks. Finally, reinforcements could be sent to the center from both Army Groups North and South to strengthen the drive on Moscow.

Hitler chose to order the conquest of both Moscow and eastern Ukraine. In the end he won neither. He gave in to his generals and allowed them to mount the major effort in the center. Army Group North's tank forces rolled southeast. Similarly, the units detached from Army Group Center for the Battle of Kiev turned to strike northeast for the capital. The now weakened Army Group South was ordered to drive east across the Ukraine. This southern advance was halted at Rostov-on-Don in late November by a combination of the Russian winter and Red Army counterattacks. The main German effort, Operation Tyfun (Typhoon), the drive to capture Moscow, was launched in early October. It was composed of three Panzer Groups (Second, Third, Fourth), three infantry armies (Second, Fourth, Ninth), and almost two million men.

The central German attack started auspiciously: multiple armored advances broke through the defensive lines and created *kessels* between Vyazma and Bryansk, containing four Soviet armies (the Nineteenth, Twentieth, Twenty-Fourth, and Thirty-Second). These pockets shrank under relentless pressure and yielded more than five hundred thousand Red Army POWs. This fighting, along with Soviet counterattacks, slowed the attackers and allowed the defenders of Moscow, now under Zhukov's command, more time to prepare. As at Leningrad, he oversaw the construction of multiple defensive lines primarily constructed by civilian labor. The weather began to deteriorate: the first snow of the season fell, melted, and turned the dirt roads of the region to mud. The German advance slowed to a crawl. At the same time, the lack of a Japanese attack, and the approach of winter, led Stalin to take the gamble of moving approximately half the strength of his Far Eastern armies to Moscow's defense via the Trans-Siberian Railway. Also, along the rails came the first supplies of aid from the United States—a stream that soon became a flood. German troops of Army Group South were surprised to encounter Soviet forces driving US vehicles, and those of

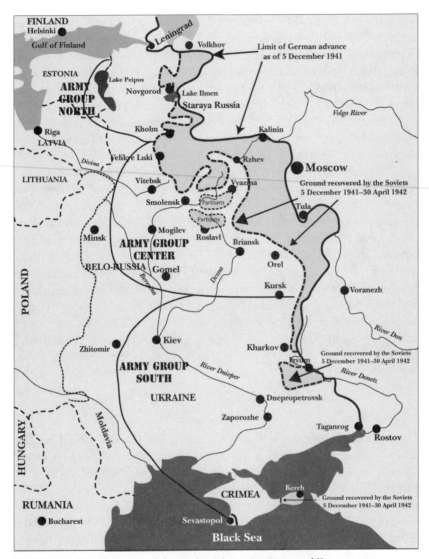

The Failure of Barbarossa and the Soviet Winter Counterattack[28]

Army Group Center in front of Moscow battled British tanks operated by the Red Army.[29]

As the thermometer dropped, the muddy roads froze, allowing the German offensive to surge forward for a time. The pace of advance slowed in the face of stiffening resistance, movement into heavily wooded terrain northwest of Moscow, and temperatures that plunged to as low as

−45 degrees Celsius. The invaders were not equipped for a winter campaign: sufficient heavy winter clothing had not been shipped to the front to protect the troops, and German artillery mechanisms and tank engines froze solid. Zhukov traded as much space for time as possible, fed enough divisions into the fight to keep the lines from collapsing, and built up reserves on the flanks of the German lines of advance. Finally, by the start of December, the invaders had reached the outer suburbs of Moscow but could push no further due to stiffening resistance, lack of supplies, and extremely cold weather.

Zhukov then launched a large-scale counteroffensive on both the northern and southern ends of the front before Moscow. The arrival of veteran Red Army divisions from the Far East greatly augmented the fighting power of the attack. In all, fifteen rifle divisions, three cavalry divisions, 1,700 tanks, and 1,500 aircraft made the trip west.[30] More than four hundred thousand of these "Siberians," equipped and trained for winter warfare, arrived after the first snowfall of 1941.[31] The arrival of such a large mass of effective reinforcements was a great shock to the *Ostheer*, which fell back from Moscow in the face of the assault. Despite severe losses in casualties and heavy equipment, the *Wehrmacht* showed itself to be as effective in defense as attack. By the end of January, the front lines had stabilized.

THE GERMAN OFFENSIVE OF 1942

Operation Barbarossa, the plan to conquer the western USSR in one season of campaigning, had failed. Many historians argue that Germany's ultimate defeat became inevitable when the invasion stalled in front of Moscow. Stalin, his generals, and the starving population of the USSR may have been hopeful after the defense of the capital, but their optimism was cautious at best. Victory was possible, but the military strength of the invaders remained immense and the Axis nations sent an additional twenty divisions to the front in 1942.

Stalin ordered a major offensive in the south near the city of Kharkov in May as a first step toward liberating the rest of occupied Ukraine. Unfortunately for the Red Army, Hitler had focused upon the same area where the Axis concentrated their forces. Operation Blau (Blue) had the objective of seizing the Don Basin to the banks of the Volga as well as a thrust to the south to capture the oil fields along the Caspian Sea.

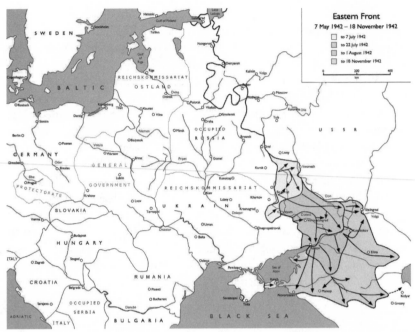

November 1942, the Furthest Reach of German Arms in the East[32]

The Soviets struck first and advanced toward Kharkov. The Germans soon launched counterattacks on either side of the Red Army vanguard, which created another enormous *kessel*. The Axis forces suffered around twenty thousand casualties versus more than a quarter million for the Red Army in yet another painful Soviet defeat. The Wehrmacht continued its offensive, and the panzer armies advanced quickly across the steppe. The Germans pushed ever further into the USSR—to the industrial center of Stalingrad on the Volga in the east and to Europe's tallest peak, Mount Elbrus, in the south. As in 1941, logistical problems plagued the invaders as they pushed forward into stiffening Red Army resistance.

After declining an urban battle in Leningrad and denied one in Moscow, Hitler allowed his forces to fight a confined attritional battle in the heart of Stalingrad. Here his army's doctrine of fast-moving armored warfare degenerated into house-to-house and hand-to-hand fighting. Once again, Zhukov rushed in to take command of a threatened city. Just as in front of Moscow the year before, the German advance slowed to a crawl while the Soviets built up reserves to launch a winter counteroffensive. This time Zhukov's double-envelopment made rapid gains: the Axis flanks, manned by Romanian, Hungarian, and Italian divisions, collapsed. This time it was the German Sixth Army that found itself surrounded and trapped in a *kessel*: more than two hundred thousand of the invaders were either killed or captured by early February 1943.

With the destruction of the Sixth Army, the German position in the south was unhinged and a massive retreat from the Caucasus ensued. The Soviets pushed forward and reconquered the eastern Ukraine before the lines once again stabilized. After the start of 1943, the *Wehrmacht* was increasingly outnumbered, underequipped, and undersupplied. In contrast, the Red Army continued to expand and equipped its soldiers with the vast output of the economies of the USSR and the United States. While Germany still held a huge amount of territory in the USSR, its days on Soviet soil were numbered. The *Wehrmacht*'s forces in the east remained massive, and years of fighting lay ahead, but the strategic initiative had passed to the Red Army. Hitler's dream to fight and win German hegemony over Europe was slowly strangled by a noose drawn tight by the combined resources of the USSR, Britain, and United States.

· 9 ·

Historical Explanations for Germany's Defeat in the East

$\mathcal{T}$he German invasion failed to conquer the USSR. That is a fact. In dispute is the reason for that failure. The final portion of this book will put forward a novel diplomatic reason for the Soviet victory. To make that argument, it is first necessary to outline the most commonly offered explanations in historical literature for Germany's defeat and discuss why they are insufficient to explain its cause. These arguments can be grouped into the following narratives:

1. The invasion was doomed from the start due to the inadequate size of the invasion force to overwhelm the massive mobilization potential of the Red Army. The Germans could not possibly defeat the USSR in one campaign season, and they failed to plan for a war that would last into 1942.
2. The war in the east would have been won if only Hitler had listened to his generals and ordered an all-out drive on Moscow in August 1941 after the German victories around Smolensk.
3. Unusually harsh weather and poor infrastructure kept the German army from capturing Moscow in November 1941 and winning the war.
4. Barbarossa only failed due to a late launch of the offensive caused by Hitler's emotional decision to first attack Yugoslavia and Greece in the spring of 1941. With an earlier start to the invasion, Moscow would have fallen and with it, Soviet resistance would have collapsed.

5. The war in the east would have been won if only Hitler had ignored his generals and ordered an all-out drive to the Volga and the Caucases after the German victories around Kiev in 1941.
6. The Nazis' genocidal policies in conquered Soviet territory stiffened resistance across the USSR to such an extent that the Red Army was able to resist and eventually drive back the invaders.

WAS THE INVASION FORCE TOO SMALL?

A common explanation given by historians for the failure of Barbarossa is that the Axis invasion force was simply of insufficient size to defeat the Red Army and conquer the vast territory of the USSR west of the Urals. This narrative explains that the Germans bet everything that Soviet resistance would collapse after the first battles along the frontier. The argument is that there was no way Germany could prevail in a long fight against the massive resources and manpower of the USSR. Consider the following statements from historian Craig Luther, and the British Imperial War Museum:

"Foremost among them, Germany's attack on the Soviet Union failed because it was fatally underpowered. The *Wehrmacht*'s eastern armies, despite their superior training, experience, and discipline, were simply too few in number—too few men, armored vehicles, aircraft, etc.—to cope successfully with the unprecedented scope and unique challenges of the Russian theater of war."[1]

"Operation 'Barbarossa' had clearly failed. Despite the serious losses inflicted on the Red Army and extensive territorial gains, the mission to completely destroy Soviet fighting power and force a capitulation was not achieved. One of the most important reasons for this was poor strategic planning. The Germans had no satisfactory long-term plan for the invasion. They mistakenly assumed that the campaign would be a short one, and that the Soviets would give in after suffering the shock of massive initial defeats. Hitler had assured the High Command that 'We have only to kick in the front door and the whole rotten edifice will come tumbling down.' But Russia was not France. The shock value of the initial *Blitzkrieg* was dissipated by the vast distances, logistical difficulties and Soviet troop numbers, all of which caused attritional losses of German forces which could not be sustained."[2]

Before considering the ratio of forces on either side of Barbarossa, it is worth perusing the annals of armed conflict regarding an argument that the Axis invasion force was too small in 1941. Military history is replete with instances of small armies conquering great expanses of territory and successfully defeating much larger opposing armies. Extreme examples of this took place in the 1500s when tiny bands of Spanish conquistadors prevailed over the mighty Aztec and Inca empires. Cortez and Pizarro certainly had too few men, cannon, and horses to cope successfully with the unprecedented scope and unique challenges of the Mexican or Peruvian theaters of war . . . yet the Spanish were triumphant.

Of course, the invaders in those cases had significant technological advantages over the native defenders that dwarfed the qualitative advantages of the *Wehrmacht* in 1941. However, throughout history there are many cases of invading forces with better discipline and élan defeating significantly larger and similarly equipped defending forces. Examples range across time and geography from Alexander the Great defeating the vast Persian Empire, to Caesar's conquest of Gaul, the Arab invasion of Egypt in 639, the US march from Vera Cruz to Mexico City in 1847, the Japanese victory in the First Sino-Japanese War, and even the Israeli victories in 1948, 1967, and 1973. The record of military history yields the conclusion that often size does not matter.

Many historians have argued that the invasion failed in the summer of 1941 when the Red Army did not immediately collapse under the initial blows of the invasion. According to David Stahel, "Although by 1941 the *Wehrmacht* was the most refined and professional fighting force in the world, its battlefield superiority at the tactical and operational level did not make it infallible strategically. Indeed the defeat of the *Ostheer* did not begin with the first retreats (and at times routs) following the launch of the Soviet winter offensive in December 1941. By this time German plans to conquer the Soviet Union had long since failed and the fact that the Soviets were now pushing the Germans back only further confirmed Germany's crisis in the east."[3]

Where today with hindsight some see an inevitable Soviet triumph, Stalin did not share such a view at the time. His actions were indicative of a man struggling to avoid abject defeat rather than one who expected ultimate victory. On at least one occasion in the second half of 1941, he put out peace feelers to see if Germany would agree to an armistice and end the war. In return for peace, he was willing to cede a huge amount of territory: his initial offer was Ukraine, the Baltics, and the lands he had seized from Finland, Poland, and Romania. "Molotov described the offer of territory in exchange for an end to the fighting as 'a possible second Brest-Litovsk Treaty,' and said that if Lenin could have the courage to make such a step, we had the same intention now."[4] Hitler seriously considered the peace proposal, and on August 18 he discussed its merits with Reich minister Joseph Goebbels.[5] In the end, the Führer chose to continue the war. Stalin also asked the United States to act as an intermediary with Finland on August 5, 1941. In this case, he offered to return all the territory taken from the Finns in the Winter War of 1939 to 1940 in return for peace.[6] Again the Soviet dictator's offer was spurned.

It is certainly correct that the Germans hoped for a collapse of Soviet resistance after the first set of massive encirclement battles west of the Dnieper. Military experts in London, Tokyo, and Washington expected just such a result. Nonetheless, it is incorrect to conclude that the Axis were incapable of fighting a long war in the interior of the USSR. Such a conclusion ignores:

1. Massive German victories of 1941 that took place over six hard months of fighting. These were titanic battles won by the *Wehrmacht* and its allies, which brought the invaders to the outskirts of Moscow, Leningrad, and Rostov-on-Don, capturing a large percentage of the industrial, agricultural, and population base of the USSR.
2. Subsequent offensives in 1942, which shattered the Red Army's front lines and pushed the Soviets back to the banks of the Volga and deep into the Caucasus.
3. The Axis's overall economic output advantage by November 1941.
4. The history of the German-Russian conflict in 1914 to 1917.
5. The reality that it took more than three years of grinding combat before the Red Army finally ejected *Wehrmacht* forces from its soil and regained its 1941 frontiers.
6. The Nazi government's diplomatic achievement of convincing allies to deploy their armies to fight on the Eastern Front.
7. Success by the invaders in raising hundreds of thousands of non-German volunteers from Iberia to the Caucasus to fight the Red Army.

As already noted, the Barbarossa invasion force was roughly comparable in manpower to that of the defending units in the western districts of the USSR. In contrast to the experience of much of the German military, more than a third of the divisions of the Red Army were raw recruits, poorly trained and equipped—they were not frontline fighting formations.[7] The forward strategic positioning of the bulk of the Red Army in border positions that had not yet been fortified, combined with the qualitative advantages of the *Wehrmacht* led to dramatic early victories for the invaders in 1941. The damage done to the military capability of the USSR in the first few months of the conflict was devastating. At the end of September, the Red Army had suffered more than two million men killed, and a similar number had become POWs compared to German dead of 150,000 and only a small number captured.[8] By the launch of Operation Tyfun, the Axis invaders in the western USSR outnumbered the Red Army defenders.[9] In excess of 20 percent of the USSR's surviving population now lived under German occupation.

In addition, the invaders had seized a great deal of the Soviet Union's economic base. By November, the Germans had captured 57 percent of the USSR's coal production, 68 percent of its pig iron, 58 percent of its steel, 60 percent of its aluminum, and 38 percent of its grain.[10] While the Soviets were exceedingly successful in evacuating industrial plant and equipment to the east by rail, many factories still fell into German hands. In addition, it was simply not possible to reposition mines and farms.

While the entire structure of the Soviet Union may not have collapsed with the first blow, the Germans certainly had "kicked in the door" and brutally damaged the USSR in both military and economic terms. In light of the territorial, matériel, and battlefield advantages gained by the launch of Operation Tyfun, it is difficult to understand how historians can conclude that Germany had already lost the war in October 1941. Marshal Zhukov relates in his memoirs that the odds were stacked against his forces during the defense of the capital: "At the time the German troops started advancing on Moscow, three fronts were defending the far approaches to the capital . . . In late September the three fronts had a combined strength of about 800,000 combatants, 782 tanks, and 6808 mortars and guns, 545 planes. . . . After regrouping his troops in the Moscow sector the enemy had a force superior to the combined strength of our three fronts. He had 1.25 times as many men, 2.2 times as many tanks, 2.1 times as many mortars and guns, and 1.7 times as many planes."[11]

The October battles of the Vyazma and Bryansk pockets yielded another half million Soviet POWs to be marched to the rear. A combination of the turn in the weather, Soviet reinforcements from Siberia, and the efforts of Moscow's civilians stopped the *Wehrmacht* advance at the outskirts of the capital. It is logical to argue that the failure to capture Moscow and the subsequent winter counteroffensive that drove the invaders back was an exceedingly serious blow to the German plan of conquest. Yet it is a fallacy to conclude that Hitler's great gamble had failed simply because the Red

Army continued to resist the German onslaught after the initial battles along the frontiers. A final Soviet victory was not inevitable even after the defeat of Army Group Center in front of Moscow in December 1941.

As already outlined, Hitler reoriented the focus of the invasion to the southeast in the spring of 1942. The German advance successfully overran the Red Army front lines and pushed into the industrial eastern Ukraine and south toward the oil wells of the Caucasus. Zhukov saw that this was potentially life threatening for the Soviet state: "Capture of the Ukraine was of particular economic importance for the Germans. They wanted to overrun the Ukraine as quickly as possible in order to deprive the Soviet Union of its foremost industrial and agricultural base and at the same time to boost their own economic potential with Krivoi Rog iron ore, Donets coal, Nikopol manganese and Ukrainian grain."[12]

The Germans extended themselves to the very limit along a supply line that reached back one thousand miles to the 1941 frontiers. They then stumbled into a savage urban battle in Stalingrad, which blunted their military advantages and played to those of the Red Army. Had Hitler halted his armies outside Stalingrad, held the territory captured in 1942, and mobilized its resources, an ultimate Soviet victory would have been much more in doubt. The German offensives to the Volga and into the Caucasus were not the actions of a nation that had lost the war in 1941.

The USSR did wear down the German armies in the east and eventually marched on Berlin, but winning such a long conflict against the Nazis was not a foregone conclusion. Today many historians point to the overbearing size of the population and economic output of the USSR versus the Axis to explain the inevitability of Soviet victory. However, such disparities were just as evident in World War I, yet the Russians were the ones to break. Hitler and his generals lived through that earlier conflict and knew that Russian resistance was not infinite. In 1914 the Triple Entente (France, Russia, and Britain) had a combined GDP 60 percent larger than that of the Central Powers (the German, Austrian, and Ottoman empires), and the imbalance increased further when the economies of allies Serbia, Belgium, and Japan were included. The Entente had an even greater population advantage with a total more than four times that of the Central Powers.[13] Despite these long odds, having its economies throttled by a British naval blockade and fighting massive battles along the trench lines in France, Belgium, and Italy, the Central Powers were able to bleed the Russian Empire white and force its collapse.

Those who argue that Germany could not win an extended conflict in the east point to the massive Soviet economy and population as determinant for a victory of the Red Army in an extended battle of attrition. Such a conclusion does not seem to take into account the previously discussed data (see table 6) that by June 1941 the economic output of the newly enlarged German Empire and its European allies was significantly larger than that of the USSR. This imbalance in the Axis's favor became greater in the second half of 1941 with the seizing of much of the Soviet nation's best agricultural land, natural resources, and industrial plant and equipment. In addition, by the start of 1942, after taking into account the millions of military and civilian casualties as well as cities and territories lost to the invasion, the USSR no longer had an advantage over its adversaries in overall population.

Killing or capturing the Red Army's soldiers, denying the USSR critical resources, and destroying its industry was a logical strategy for victory after the initial resilience shown by the Soviet state in 1941. Recent history had shown that the Russians would eventually sue for peace after a long war. Logically such a surrender could be accelerated if Germany inflicted enormous casualties and seized large amounts of Soviet territory early in a conflict. The Soviets only prevailed in a long war of attrition through the most ruthless conversion of all their remaining national output to the war effort combined with massive and sustained material assistance from Britain and the United States.

The butcher's bill for the Red Army is almost unimaginable today. Almost as astounding is the relentless progression of human losses over the course of war. Most today hold the impression that the Soviets suffered the worst losses in 1941 in the early months of the invasion, or in 1942 in the maelstrom around Stalingrad. Yet 1943 was the Red Army's bloodiest year when it suffered nearly eight million total casualties. The following year was only slightly less terrible with almost seven million additional casualties. In fact, less than half of the USSR's military losses in World War II took place in 1941 and 1942. While the battles of Moscow and Stalingrad were terrible defeats for Germany, the fighting was far from done. The USSR only won the war in the long, grinding months of combat that

Table 8.   Red Army Losses 1941–1945[14]

Time Period	Irrecoverable Losses	Wounded and Sick	Total Losses
1941	3,137,673	1,336,147	4,473,820
1942	3,258,216	4,111,062	7,369,278
1943	2,312,429	5,545,074	7,857,503
1944	1,763,891	5,114,750	6,878,641
1945	800,817	2,212,690	3,013,507
Totals	**11,273,026**	**18,319,723**	**29,592,749**

Note: This data does not include 36K casualties suffered in the Far East in 1945

stretched from the start of 1943 to the middle of 1945. Against the more than 29 million casualties suffered by the Soviet military, the Wehrmecht recorded dramatically lower losses of "only" 5.3 million dead in World War II of which close to 4 million died in the fight against the USSR.[15] Unfortunately for its enemies in World War II, just as in 1914 to 1918, the German military was a terribly effective killing machine.

Working against an "inevitable" USSR victory was the success Germany had in raising local levies in captured Soviet territory, motivating allied nations to deploy troops to the Eastern Front, and recruiting willing soldiers from across the rest of Europe. Several other European nations were willing to send their men to fight and die in the vast interior of the USSR. By the time of the great struggle around Stalingrad, more than one in four divisions in the invading forces were non-German. These formations were of varying quality, but many were quite effective on the battlefield (Finland's army, for example), and even weaker units could still hold quiet portions of the front. Many today believe that these allies of the Nazis did little fighting and added only marginally to the Axis's effort in the east. The more than seven hundred thousand Romanian, Hungarian, and Italian soldiers who died fighting the Red Army refute such a conclusion.[16]

The Nazi's *Waffen-SS* military organization also attained high levels of recruitment into its ranks from outside Germany. In many cases, these were volunteers swept up in the Nazi's warped ideology. The recruits came from all across Europe—from Spain to Armenia, from Norway to Albania. More than 140,000 men from occupied portions of the USSR and 180,000 from across the rest of Europe joined and fought in the *Waffen-SS*.[17] Many of these units, such as the 33rd *Waffen-Grenadier* Division (Frenchmen), the 11th *SS-Freiwilligen Panzergrenadier* Division (Scandinavians), and the 23rd *SS-Freiwilligen Panzergrenadier* Division (Dutch), fought for years on the Eastern Front. Such men were among the final fanatical defenders of Hitler's Berlin bunker at the end of the war.

As the war in the east extended past 1941, the *Wehrmacht* allowed hundreds of thousands of Soviet citizens to join in the fight against the Red Army. These men served in many capacities in the German war effort and were referred to by various titles such as "volunteer assistants" (*Hilfswilliger*, known as *Hiwis*) or "eastern troops" (*Osttruppen*). Some were true volunteers, but others were Red Army POWs who joined solely to avoid slave labor or death by starvation. They served in rear area security units in antipartisan roles, as concentration camp guards, or joined frontline fighting formations of the German army. Regardless of the reason they joined,

Table 9. German/Allied Forces on the Eastern Front by Division/Division Equivalents[18]

Date	Germany	Romania	Hungary	Italy	Slovak Republic	Finland	Spain	Total	Total Non-German	Percent Non-German
June 1941	121	15.5			0.5	16	1	153	32	21%
September 1941	137	15.5	1.5	3	2	16	1	176	39	22%
January 1942	149	7	3	3	2	16	1	181	32	18%
June 1942	171	13	9	3.5	1	16	1	214.5	43.5	20%
November 1942	173	27	12	11.5	1	16	1	241.5	68.5	28%
April 1943	177	10	5		1	16	1	209	33	16%
December 1943	173	9	9		1	16		155	36	17%
September 1944	134		21					155.5	21	14%
November 1944	139		16.5					190	16.5	11%
March 1945	179		11						11	6%

the NKVD referred to these men as "former Russians," and they awaited certain death or transport to the Gulag if captured.

One metric of the success of German recruitment of these local auxiliaries is that more than fifty thousand Hiwis were serving in the *Wehrmacht's* Sixth Army in late 1942 when the Soviets surrounded it around Stalingrad.[19] This represented more than 25 percent of that army's total manpower, and some units such as the 76th and 71st Infantry divisions had as many Hiwis as Germans. These "former Russians" often fought to the death and served to increase the killing power of the *Wehrmacht*.

Table 10.   Hiwi's in the 6th Army[20]

Division	Germans	HIWIs	% HIWIs
295th Infantry	6,899	50	1
24th Panzer	10,950	1,675	13
16th Panzer	11,051	1,843	14
384th Infantry	8,821	1,804	17
44th Infantry	10,613	2,365	18
60th Motorized	8,933	2,071	19
305th Infantry	6,683	1,562	19
100th Jaeger	8,675	2,132	20
79th Infantry	7,980	2,018	20
389th Infantry	7,540	2,379	24
94th Infantry	7,269	2,581	26
376th Infantry	8,187	4,105	33
3rd Motorized	8,653	4,530	34
113th Infantry	9,461	5,564	37
71st Infantry	8,906	8,134	48
76th Infantry	8,023	8,033	50
14th Panzer	588	934	61
Totals	**139,232**	**51,780**	**27**

So, for many reasons it is difficult to conclude that the invasion of the USSR failed due to insufficient size of the attacking force. While it was necessary that the Red Army continued to fight, such resistance did not automatically ensure an ultimate victory for the USSR. The *Wehrmacht* won dazzling victories in 1942, and was able to inflict huge numbers of casualties in 1943 and 1944 while still fighting in occupied territory. Germany and its allies controlled an economic preponderance over the USSR in June 1941 that only increased as the *Wehrmacht* rolled east into Soviet territory. While the Red Army could draw upon a massive pool of manpower, so too did the Germans, who were able to rally entire allied armies and well over a million non-German recruits to fight in the east.

World War II: a conflict of devastation like no other. Tens of millions died and scores of cities suffered similar fates to that of Rotterdam, seen here after the German aerial bombardment of June 1940. Source: National Archives.

Arguably the most famous image of the war: The "Big Three" of Churchill, Roosevelt, and Stalin at Yalta in February 1945. Thankfully, no similar summit of the German, Finnish, and Japanese leaders took place prior to the invasion of the USSR in 1941. Source: National Archives.

Kaiser Wilhelm III with his generals Paul von Hindenburg (left) and Erich Ludendorff (right) in 1917. The policy of the kaiser's government, the Septemberprogramm, was the conquest of much of the northern European Plain with designs on large parts of Russia, France, and the Low Countries. Photo by Robert Sennecke (1885–1940) from the Huis Doorn fotocollectie as uploaded to Wikimedia, https://commons.wikimedia.org/wiki/File:Hindenburg,_Kaiser,_Ludendorff_HD-SN-99-02150.JPG.

Hitler in occupied Poland, September 1939. Several years of negotiation, bluff, and audacity gained Hitler significant territorial gains for Germany. The era of peaceful diplomacy ended with the invasion of Poland and declarations of war from France and Britain. Photo by Josef Gierse as uploaded to Wikimedia, https://commons.wikimedia.org/wiki/File:Hitler_Polen_Sep._39_Josef_Gierse.JPG.

Vyacheslav Molotov (seated) signs the Soviet-German Non-Aggression Pact in Moscow while Joachim von Ribbentrop looks on (behind in suit). Joseph Stalin (in white uniform) expected the agreement would lead to a lengthy war in the west that would exhaust Germany, France, and Britain. Source: National Archives.

British soldiers march off into captivity after the battle of Dunkirk, June 1940. While bloodily defeated on the Continent, Britain remained resolute behind its channel moat and prepared to repel a German invasion. Source: National Archives.

Hitler in Paris, June 1940. France, Poland, and the Low Countries had been conquered. Like Napoleon before him, the German leader dominated Western Europe, but to solidify his gains he had to deal with a determined British foe and Russia (now the USSR) looming as a threat in the east. Source: National Archives.

Romania's oil fields at Ploesti, the Achilles' heel of the Third Reich. Hitler feared an air strike on these facilities could cripple the German economy. The Wehrmacht's invasion of Greece and the USSR precluded such an event until August 1943 when US B-24s based in Libya bombed the area. Source: 44th Bomb Group Photograph Collection as uploaded to Wikimedia by the United States Army Center of Military History.

Stalin and Molotov. Thankfully for world civilization they turned down an offer to join the Axis coalition in November 1940. Instead of acting on Hitler's encouragement to move south and conquer British holdings in the Middle East, they demanded Germany accept Soviet military control of Finland and Bulgaria. The two totalitarian empires moved ever closer to war. Source: May 30, 1932, issue of Projector *(Spotlight) as uploaded to Wikimedia, https:// commons.wikimedia.org/wiki/ File:Vycheslav_Molotov_and_ Joseph_Stalin_May_1932.jpg.*

Hitler viewed Soviet and British support of Yugoslavia and Greece as a threat and ordered an Axis invasion of these two Balkan nations in April 1941. Forces of Germany, Italy, Bulgaria, and Hungary jointly invaded Yugoslavia and Greece and secured the Axis's southern flank before the launch of Operation Barbarossa in June. Here Bulgarian troops advance in northern Greece. Source: Bulgarien—Land, Volk, Geschichte, Kultur, Wirtschaft *by von Kurt Haucke, photographer unknown, as uploaded to Wikimedia, https://commons.wikimedia.org/wiki/File:Bulgarians_1941.jpg.*

Captured Soviet equipment and fallen soldiers near Suomussalmi. The pathetic performance of the Red Army in its invasion of Finland in November 1939 convinced Hitler and many others that the USSR was a colossus with feet of clay. Source: Sa-kuva (Finnish Armed Forces photograph), photographer unknown, as uploaded to Finna.fi, https://finna.fi/Record/sa-kuva.sa-kuva-105710.

Hitler met with the leaders of several Allied nations (here seen with Italy's Benito Mussolini). German diplomacy successfully assembled a large European coalition that committed significant armed forces to fight with the Wehrmacht in the USSR. Source: Ladislav Luppa, photographer, as uploaded to Wikimedia, https://commons.wikimedia.org/wiki/File:Mussolini_a_Hitler_-_Berl%C3%ADn_1937.jpg.

Yosuke Matsuoka, Japan's Minister of Foreign Affairs 1940–1941. While an ardent proponent of his nation joining Germany in a war on the USSR, he was told nothing of the Barbarossa invasion plan when he traveled to Berlin in late March 1941. Hitler's failure to coordinate strategy with his most militarily powerful ally was a major cause of the final Axis defeat. Source: Wikimedia, https://commons .wikimedia.org/wiki/File:Yohsuke_matsuoka1932.jpg

Marshal Zhukov, arguably the most successful and consequential general of World War II. Here he is pictured in early September 1941 immediately before assuming command of the faltering defenses of Leningrad. Later he would take on similar roles in the battles of Moscow and Stalingrad and then lead Soviet armies in the counteroffensives that led to final German defeat. Source: RIA Novosti archive, image #2410 (Russian International News Agency), P. Bernstein photographer, as uploaded to Wikimedia, https://commons.wikimedia.org/ wiki/File:RIAN_archive_2410_Marshal_ Zhukov_speaking.jpg.

With the defenses of Leningrad stiffening in September of 1941, Hitler chose to besiege the city rather than opt for a costly frontal assault. Leningrad's population suffered through a nine-hundred-day siege in which more than a million of the city's inhabitants died. In this photo from October 1942, men labor to bury the victims. Source: RIA Novosti archive, image #216 (Russian International News Agency), Boris Kudoyarov photographer, as uploaded to Wikimedia, https://commons .wikimedia.org/wiki/File:RIAN_archive_216_The_Volkovo_cemetery.jpg.

Zhukov assumed command of the defenses of Moscow in early October 1941. Under his direction, more than one hundred thousand civilians labored to dig ditches and build obstacles that stretched in excess of one hundred miles to impede the German advance. Source: United States Information Agency as uploaded to Wikimedia, https://commons.wikimedia.org/wiki/File:Battle_of_Moscow.jpg.

As the German effort to take Moscow stalled, just west of the city, the Red Army launched a counteroffensive comprised of newly recruited reserve armies leavened by seasoned formations arriving from Siberia. Here, Soviet tanks and infantry attack in early February 1942. Source: RIA Novosti archive, image #301 (Russian International News Agency), Maksimov photographer, as uploaded to Wikimedia, https://commons.wikimedia.org/wiki/File:RIAN_archive_301_An_attack.jpg.

German forces advanced east and south to the outskirts of the Soviet oil fields in the Caucasus in 1942. Here Wehrmaht infantry attack toward burning oil storage facilities in Maikop, a remarkable 1,500 miles from Berlin. This was the high tide of the German advance as the Soviet victory at Stalingrad began the Red Army's long push west that culminated in the fall of Berlin. Source: Waralbum. ru/46226, photographer unknown, as uploaded to Wikipedia, https:// commons.wikimedia.org/wiki/ File:German_soldiers_Maikop.jpg.

Italian POWs march into Soviet captivity in Ukraine in early 1943. Military formations of Germany's allies made up more than a quarter of the invading forces in the USSR by late 1942. Source: Ukrainian public domain photo scanned from L'Amata Rossa e la dsifatta italiana, di G. Scotoni, Casa Editrice Panorama, 2007, as uploaded to Wikimedia, https://commons.wikimedia.org/wiki/File:Italiani_-ARMIR.jpg.

Vidkun Quisling inspects troops of the Norwegian Hirden. Hundreds of thousands of such men from across Europe volunteered to join the Waffen-SS and fight in the East. Source: Image from Riksarkivet (National Archives of Norway)/Filmavisen 1943 #66 Norsk Film AS as uploaded to Wikipedia, https://commons.wikimedia.org/wiki/File:Vidkun_Quisling_og_Oliver_Møystad_(hirdsjef_og_sjef_for_sikkerhetspolitiet)_inspiserer_Rikshirden.jpg.

Stalin had no intention of surrendering Moscow intact and planned a scorched-earth defense similar to what played out in the Battle of Stalingrad. More than one thousand of the city's major buildings, such as the Bolshoi Theater (pictured here in 1942), were mined with explosives, and guerrilla formations were organized to fight from the sewers. Source: RIA Novosti archive, image #42402 (Russian International News Agency), Alexander Krasavin photographer, as uploaded to Wikimeida, https://commons.wikimedia.org/wiki/File:RIAN_archive_42402_Protective_camouflage_on_the_building_of_the_Bolshoi_Theater.jpg.

Hundreds of thousands of Red Army soldiers continued to surrender after 1941 despite the inhumane German treatment of such POWs that led to millions dying of starvation and exposure. Here, soon after the start of the invasion, Heinrich Himmler and entourage inspect Soviet captives held in open fields behind barbed wire fences. Source: US National Archives and Records Administration, NAID 540164, collection of Heinrich Hoffman, as uploaded to Wikimedia, https://commons.wikimedia.org/wiki/File:Himmler_besichtigt_die_Gefangenenlager_in_Russland._Heinrich_Himmler_inspects_a_prisoner_of_war_camp_in_Russia,_circa..._-_NARA_-_540164.jpg.

While partisans harassed German rear areas, hatred of the Stalin's government was such that more than a million Soviet citizens volunteered to fight on the side of the Axis. Pictured, a group of partisan hunters near Novgorod in 1942. Source: Personal collection from former German sergeant fighting in the Luftwaffen Division Meindl in the USSR in 1942–1943 as uploaded by his son to Wikimedia, https://commons.wikimedia.org/wiki/File:Antisovjet_russian_partisan_hunters_1942.jpg.

Japanese soldiers posing with captured Red Army equipment during the Battle of Khalkhin Gol in 1939. Throughout the 1930s, warfare repeatedly broke out along the border of the USSR and Japanese-controlled Manchuria. Many in Tokyo agitated for a general war of conquest against the Soviets. Image from Contemporary Military Historian from a photograph in the public domain in Japan and the United States. Source: unknown photographer, as uploaded to Wikimedia, https://commons.wikimedia.org/wiki/File:Battle_of_Khalkhin_Gol-Japanese_soldiers.jpg.

Emperor Hirohito presiding over a meeting at Imperial General Headquarters in Tokyo, 1943. Hirohito's intervention to reverse the troop build-up in Manchuria in the summer of 1941 was critical in the successful defense of Moscow and the Japanese decision to attack Pearl Harbor, Manila, and Singapore. Source: Asahi Shimbum, photographer unknown, as uploaded to Wikimedia, https:// commons.wikimedia.org/wiki/File:Imperial_general_headquaters_meeting.jpg.

The prodigious output of the US economy was able to supply the USSR with everything Stalin requested except the Red Army soldiers willing to do the fighting and dying. Here workers inspect the nose cones of A-20 HAVOC light bomber aircraft. The Soviets received 2,900 of these planes representing almost 40% of those built. Source: National Archives.

US Lend-Lease deliveries of more than four hundred thousand trucks and jeeps as well as the petrol to fuel them had a dramatic impact on the mobility of the Soviet forces as they advanced westward. Here, soldiers of the First Polish Army fighting under Red Army command in Warsaw stand next to their Jeep, which likely arrived from the United States via the Soviet port of Vladivostok. Source: Marek Tuszyński, photographer, 1945, as uploaded to Wikimedia, https://commons.wikimedia.org/wiki/File:Aleje_Jerozolimskie_waf-2072-1002-40_(1945).jpg.

Finnish president Risto Ryti (right) and Marshal Carl Mannerheim (left) walk with Hitler after he landed in their country on June 1942. Hitler reiterated previous German requests that Finland's armed forces aid in the siege of Leningrad and seize the railway line leading to Murmansk. Nothing came of these efforts, and the Finns remained in static positions across the front. Source: SA- Kuva (Finnish Armed Forces photograph), photographer unknown, as uploaded to Wikimedia, https://fi.wikipedia.org/wiki/Tiedosto:Hitler_visit_Finland_1942.jpg#/media/File:Hitler_visit_Finland_1942.jpg jpg.

Overwhelming Red Army forces launched an offensive along the Finnish front lines in June 1944. Germany rushed aid to their ally, such as the Panzerfauste these Finns are carrying as they pass a destroyed Soviet T-34 tank during the Battle of Tali-Ihantala. Nevertheless, the Finns were driven back and forced to accept a humiliating peace treaty with the USSR. Source: Military Museum of Finland/ SA- Kuva (Finnish Armed Forces photograph), Hedenström photographer, as uploaded to Wikimedia, https://commons.wikimedia.org/wiki/File:Tali-Ihantala.jpg#/media/File:Tali-Ihantala.jpg.

Contrary to the myth of the Blitzkrieg, the German army relied heavily on horses—and was never as motorized or mechanized as popularly believed. Source: Michael Olive and Robert Edwards, Operation Barbarossa 1941 (Mechanicsburg, PA: Stackpole Books, 2012), 8.

· *10* ·

An Early Drive for Moscow

$\mathcal{A}$s previously discussed, many of Hitler's generals argued that the focus of Barbarossa should be the earliest possible capture of Moscow. After the destruction of the Soviet 16th, 19th, and 20th armies around Smolensk at the end of July, the road to the capital appeared to be open, and the generals of Army Group Center and OKH wanted to push east immediately. These military officers seemed to believe that the conflict in the USSR was simply a more modern version of the wars Clausewitz experienced in the 1800s: defeat the opponent's main army in the field, capture its capital, and the enemy leadership will sue for peace. Of course, within the first month of Barbarossa, the Germans had already made the war one of great brutality, which turned Eastern Europe into an enormous abattoir. This was a conflict between opposing ideologies, entire peoples, and masses of resources to be conscripted into battle. The war in the East was most certainly not a game of "capture the flag."

Hitler disagreed with his military commanders. He worried that such a bold advance on Moscow would expose his forces to flank attacks from both the north and the south. Greater importance was assigned to the destruction of the Soviet armies around Kiev and conquest of the Ukraine, and in the north to surrounding Leningrad and linking up with the Finnish army. After a number of conferences, memos, and heated debates with his generals, Hitler chose to detach significant forces of Army Group Center to the north and south. After the fighting ended, several of the surviving *Wehrmacht* military leaders blamed this decision for the loss of the war in the east. Many historians agree that a strike for Moscow in August 1941 would have led to a German victory over the

USSR. Consider the following statements from R. H. S. Stolfi, Andrew Roberts, and Theodore Ropp:

"As the German army stood immobilized by Hitler's concern for indecisive gains on the wings of the advance, a campaign and a war that could have been won in August 1941 irrevocably slipped away. At this moment, around the end of July 1941, the Germans came closer to defeating the Soviet Union and winning the Second World War in Europe than at any other time. . . . Surely, had the Germans reached Moscow in August 1941 they would have won the campaign and war."[1]

"The Germans were unlucky with the weather, it is true, but they did not devote enough troops to this great assault on Moscow, and they had already lost 750,000 casualties, including 8,000 officers and nearly 200,000 men killed, since the launch of Barbarossa. It is no exaggeration to state that the outcome of the Second World War hung in the balance during this massive attack, but by 5 December the 3rd and 2nd *Panzer* Groups had to be withdrawn to the Istria-Kiln and Don-Ulla Lines respectively and put on the defensive. Could the Germans have taken Moscow if Hitler had not drawn Guderian's Second *Panzer* Army and the Second Army more than 250 miles south between 23 August and 30 September? We cannot know for certain, but must suspect so."[2]

"Hitler decided, instead, to detach some forces from Bock's wings to aid Leeb and Rundstedt. In the Ukraine Rundstedt captured Simeon Budenny's whole group of armies. This was Hitler's greatest single victory and, perhaps, his greatest blunder . . . his August postponement of the drive on Moscow cannot be defended."[3]

To analyze this argument, we must consider the following two questions:

1. Could Army Group Center have successfully pushed east in August and September of 1941 to capture Moscow?
2. Is it reasonable to assume that Germany would have won the war had it taken the Soviet capital?

First, let us consider the state of Army Group Center in early August 1941. It had successfully battered its way through the frontier fortifications around Brest and two lines of Soviet field armies to take up positions east of Smolensk. OKH's planners had scheduled a stop at this geographic point to allow the logistics train to bring up necessary munitions, fuel, and supplies to continue the offensive. Of course, in reality the *Wehrmacht* in

Barbarossa had expended much more in munitions than expected due to Red Army resistance, and the poor road network led to petrol consumption being twice the budgeted amount.[4]

Several German generals clamored for an immediate advance on Moscow, but the *Wehrmacht*'s supply lines were already stretched to the breaking point. Van Creveld's study of *Ostheer* Quartermaster records under General Wagner concludes that the logistical train network would not allow for a continued general advance:

> From the middle of July, the supply-situation of Army Group Centre was developing signs of schizophrenia. On one hand Wagner and Halder were aware of some "strain," but nevertheless confident of their ability to build up a new supply basis on the Dnieper, from which further operations were to be launched around the end of the month. They appeared not to hear the loud cries for help from the armies. The consumption of ammunition throughout this period was very high, and could be met only—if at all—by means of a drastic curtailment in the supply of fuel and subsistence. . . . Around the middle of August, both 9. and 2. Armies were living from hand to mouth, with stocks of ammunition still falling instead of rising in preparation for a new offensive. Moreover, the supply of POL (petrol, oil, and lubricants) was quite insufficient, and did not take into account the worn state of the engines. The continued resistance of the Russian troops trapped inside the Smolensk pocket delayed the refreshment of the armored formations and this finally required almost a month, instead of the three or four days Guderian thought would be needed. . . . Meanwhile, even though the Smolensk pocket had finally been liquidated, Army Group Center was still engaged in heavy fighting. Throughout August it had to face enemy counter-attacks from the east, causing heavy expenditure of ammunition that could only be met by cutting back on subsistence. Stockpiling for a new offensive was impossible.[5]

By the time the Germans reached the Dnieper River east of Smolensk, the operational rail and road networks could only supply a portion of the Army Group with sufficient matériel to continue its advance. A lengthy period was required to establish supply dumps near the front to support the entire force in a final offensive on the Soviet capital. Van Creveld tells us that Army Group Center was only getting enough through the transportation networks to allow a limited detachment to continue a fighting advance. There were just not enough supplies making it to the front to feed the needs of a fighting force of more than three-quarters of a million men.

There is no doubt that the logistic situation would not have allowed an advance by Army Group Centre on Moscow at the end of August. At the very best, a force of between 14 and 17 armoured, motorized and infantry divisions might have been so employed, and whether this would have been enough, even in September 1941, to break through the city's defenses is very much open to question. . . . The delay imposed by Hitler's decision to give the Ukraine priority over Moscow was therefore far shorter than the usual estimate of six weeks. The postponement, if there was one, can hardly have amounted to more than a week or two, at the very most. The difficulties experienced in building up a base for the attack on Moscow also rule out another suggestion that is sometimes made, namely that Hitler, instead of dissipating his forces in simultaneous offensives along three divergent axes, ought to have concentrated them for a single attack against Moscow. The logistic situation ruled out such a solution as the few roads and railroads available would not have allowed such a force to be supplied. Even as it was, the concentration of seventy divisions for the attack early in October gave rise to very great difficulties, especially with the railways and the supply of fuel. It would have been utterly impossible to construct an adequate forward base for a force twice that size.[6]

Had Hitler ordered such a stripped-down advance on Moscow in September, the strike force would have confronted several Soviet formations that historically suffered enormous losses in later counterattacks against the static German front lines around Vyazma and Yelnya at the same time that the Battle of Kiev was taking place further south. David Glantz points out that an earlier rush to take Moscow, rather than being easy, would have been problematic at best: "Some claim that had Hitler launched Operation Typhoon in September rather than October, the *Wehrmacht* would have avoided the terrible weather conditions and reached and captured Moscow before the onset of winter. This argument too does not hold up to close scrutiny. Had Hitler launched Operation Typhoon in September, Army Group Center would have had to penetrate deep Soviet defenses manned by a force that had not squandered its strength in fruitless offensives against German positions east of Smolensk."[7]

The Red Army defenders west of the capital would not have been the only threat to a successful German advance. A September push to take Moscow would have extended what was already an exposed salient in the front line. If the *Wehrmacht* had pushed east for the capital, the Soviet armies to the south of Army Group Center (50th, 13th, 40th, and 21st) would have found themselves perfectly positioned to attack north into the German flank. Similarly, the armies defending the northern section of the

USSR's front (22nd, 27th, and 34th) would have been able to strike the other flank of the invaders' advance.

Many hastily mobilized Red Army reserve formations would have joined such a counterattack. Historically these units deployed into the Ukraine to rebuild a semblance of a front after the massive German victory there. If Hitler had not ordered his pincer attack around Kiev, these new Soviet divisions would have been available to feed into the fight on the exposed wings of a *Wehrmacht* advance as it closed in on Moscow. Zhukov tells us he would have ordered exactly such an operation: "As for the temporary suspension of the Moscow offensive and the drawing off of part of the forces to the Ukraine, we may assume that without that operation the situation of the German central grouping could have been still worse than it turned out to be. For the GHQ reserves, which were used to fill in the gaps in the south-western sector in September, could have been used to strike at the flank and rear of the 'Center' group of armies advancing on Moscow."[8] The Red Army was by no means passive in the face of the German advance in 1941: it counterattacked often, repeatedly, and without regard for casualties. Such attempts to drive back the invaders were especially fierce against the front lines of Army Group Center around Vyazma and Yelnya in August and September. It is difficult to believe that multiple Soviet armies would have remained in static positions when offered a chance to attack the flanks of a panzer striking force closing in on Moscow.

Finally, as the forward elements of Army Group Center neared the capital, they would have had to fight through ever more fresh Red Army units brought in by rail from Siberia. As we will see, the Japanese began to unwind their buildup of forces along the Manchuria border in August, specifically to signal to the USSR that it could safely shift its Far Eastern armies to Europe. The drawdown of Japanese troops along the Soviet frontiers and an imminent fall of his capital would have likely convinced Stalin of the need to gamble and rush large numbers of his Far Eastern divisions to the defense of Moscow. Historically, many of these Red Army soldiers did not move west until later in 1941, but their presence would have been just as useful against a smaller Army Group strike force in August or September.

So, to close a discussion regarding the chances of an early Army Group Center thrust at Moscow: the logistical situation would have only allowed a stripped-down German force to advance. This smaller vanguard would have had to fight its way through still-intact defending armies while exposing itself to crippling flanking attacks by much larger Soviet forces. If successful in its advance, it would have arrived at Moscow concurrently with Red Army reinforcements of similar size detraining from the Far East. While all is possible in counterfactual history, the likelihood of a detached strike force of Army Group Center taking and holding Moscow in the early autumn of 1941 is slim.

Nevertheless, what if such a gambit had been successful? Would Soviet resistance have collapsed, as has been argued repeatedly by German generals and later historians? The facts argue against such a surrender by the Russian people upon the loss of their capital. Consider the defenders of Leningrad: they withstood a multiyear siege lasting from late 1941 to early 1944. The city's inhabitants and garrison suffered continual bombardment and starvation to such an extent that many resorted to cannibalism to survive. Yet through three brutal winters they did not surrender. Is it logical to assume that these same stoic Soviets would have given up upon receipt of the news of Moscow's fall in 1941? It seems unlikely.

What about the great assemblage of Soviet armies in the Ukraine around Kiev? Had Hitler ordered a successful early drive on Moscow, these formations would have been intact upon the capture of the capital. In actuality, many tens of thousands of these Red Army soldiers fought to the death even after being surrounded and hopelessly cut off by the linking up of the First and Second Panzer Groups in the middle of September. Why is it reasonable to assume that these same Soviet soldiers, comprising upward of a million men, controlling Kiev and much of the most productive industrial and agricultural lands of the USSR, would have capitulated upon receiving news that Moscow had fallen?

The Soviet strategy in 1941 was similar to that employed by Russia's defenders in other invasions from the west over the centuries: trade space for time, wear down the enemy, and wait for the onset of winter cold. Stalin and the Politburo prepared detailed plans to continue the fight if the Germans captured Moscow. The central government would be relocated to the strategic city of Kuybyshev (now Samara) on the Volga. As the Germans pushed east from Bryansk and Vyazma, thousands of train cars carried the contents and workers of government offices out of Moscow to the new capital. Even Lenin's mummified body made the trip east. Russian resistance did not disintegrate in 1812 when Napoleon's forces captured Moscow. The French arrived in a city ravaged by fires set by the retreating forces bent on continuing the fight. The Soviet plan in 1941 was to lure the Germans into attritional urban fighting, ensure the invaders would capture little of value, and prepare a winter counterattack. A special brigade of the NKVD, the OMSBON, was created with the specific mission to mine, booby trap, and demolish 1,200 of the capital's most prominent buildings. These included Lubyanka Prison, the Bolshoi Theater, and the Kremlin. Also rigged for destruction was much of the city's telephone, water, and power infrastructure.[9] Moscow would be defended block by block using guerilla tactics and movement through the sewer tunnels. While a striking force detached from Army Group Center might have reached Moscow in the autumn of 1941, the Germans would have encountered the sort of grinding urban engagement there that took place in the Battle of Stalingrad in 1942. The captured capital would have been in ruins at the end of the fighting, leaving little in the way of comfortable winter quarters for the invaders.

Panzers parked in front of the Kremlin flying the swastika banner has appealed to many as an imagined image equating to a complete Nazi victory. The capture of Moscow would have been a grave blow to Stalin's regime, causing significant disruption to communications, transport, and industry. However, in such a scenario, large intact Soviet armies would have remained along a front in a great arc from Leningrad to the Volga to Kiev. In recent years, more historians have spoken up to contest the "accepted" opinion that a German capture of Moscow would have resulted in a Nazi victory. Historian Ben Shepherd argued in 2016 that the fall of the Soviet capital would not have been decisive: "The Germans' final drive on Moscow had failed, though it is unclear how much good it would have done them had they reached the city. Moscow's fall would probably not have been fatal to the Soviet effort on its own. Its loss as a major transport and administration hub would certainly have caused disruption, but the Soviet administration would still have functioned, and so too would the arms factories beyond the Urals. And the Red Army, with its rail network intact, would probably have had little difficulty in establishing a new defense line further east."[10]

Another recent history by Robert Kirchubel agrees,

> Many commentators have taken the German leadership to task for not capturing the city. While taking the enemy's capital has the false ring of sound military judgement, there is no proof that occupying Moscow would have led directly to the collapse of the USSR shopworn clichés about the "seat of centralized Soviet power" or the "hub of the Soviet transportation net" notwithstanding. . . . During Typhoon the Soviet defense crumbled as before but it did not devolve into a confused rout. As Timoshenko told the Supreme Defense Council: If Germany succeeds in taking Moscow that is obviously a grave disappointment for us but it by no means disrupts our grand strategy; that alone will not win [them] the war.[11]

Historian Laurence Rees went even further to argue that an early push on Moscow would have been catastrophic for the Germans: "Perhaps even if Stalin had deserted the capital, the Germans would have been surrounded and trapped inside Moscow—that's almost certainly what would have happened if Army Group Centre had moved on the Soviet Capital in August while the threat from the flanks remained."[12]

The Russian people had historically shown that they would fight on after initial severe military losses and military defeats. The Tsar's army suffered repeated defeats in World War I, but its will to fight only faltered after a long war of attrition in three years of combat in which it recorded more than five million men killed or wounded.[13] Similarly, the will of the people of the Russian Empire to fight did not falter when Moscow fell to the French in 1812. Had the Soviet government been forced to relocate to Kuybyshev, the population could also look to the Chinese state's ongoing resistance against the Japanese after Chiang Kai-shek moved his capital to Chungking in 1937. Years of purges and the iron discipline of Stalin's state allowed no room to mutiny. Those who refused to fight or spoke of surrender were shot, transferred to penal battalions, or shipped off to the Gulag.

Thus, while the German military believed the Soviet military effort would have crumbled with the capture of Moscow, such an outcome was highly unlikely. If Army Group Center had taken Moscow quickly by the autumn of 1941, the Axis invaders would still have had to deal with large, undefeated Red Army formations in the Ukraine and around Leningrad. At the same time, new reserve armies were being raised and hundreds of thousands of well-trained troops were streaming to the front across the USSR's railways from Siberia. Perhaps Zhukov would have launched his winter counteroffensive from further east than occurred historically, but it is still likely that it would have taken place.

In conclusion, it can never be disproven that had Army Group Center taken Moscow in the autumn of 1941, the USSR would have collapsed and the Axis would have won World War II and conquered the globe. However, logic argues against this counterfactual for the following reasons:

1. Army Group Center's supply lines were so stretched that only a portion of its forces could have pushed east in August.
2. Such an advance would have exposed the Germans to flank attacks from both the north and south, potentially leading to the encirclement and defeat of the invaders' vanguard.
3. As the Germans closed in on Moscow, large numbers of fresh Soviet troops would have rushed to the battlefield from Siberia.

4. A battle to take Moscow itself would have degenerated into the sort of attritional urban warfare in which the larger Red Army was advantaged and the *Wehrmacht*'s qualitative advantages of movement and tactical skill were reduced.

5. The invaders would have eventually taken control of a city left a smoking ruin by its defenders, with the Soviet government relocated more than five hundred miles east in Kuybyshev to continue the fight. German hopes for comfortable winter quarters would have been dashed.

6. A deviation from history and such an early strike at Moscow would have left Leningrad's supply lines intact in the north. In the south, most of the Ukraine would have remained in Soviet hands protected by the largest collection of Red Army units in the western USSR.

7. Had the invaders captured Moscow, while the Germans waited for the "inevitable" collapse of Soviet resistance, the Red Army would have prepared to launch its winter counteroffensive. Stalin would have been able to attack anywhere along the front: from the Baltic in the north, to the extended central salient created by the "early" advance on Moscow, to an attack in the south aimed at Romania and its oil fields.

Advancing hell-bent for Moscow after the fall of Smolensk was neither strategically nor logistically the obvious correct decision as argued by many since the end of World War II. One could just as easily make the case that surrounding Leningrad and seizing Kiev and much of Ukraine in the late summer of 1941 brought Germany closer to winning the war in the east than would have resulted from an underpowered thrust at the capital. Logically, the best chance of taking Moscow in 1941 may have been as it played out historically: waiting until after resupplying and reinforcing Army Group Center, clearing its flanks of large enemy formations, and then proceeding east in Operation Tyfun.

· 11 ·

Cold, Snow, and Mud

$\mathcal{N}$ext, we consider the impact of the weather and infrastructure of the USSR on the German invasion. Many have argued that the severe cold, poor roads, and inadequate railways encountered by the *Wehrmacht* in 1941 were the prime factors in the German defeat. If only the winter was milder, the dirt roads had not become impassable in the autumn rains, and the railways worked better, Army Group Center would have taken Moscow and Soviet resistance would have collapsed. Senior German commanders on the Eastern Front such as Field Marshals von Rundstedt and Ewald von Kleist held to this view when interviewed by British historian Captain Liddell Hart after the war:

> The next question I explored was how the plan went wrong. Kleist's answer was: "The main cause of the failure was that winter came early that year, coupled with the way the Russians repeatedly gave ground rather than let themselves be drawn into a decisive battle such as we were seeking." Rundstedt agreed that this was "the most decisive" cause. "But long before winter came the chances had been diminished owing to the repeated delays in the advance that were caused by bad roads, and mud. The 'black earth' of the Ukraine could be turned into mud by ten minutes' rain—stopping all movement until it dried. That was a heavy handicap in a race with time. It was increased by the lack of railways in Russia—for bringing up supplies to our advancing troops."[1]

The winter of 1941 was the coldest in Europe in the twentieth century, and surface temperatures between −20 and −30 degrees Celsius prevailed over the battlefront for much of December.[2] Winston Churchill took to the airwaves in the spring of 1942 to mock Hitler for his defeat:

133

He forgot about the winter. There is a winter, you know, in Russia. For a good many months the temperature is apt to fall very low. There is snow, there is frost, and all that. Hitler forgot about this Russian winter. He must have been very loosely educated. We all heard about it at school; but he forgot it. I have never made such a bad mistake as that. So winter came, and fell upon his ill-clad armies, and with the winter came the valiant Russian counterattacks. No one can say with certainty how many millions of Germans have already perished in Russia and its snows.[3]

It is not surprising that the German commanders of Barbarossa argued what they did. They believed that successfully taking Moscow would force the Red Army to expend its reserves and lead to a complete victory in the east. Blaming their defeat in front of the capital on weather and poor infrastructure was easier to accept than a deficiency in the *Wehrmacht*'s operational skill and the ability of its fighting men. Certainly, they had a point that the cold took a great toll on the invaders. The Germans suffered more than two hundred thousand frostbite casualties in the Battle of Moscow brought about by exposure to the terrible cold on soldiers who had not received sufficient winter clothing. *Wehrmacht* military equipment performed no better, as artillery recoil mechanisms, tank engines, and machine gun lubricants all froze solid. The invaders' locomotives also became unusable. Compared to Soviet models, those used by the Germans had their water tanks mounted on the locomotive's exterior, and they burst when they froze.

A subset of the argument regarding the lack of winter clothing supplied to the German army in late 1941 is who was at fault for its deficiency. Some have argued that Hitler refused to allow shipment of winter equipment to the front and that he deserves the blame for the damage done by the bitter cold on the German forces. Historian Trumbull Higgins writes that in early August, "The OKH also submitted a request to the Fuehrer for a public collection of winter clothing from the German civilian economy for the sake of the army in Russia. The infuriated Nazi dictator rejected this suggestion on the grounds that he had promised the German people that their soldiers would be home for Christmas and that in any event there was not going to be a winter campaign in Russia."[4]

Hitler wanted to believe that Soviet resistance would disintegrate, but even if the conquest of the western USSR was not completed in 1941, he did not wish to alarm the German people. There were many ways to procure winter clothing for the *Ostheer* other than donations from the civilians of the Third Reich. Seizing cold weather gear from conquered armies and occupied populations from France, Poland, or Ukraine was one obvious solution. When the Soviets did not capitulate after the first six weeks of fighting, preparations began in August to equip the invading armies on the Eastern Front for a conflict that continued into the winter. Van Creveld makes it quite clear that any argument that Hitler forbade the German High Command from shipping cold weather gear to the men of Army Group Center is not sustained by the facts:

> Anyone who has studied the documents cannot fail to be impressed by the hundreds of orders, directives and circulars concerning winter supplies that began to emanate from OKH from early August onward, covering every detail, from the reconnoitering of suitable shelters to the provision of freeze-proof POL, from winter clothing to veterinary care for horses. To what extent these documents represent a concrete reality is very difficult to say, but there is no reason to suppose that OKH was engaging in mere mental gymnastics. Moreover, we have the evidence of Wagner and his subordinates that winter equipment was available in "sufficient" quantities but could not be brought up owing to the critical railway-situation. It is certain that the railroads, hopelessly inadequate to prepare the offensive on Moscow and to sustain it after it had started, were in no state to tackle the additional job of bringing up winter equipment.[5]

Some cold weather gear did make it to the front, but not enough to outfit the vast majority of the *Ostheer* as the supply system strained to deliver sufficient ammunition, fuel, and food to sustain the drive on Moscow.[6] What resulted was a significant gap between the quantities of winter gear Hitler was told had been sent to the front versus what actually arrived there. This is clear from the discussion between the commander of the Second Panzer Group, General Guderian, and the German dictator on December 20, 1941:

> I: "Naturally it is my duty to lessen the suffering of my soldiers so far as that lies within my power. But it is hard when the men have even now not yet received their winter clothing and the greater part of the infantry are still going about in denim uniforms. Boots, vests, gloves, woolen helmets are either non-existent or else are hopelessly worn out."
>
> Hitler shouted: "That is not true. The Quartermaster-General informed me that the winter clothing had been issued."
>
> I: "I dare say it has been issued but it has never arrived. I have made it my business to find out what has happened to it. At present it is in Warsaw station, where it has been for the last several weeks, since it cannot be sent on owing to a lack of locomotives and obstructions to

the lines. Our requests that it be forwarded in September and October were bluntly refused. Now it's too late."

The Quartermaster-General was sent for and had to admit that what I had said was correct.[7]

General Guderian is quite explicit as to where the blame lay: "It is frequently maintained nowadays that Hitler and only Hitler was responsible for the lack of winter clothing in the army of 1941. I can in no way subscribe to this belief. Proof of this is that the *Luftwaffe* and the *Waffen-SS* were well and adequately equipped and had laid in the necessary stocks in plenty of time. But the supreme command was sunk in its dream of defeating the Russian Army in eight or ten weeks; this defeat would result, they thought, in the political collapse of the Soviets."[8]

When confronted with the desperate need to supply the armies with fuel, ammunition, and replacement parts along a tenuous transportation network, not only was it Hitler but also the German army's senior officers who failed to prioritize the early shipment of winter clothing and equipment. This was a remarkable oversight by the leaders of OKH and the *Ostheer*. They had not only read about the ferocity of the winter in the east from histories of Napoleon's invasion, many of them had experienced it firsthand when the German army fought its way into Russian territory in World War I and stayed there until 1919. Thus, it is difficult to comprehend how these senior officers could be surprised by the topography, weather, and infrastructure of the USSR. Still they claimed they were.

What if the USSR had experienced a mild winter in 1941? Would the Germans have taken Moscow and won the war? Perhaps the invaders would have moved a little faster and made it to the city. Had the Germans arrived outside of Moscow in a somewhat less cold winter, they would have had to defeat a Red Army which planned to engage in house-to-house fighting with NKVD troops dynamiting and mining hundreds of buildings. The Germans would assuredly have suffered high casualty rates before they captured the ruined shell of the city. And then? As already discussed, the fall of the capital in and of itself was unlikely to lead to the collapse of Soviet resistance and German triumph. Even with Moscow in German hands, there is no reason to believe that Zhukov's counterattack would have failed to take place. It is possible that the invaders would have held onto Moscow if faced with a Soviet winter offensive in slightly less cold temperatures, but still the war would have hung in the balance.

While the bitter cold of late 1941 has received a great deal of attention, Liddell Hart concluded instead that the USSR's dirt roads proved the decisive reason for the invasion's failure:

What saved Russia above all was, not her modern progress, but her backwardness. If the Soviet regime had given her a road system comparable to that of western countries, she would have been overrun in quick time. The German mechanized forces were baulked by the badness of her roads. But this conclusion has a converse. The Germans lost the chance of victory because they had based their mobility on wheels instead of on tracks. On these mud-roads the wheeled transport was bogged when the tanks could move on. *Panzer* forces with *tracked* transport might have overrun Russia's vital centres long before the autumn, despite the bad roads.[10]

Better roads would have been to the advantage of the invaders, but the Soviet road network of 1941 was poorly developed, and the local economy was more dependent on railways. By accident or design, the USSR was harder to invade than Poland and France when the rains began to fall. In Hart's scenario, such limited infrastructure could have been overcome if the Barbarossa invasion force had been equipped with tracked transportation. Of course, this was not how the German army of 1941 advanced. Not only did it not have tens of thousands of tracked vehicles to haul the petrol, ammunition, spare parts, and infantry needed to support the panzers, it did not even have enough in the way of traditional wheeled trucks to do the job. As it was, more than a hundred different truck models were employed in the invasion, including thousands seized in France or purchased from Switzerland.[10] Due to a lack of trucks, the Germans moved east with 750,000 horses, with many pulling more than fifteen thousand wooden carts filled with supplies.[11]

Had the Third Reich configured its industrial base to build the tracked transport in the late 1930s necessary to transport the Barbarossa invasion force, the *Wehrmacht* would not have had enough fuel to power its movement. This was due to the German's dearth of petroleum supplies and owing to the lower energy efficiency and heavier weight of tracked vehicles versus ones using wheels.[12] No army in World War II fielded a completely motorized military, not to mention one that transported its infantry and supplies in tracked vehicles. Despite its dearth of motorized transport vehicles in 1941, the *Wehrmacht* penetrated many hundreds of miles into the Soviet interior to Leningrad, Moscow, and Rostov-on-Don.

While it is likely that the Germans would have pushed further with a large fleet of tracked supply vehicles, one could use the same argument for squadrons of attack helicopters, or drones firing laser-guided munitions. As a recent US Secretary of Defense put it, "You go to war with the army you have, not the army you might want or wish to have at a later time."[13]

While poor weather and infrastructure hindered the invasion, were these factors truly the cause of its failure? Even van Creveld, after sifting through a massive body of data, concluded that the inability of the German general staff to supply its soldiers at the front in 1941 was not the primary reason for the Soviet victory.

> This war was lost on grounds other than logistic, including a doubtful strategy, a rickety structure of command and an unwarranted dispersion of scare resources. While recognizing the magnitude of the achievement—among other things, logistic—that brought the *Wehrmacht* almost within sight of the Kremlin, the above-listed factors certainly played an important role in its failure, and for this it is OKH, not Hitler, who must be held responsible. In logistics, as in everything else lying between minor tactics and strategy, the *Führer* had no interest whatsoever. Apart from one or two points, any errors that were committed in these fields—which is said to comprise nine-tenths of the business of war—must be laid squarely at the door of Halder and the General Staff. Even the most important decision Hitler made during the campaign of 1941, namely the sending of Guderian into the Ukraine instead of towards Moscow, was justified on logistic grounds and certainly had little to do with the postponement of the drive on the Russian capital. In war it is often the small things that matter, and in many of these the *Wehrmacht* had been weighed, counted, and found wanting.[14]

No matter how bad the roads, no matter how cold it became, it was the fighting soldiers of the Red Army and the civilians supporting them who prevailed at the end of 1941 while enduring the same conditions as their opponents. Zhukov wrote forcefully that it was the Soviet population and their resolve that won the Battle of Moscow:

> Other generals and bourgeois historians put all the blame on slush and lack of roads. But I was there to see thousands upon thousands of Moscow women, not particularly suited for the arduous job of sapping, who had left their comfortable homes to dig anti-tank ditches and trenches, put up barricades, construct "asparagus" and other obstacles and carry sandbags. . . . It was neither rain nor snow that stopped the fascist troops near Moscow. . . . The grouping of picked Hitlerite troops, over one million strong had been routed by the courage, iron staunchness and valour of the Soviet troops which had the people, Moscow and Motherland behind them.[15]

· 12 ·

The "Fatal" Delay of Marita
and a Southern Tyfun

Since 1945, many historians have claimed that if only Hitler had ignored the Balkans in the spring of 1941 he could have ordered an earlier invasion of the USSR, which would have led to victory in the east. Consider the following quotes from William Shirer, Chris Bellamy, and Winston Churchill:

"And then, according to an underlined passage in the top-secret OKW notes of the meeting, Hitler announced the most fateful decision of all. 'The beginning of the Barbarossa operation,' he told his generals, 'will have to be postponed for up to four weeks.' This postponement of the attack on Russia in order that the Nazi warlord might vent his personal spite against a small Balkan country which had dared to defy him was probably the most catastrophic single decision in Hitler's career. It is hardly too much to say that by making it that March afternoon in the Chancellery in Berlin during a moment of convulsive rage he tossed away his last golden opportunity to win the war and to make of the Third Reich, which he had created with such stunning if barbarous genius, the greatest empire in German history and himself the master of Europe."[1]

"Barbarossa was delayed—almost certainly with disastrous consequences for the Germans—because of the 27 March 1941 coup in Yugoslavia, and Hitler's subsequent invasion to deal with it."[2]

"In Yugoslavia, when a popular revolt upset Hitler's plans for peaceful conquest, the Germans wiped out the Yugoslav army in 11 days. The Greeks lasted barely longer. . . . Fast as they were, these victories were too slow. They postponed Hitler's assault on Russia, and thus probably saved Moscow and changed the whole course of the war."[3]

139

There are three primary points I would suggest one needs to consider when evaluating this argument. The first is that the spring thaw in Eastern Europe in 1941 came unusually late and would have delayed the launch of Barbarossa regardless of events in the Balkans. The second, as has already been discussed, is that driving Britain's forces out of Greece was a German strategic imperative rather than a rash decision driven by personal spite. A British bomber offensive launched from the Balkans aimed at the Romanian oil fields at Ploesti would have been a grave threat to Hitler's war machine. Finally, as previously discussed, it is not clear that the capture of Moscow in 1941 would have won the war for the Germans.

Multiple German military sources note that the Bug River was still in flood and the ground sodden along the central frontier with the USSR in the first couple of weeks of June.[4] The success of the invasion plan depended upon rapid and deep panzer advances to surround and destroy the Red Army forces close to the border. As the *Wehrmacht* found in the autumn of 1941, mud was a great enemy of *Blitzkreig*. John Keegan argues that Marita was of little consequence to the actual launch date of Barbarossa:

> The Balkan campaign, often depicted by historians as an unwelcome diversion from Hilter's long-laid plan to attack the Soviet Union and as a disabling interruption of the timetable he had marked out for its inception, had been in fact no such thing. It had been successfully concluded even more rapidly than his professional military advisers could have anticipated; while the choice for D-Day for *Barbarossa* had always depended not on the sequence of contingent events but on the weather and objective military factors. The German Army found it more difficult than expected to position the units allocated for *Barbarossa* in Poland; while the lateness of the spring thaw, which left the eastern European rivers in spate beyond the predicted date, meant that *Barbarossa* could not have been begun very much earlier than the third week in June, whatever Hitler's intentions.[5]

Many have noted that Hitler's invasion of Russia launched within just a few days on the calendar as Napoleon's. The French emperor had to wait until the grass in the area had grown in enough to act as fodder for his horses. The panzers certainly had no need for grass, but, of course, only a small portion of the German army was mechanized in 1941. The 750,000 horses that accompanied the Axis forces into the USSR needed to eat, just as did those with the *Grande Armée* in 1812.[6] Had the Germans launched Barbarossa across muddy land not yet ready to support the feeding of their horses, the pace of the invasion would have slowed much sooner than actually occurred.

Finally, those who argue that Operation Marita cost Hitler his empire downplay the importance of securing the Balkans before turning east to deal with the USSR. With the launch of Barbarossa and the end of trade with the USSR, Germany would become entirely reliant on Romanian oil supplies. Any aviation threat to the petroleum industry around Ploesti would constitute a severe danger to the *Wehrmacht* and the German economy. This meant that the British could not be allowed to base RAF bombers anywhere in the Balkans. Upon coming to power, the new Yugoslav government immediately requested that Moscow enter into a military alliance. The Serbian military junta also discussed an alliance with the Greeks to drive the Italians out of Albania. The British had been working hard to establish such an anti-Axis "Balkan Front," the organization of which would have constituted a significant threat to Germany, especially after it had sent the bulk of its military forces into battle in the USSR.

Logical analysis yields the conclusion that Hitler had to conquer the Balkans in early 1941 as a result of the coup in Belgrade, the failure of the Italian invasion of Greece, and the landing there of a British expeditionary force. Rather than a decision made in an irrational rage, the launch of Marita was supported by clear geopolitical factors. The attack on Yugoslavia almost certainly resulted in a faster conquest of Greece than would have otherwise taken place had the Germans invaded solely via Bulgaria. After quickly defeating the Yugoslav army, the *Wehrmacht* was able to outflank the Greek "Metaxas Line" defensives and rapidly descend on Athens and the Peloponnese. The conquest of Yugoslavia and Greece yielded the Axis significant strategic gains at small cost, and the late spring thaw in 1941 would have delayed the launch of Barbarossa into June even had the crisis in the Balkans not erupted.

To truly examine the counterfactual implicitly posed by Shirer and Churchill, let us consider what would have transpired if Hitler had ignored the Balkans, the thaw in the east came early in 1941, and Barbarossa had been launched on the first of June rather than on the 22nd of that month. This would have led to an earlier conclusion of the Battle of Kiev and encirclement of Leningrad and allowed Operation Tyfun to begin in early September rather than October 2. What would have been the result of this accelerated timetable?

An earlier launch of Tyfun would have run into tens of thousands of additional Red Army soldiers who historically became casualties in often-suicidal counterattacks on Army Group Center in September. Thus, the

Germans would have had a more difficult time encircling and then reducing the Soviet armies in the Vyazma and Bryansk *kessels*. However, in time, these pockets of resistance would have been wiped out, and the advancing panzers would have made headway on still dry roads. Perhaps the leading units of the offensive would then have made it to Moscow, but this could have been a disaster for Army Group Center: the Soviets would have executed their plan to engage in a drawn-out attritional urban battle in the capital punctuated with the booby trapping and mining of hundreds of buildings.

In the midst of this fighting, the extended German supply lines would have been obstructed as the autumn rains turned the roads to quagmires of mud. The *Rasputitsa's* arrival at the same time the lead elements of Army Group Center were slugging it out in Moscow against Red Army forces receiving supplies and reinforcements via existing rail lines would have placed the Germans at a significant disadvantage.

At the same time, Zhukov would have been positioning the newly raised conscript armies, stiffened by the arrival of seasoned "Siberian" divisions, to the north and south of the city in preparation for a winter counterattack. Thus, such an earlier start to Barbarossa would most likely have resulted in something akin to the Battle of Stalingrad taking place in Moscow at the end of 1941. Had the Germans taken Moscow and hung onto the city through Zhukov's counteroffensive, this would not have guaranteed the collapse of Soviet resistance. While an earlier launch of Barbarossa would have delivered advantages to the invaders, the theory that Hitler's decision to invade Yugoslavia and Greece directly resulted in German defeat in the USSR does not hold up under rigorous investigation.

What would the British in Greece have been doing as the panzers rolled east? At the very least, at Stalin's urging, the RAF would have bombed Ploesti. A disruption of oil supplies to the German armies' operations hundreds of miles inside the USSR could have been catastrophic to the invaders.

A SOUTHERN TYFUN

In recent years, a few historians have argued that the path to German victory ran through a continued offensive across the Ukraine after the Battle of Kiev in 1941. If only Hitler had ignored Moscow, he could have ordered Army Group South to push east to the Volga and south to the Caspian Sea, thus capturing a large portion of the USSR's agricultural, industrial, and natural resources for the Reich. The following is from the historian Bryan Fugate:

The *Wehrmacht* could perhaps have won a strategic victory in 1941 had the upper-level leadership been decisive and resolute in consolidating the German gains in the southern part of the Soviet Union, but this was not to be. In early September the German high command undertook the planning of an operation that was guaranteed to save Russia—an assault on a strongly fortified Moscow in the fall of 1941.... Germany could have won a strategic victory over the Soviet Union in 1941, however, by concentrating on gains in the south of the country, in the Ukraine and in the Caucasus, and by foregoing an assault on Moscow in the fall of the year.[7]

This line of reasoning is an intriguing counterfactual. At the conclusion of the Battle of Kiev, Hitler had his strongest concentration of armored force (the First and Second Panzer groups) positioned in the south. Unlike the forested areas around Moscow, Ukraine was generally flat agricultural land punctuated by the occasional river—perfect for the advance of an armored force. Red Army defenses east of Kiev had been shattered and few Soviet formations were in position to defend against an advance by Army Group South. Historically, the German offensive in the Ukraine from September to December 1941, led by a single panzer group (the First), pushed as far as Rostov-on-Don. Could much more have been achieved if Army Group South utilized General Guderian's Second Panzers in a race to the Volga?

Hitler laid out such a plan of attack in the directive he issued on August 21, 1941, which sent the Second Panzer Group south to the Battle of Kiev: "The most important objective to be achieved before the onset of winter is not the capture of Moscow, but the occupation of the Crimea and the industrial and coal region of the Donets [Donbas] together with the isolation of the Russian oil regions in the Caucasus. In the north, [it is] the encirclement of Leningrad and union with the Finns."[8] Had Hitler ignored his generals' clamoring for a strike on the capital and decided upon a "Southern Tyfun" strategy, the region west of Moscow would have remained in Stalin's hands. However, every extra mile conquered in the Ukraine deprived the Soviets of more agricultural, industrial, and natural resource output in what was rapidly becoming a war of attrition.

A shift in the direction of advance to the south would have had an impact on the manpower balance. As discussed previously, large numbers of Ukrainians received the invaders with enthusiasm. Many other restive minority groups lived in the lands east and south of Rostov-on-Don and proved to be willing recruits for the arriving German forces. Had enlistment of these non-Russians taken place earlier, the balance of forces on the front would have tilted that much further away from the Red Army.

As it was, the territories occupied by the Axis in 1941 reduced the USSR's nonagricultural workforce from 31.5 million to 18.5 million, and industrial workers from 11 million to 7 million.[9] An early conquest of the rest of the Ukraine and the Caucasus would have resulted in an even greater impairment in the USSR's war-fighting ability in 1942.

With no need to launch a strike at Moscow in 1941, the Third Panzer Group would have been free to continue supporting Army Group North in cutting off Leningrad and linking up with the Finns. At the same time, rather than wasting themselves in an overextended advance into the teeth of the Russian winter, Army Group Center could have prepared reasonable defensive positions to hold off Soviet counterattacks. So could such a drive through the Ukraine have resulted in German victory?

The problems with this scenario are the distances involved and the likely response of the Red Army to such a directional change in the advance of the invaders. In the dry summer weather of 1942, it took the resupplied and refitted German forces from late June to the end of August to reach Stalingrad on the banks of the Volga, and another month to advance to the edge of the Soviet oil fields around Grozny. By early September 1941, Army Group South had already pushed more than four hundred miles into the USSR, suffered significant casualties, worn out much of its equipment, and was operating on tenuous supply lines. To advance hundreds of miles further east to the banks of the Don was one thing, but pushing even further to the Volga and into the Caucasus as the weather deteriorated would have represented a monumental task for the mostly unmotorized invading force. Again, anything is possible in counterfactual history, and had Hitler struck south in late 1941 with a second panzer group, his armies would at least have driven further east across Ukraine than actually occurred.

However, the further the Axis advanced in this "Southern Tyfun" scenario, the more exposed they would have been to a Red Army winter counteroffensive. With no attack on Moscow, it is logical to assume that Stalin's newly formed reserve armies and the experienced divisions moving west from Siberia would have been shifted south rather than being concentrated around the capital. The Soviets, operating on interior lines of communication and intact rail systems servicing the Eastern Ukraine, would have been at an advantage compared to the Germans and their allies pushing ever further away from logistics bases accessed primarily by dirt roads.

In 1939, Zhukov launched a two-pronged attack in his defeat of the Japanese at Nomonhan. In 1941, he attempted a similar but much larger operation in an attempt to envelop Army Group Center's forces around Moscow. In 1942, Zhukov's strategy was successful on a grand scale as it surrounded an entire German army at Stalingrad. Logically one can conclude that such a double-pronged counterattack would have taken place in late 1941 in Ukraine had Hitler opted to ignore Moscow in favor of a "Southern Tyfun."

How would 1941 have ended under such a scenario? Along the Baltic, it is possible that Army Group North operating with an extra panzer group would have cut off Leningrad's critical supply line across Lake Ladoga. Just as possible would have been a Soviet winter counterattack that pushed the invaders back and reopened the so-called Road of Life to the city. In the south, the Germans could have advanced to the banks of the Donets, Don, or the Volga. Nevertheless, the further east the invaders advanced, the greater the chance a Soviet counterattack would have cut off and savaged the extended German formations operating on insufficient logistics networks. Historically, Hitler's proclivity on the Eastern Front was to push his armies in a relentless advance and never allow a retreat to favorable defensive positions no matter the weather or supply situation. This argues for a more successful Red Army counterattack.

The most likely result of this counterfactual is that at the end of 1941 the USSR would have been a bit weaker and the *Wehrmacht* a bit stronger than in the historical record. Perhaps the Axis would have overrun the Caucasus and their oil fields in 1942 and the USSR's resistance would have crumbled as a result. Alternatively, just as likely, the Red Army would have continued to fight with increased petroleum imports from the United States. Alternatively, the Germans could have struck for Moscow after the spring thaw and been defeated there similarly to the historic disaster at Stalingrad. In conclusion, while a "Southern Tyfun" option could have improved the invaders' cause compared to a late-season advance on Moscow, there is little evidence to suggest that this change in history would have led to an obvious German triumph in the east.

· *13* ·

Nazi Genocide, Ideology, and the Loss of Hearts and Minds

$\mathcal{N}$ext, we consider commentators who argue that German policies in the conquered areas of the USSR were so heinous, murderous, and evil that they drove the Soviet people to fight tenaciously, often suicidally, and eventually victoriously against the invaders. Historians Max Hastings and Christian Hartmann explain this thesis:

"The Germans made a grave error in inflicting barbarism indiscriminately upon those who welcomed them, just as they did upon those who resisted. Many Ukrainians and other Russian subject peoples detested Stalin and Moscow's tyranny and were perfectly willing to assist the cause of Germany. Yet when they too found themselves victims of wholesale brutality, there seemed no choice save to resist. Through the years that followed, partisan war behind the front imposed mounting pressure on German supply lines. Attempts to suppress this by mass murder, hostage-taking, and devastation of civilian communities foundered on the Soviet peoples' extraordinary capacity for suffering."[1]

"Ironically enough, ideology did ultimately tip the balance, but in a quite different way from the one expected by the German planners. Long before, Clausewitz and Caesar knew that there are three things one needs to master in winning a war: the enemy's armed forces, his territory, and, lastly, his people's will to resist. The armed forces had to be destroyed and the country occupied but it was only when the opponent's will to resist had been broken or won over that the war would truly be at an end. The German leadership, by contrast, were so foolhardy that they waged war from the beginning, not only against the Soviet Union with its superior resources, but also against almost all of its peoples at the same time. Hitler and his entourage did not think it necessary to make even tactical allowances for the scale of the task, and steadfastly ignored the enormous political opportunities that presented themselves, especially in summer 1941, when the *Wehrmacht* was often being joyfully received in the Soviet Union's westernmost territories and desertion was threatening to undermine the very existence of the Red Army. The German leaders, however, were determined not to make any alteration to their idea of how the war would be conducted, which meant destruction, exploitation, and oppression."[2]

As previously discussed, Hitler, his government ministers, and his army commanders planned to murder millions of Soviet Jews, commissars, intellectuals, and Communist Party officials in the first months of the invasion. After that, tens of millions more would be starved to death in what would become a vast, depopulated territory to be settled by Germanic peoples. The killings began as soon as the invaders crossed the border, and they continued until 1944 when the *Ostheer* was finally expelled from the territory of the USSR. Could not such wanton criminal slaughter have been the motivating force behind the heroic efforts of the Soviet people that spurred them on to final victory?

The Nazis most certainly did engage in massive war crimes in the USSR, but it is by no means clear that these actions led to the *Wehrmacht's* defeat in the east:

1. The treatment of Soviet soldiers and population by Stalin's government was barely better than that of the Nazi invaders.
2. There is little evidence that Red Army frontline forces and the civilians who supplied them were fighting because of specific brutal acts of the Nazis. Yes, the Soviet population fought to take revenge and recover their motherland, but their resistance was not necessarily due to the war crimes of the invaders. While the average Red Army soldier was motivated to fight by patriotism, he also marched forward due to fear of the NKVD's wrath to his rear.
3. While partisan activity in Axis-occupied regions of the USSR generally intensified over the course of the war, this irregular warfare was not a deciding factor in the *Wehrmacht's* defeat.
4. Sadly, those same Nazi policies that were so brutal to Soviet POWs, communist officials, Jews, Roma, and others, found support in large segments of the populations across Axis-controlled territory. Germany was quite successful in mobilizing hatred and prejudice to raise additional combat troops and allies that extended the duration of the war in the east.

(1) It seems obvious that Hitler's genocidal policies against the Soviet people would lead them to rise up against his evil. Yet during the war it was difficult for most civilians to discern that life under Nazi rule was significantly worse than under Stalin's. In the years immediately prior to Barbarossa, the Soviet population endured forced starvation, summary execution, and imprisonment in a vast network of slave labor camps. In countless cases, the state security apparatus targeted citizens who showed initiative or any indication of independent thought. Those left in positions of authority were reflexively subservient to the ruling regime, but were often incompetents living in fear of the NKVD.

Once the invasion began, civilian living conditions in areas remaining under Soviet control deteriorated markedly. Men of fighting age were conscripted, resulting in a majority civilian workforce of women, augmented by old men and teenagers.[3] Tens of millions of these workers were caught up in history's largest human migration as thousands of factories were relocated east of the war zone. Once at their new labor camps, all holidays and vacations were cancelled and workers endured fixed factory shifts of twelve to sixteen hours a day. Soviet workers had to endure this increased work regimen while receiving significantly reduced food rations that equaled only a quarter of what was received by those in Germany and one-fifth available to British civilians.[4] Many industries were placed under military law. Those who missed work shifts, became ill, or did not meet increased production quotas faced arrest and shipment to the Gulag. A combination of such difficult conditions along with patriotism and pressing military needs led to more than one million women joining the Red Army, many in frontline combat roles.

This "good life" of the Red Worker was only available to ethnic peoples of the USSR not collectively under suspicion of being potential collaborators with the enemy. Entire populations from the southern areas of the country were forcibly deported to remote regions of Siberia where mortality rates soared. This ethnic cleansing included removal of the Kalmyks, Karachi, Chechens, Balkars, and the Tartars. Only many years after the war and Stalin's death were some of these citizens allowed to return to their ancestral homes.

Conditions in the Red Army were pitiless. Frontal-wave attacks similar to those used in World War I were common. Units were often sent into battle with many fewer rifles than soldiers. Those who were unarmed were ordered to advance under fire and pick up weapons dropped by those wounded or killed. Attempts at desertion were common, but so was summary execution of those who fled the front lines. In the first four months of fighting, the NKVD recorded that 667,364 deserters were arrested, of whom more than 10,000 were shot, 25,000 were imprisoned, and 630,000 were formed into new "penal battalions" that were assigned roles such as marching through minefields to clear them.[5] More than four hundred thousand Red Army soldiers served in "punishment battalions" to impose military justice immediately behind the front lines. This justice was severe, and more than 135,000 Red Army soldiers were executed by their own side by the end of the war.[6]

The people of the USSR found themselves living either under Axis rule consisting of a starvation diet, summary executions, and mass deportations to grueling work camps, or continued Soviet law, which . . . was much the same. Civilians residing east of the front lines could at least take heart from the constant barrage of patriotic messages that their efforts were critical, valued, and that all were fighting—soldiers, workers, and farmers alike—for the Russian motherland against barbarous invaders. Nevertheless, the ruthless rule of Stalin's government before and during World War II helps explain why millions of Soviet citizens actively collaborated with the Axis.

(2) Next we need to consider the impact of German treatment of Soviet POWs on the course of the war. Despite protests of innocence in the years that followed World War II, the proof is devastating that large numbers of the officer corps and the rank and file of the *Ostheer* either actively engaged in carrying out criminal programs against POWs and civilians or at least knew of their ongoing implementation.[7] The Germans expected an invasion of the USSR would quickly yield a vast haul of prisoners. After all, in World War I, the Central Powers took three million Russian POWs by the end of 1916.[8] Prior to the launch of Barbarossa, OKH war games concluded that more than half a million Red Army prisoners were likely to be captured in the early weeks of the campaign. Of course, the Soviets were "rounded up in droves" and more than three million surrendered by just the twelfth week of the invasion.

Little planning took place to manage the transport, clothing, and feeding of these captured soldiers. In other words, the German army's official policy was to execute tens of thousands of Soviet POWs in mass shootings and impose conditions on the remainder that would result in their death by starvation, disease, and exposure. Admiral Wilhelm Canaris, head of the *Abwehr* (Military Intelligence), did complain that such treatment of prisoners was immoral and against the laws of war. These objections were overruled by Field Marshal Wilhelm Keitel, head of OKW, who wrote that the admiral's thinking was grounded in "traditional ideas of gentlemanlike warfare, but this war is an ideological war of extermination."[9] The Germans captured more than five and a half million Soviet soldiers during the war. Almost two-thirds, more than three million prisoners, died in captivity due to starvation, disease, or a bullet to the back of the head.[10]

So did these criminal policies result in a decisive increase in resistance and a refusal to surrender by the rank and file of the Red Army? Several facts seem to argue against such a conclusion. As early as the first few days of the fighting, the Germans were repeatedly surprised by what they thought to be foolhardy, suicidal last stands by surrounded pockets of defenders. The intensity of combat was significantly higher than what the *Wehrmacht* had encountered in Poland or France in 1939 and 1940. One well-known example of this is the frontier battle of the Brest Fortress that began the first day of Operation Barbarossa. Despite being massively outnumbered, surrounded, and outgunned, the Soviet garrison continued to fight back for more than a week. The Germans had to employ heavy artillery, flame-throwers, and multiple airstrikes to overcome the defenders. Such determined Soviet resistance took place despite no initial knowledge that the *Wehrmacht* planned abominable treatment for those they took prisoner in the east.

Conversely, large numbers of Red Army soldiers continued to surrender in the years after 1941 despite the treatment previously meted out by the Germans to POWs in the east. Poor generalship by those in command of the Red Army allowed the *Ostheer* to surround large Soviet formations on a regular basis. When encircled, running low of ammunition and/or food, and under constant artillery barrage, even patriotic Soviet soldiers often chose to lay down their arms rather than fight to the death. In May 1942, the Germans took 170,000 prisoners on the Kerch peninsula in the Crimea.[11] An additional 250,000 Red Army soldiers were taken captive in a *kessel* near the city of Kharkov that same month.[12] The 2nd Shock Army was encircled east of Leningrad, leading to more than thirty thousand Soviets surrendering in June. Among those captured was that army's commander, General Andrei Vlasov, who switched sides to lead the Russian Liberation Army in the fight against Stalin. While German treatment of POWs in the east likely led to more sustained resistance by Red Army soldiers, it most certainly did not end large capitulations of surrounded Soviet formations.

Was such treatment instrumental in the final victory of the USSR? Letters written home from the front repeatedly describe patriotism as the motivating force for the average Soviet soldier. When under heavy fire and considering retreat, it seems that those in the Red Army who chose surrender may have been more concerned by the "fast justice" meted out by the NKVD and "punishment battalions" than the risk of death if taken prisoner. Surrender was considered such a threat to the Soviet state that Stalin issued Order No. 270 in August 1941 that classified all Red Army POWs as traitors and the soldier's families would either have their ration cards confiscated or be arrested and sent to the Gulag. Marshal Zhukov took this a step further during his command of the besieged forces in Leningrad when he announced that not only would deserters be shot but their families as well.[13]

While the Nazis were unboundedly barbaric in their methods, the resistance they encountered appears to have been driven by traditional patriotism and a desire to expel what represented another in a long line of armies that had invaded Russia. A historian, Roger Reese, concluded: "Most likely the fundamental reason why Soviet citizens fought was that their country had been invaded. Hitler handed Stalin and the Soviet population a just war by invading and violating the 1939 Nazi-Soviet Nonaggression Pact."[14] As an example, consider the reaction of Marshal Zhukov in late 1941 when he looked across the front lines. "We did not know what was burning, but the sight of the fires was depressing. Perishing in the flames was national property, the fruits of many years of labour by Soviet men and women. I asked myself how and with what should the Soviet people repay the enemy for the suffering he was leaving behind in his bloody wake? With the sword and with the sword alone, by ruthlessly destroying the enemy brute, was the only answer."[15] These are the words of a man enraged that his country has been invaded and despoiled rather than outraged by specific German policies that constituted massive war crimes. Substitute *Russian* for *Soviet* in the above quote, and this could have easily been a Russian general expressing his feelings toward the French invasion in 1812 or the Swedish one in 1708.

Stories of the invaders' atrocities did filter back to the Soviet front lines. Nonetheless, in the chaos of battle in the first year of fighting it was difficult for Stalin's regime to convince its soldiers that surrender would likely result in a slow death in captivity as the average citizen of the USSR was inured to official lies emanating from the government. The Nazis were also effective in spreading false information: "As a result of German propaganda leaflets showing captured Red Army men eating bread and drinking beer, many soldiers began to believe that the Nazis treated prisoners well, or at least they doubted the claims of their *politruki* [political commissars] to the contrary. Rather than address the questions, the army, security and political authorities ordered all Nazi propaganda leaflets immediately destroyed and criminalized the possession of them."[16]

While treating captured soldiers well might have led to a greater haul of prisoners, it is not clear that this was militarily the correct choice for the *Wehrmacht*. Millions of surly but healthy prisoners massed together in camps behind the front would have represented a serious potential security threat. In addition, proper care of millions of Red Army POWs would have required the German provide them with great quantities of clothing, food, guards, and doctors. Instead, the invaders directed these resources to the front to increase their military striking power. While it is likely that the criminal treatment of prisoners hurt the German chance of victory, we will never be able to prove it definitely, and it is even harder to know if it was a primary cause of the invaders' defeat.

(3) The Nazi's evil and genocidal policies convinced many otherwise apolitical civilians in conquered territory to take up arms against the invaders. However, if this were the primary cause of the German defeat, then partisan activity should have risen to such high levels as to force the *Wehrmacht* to redeploy large formations from the front to rear area security duties. Throughout the period from the launch of Barbarossa to the invaders' ejection from Soviet territory years later, the *Wehrmacht* was able to concentrate its best troops on the front lines. To control and pacify overrun territory, the Germans primarily employed a mixture of weak army security divisions, police battalions, SS death squads, allied formations, and units of local collaborators.

Partisan activity began almost immediately after the launch of Barbarossa. This was understandable in light of the tens of thousands of Red Army soldiers wandering the countryside after their units were smashed by the rapid German advance. Many of these lost men expected that they would be shot if they surrendered to the invaders . . . or shot as deserters if they retreated east to their own front lines. Their only means of survival was to live, and fight when necessary, in the forests and swamps behind the front. While supply lines did suffer repeated attacks that certainly weakened the fighting strength of the *Wehrmacht*, German field commanders spent more time complaining about the mud, cold, poor infrastructure, and equipment shortages than about partisan activity. First-echelon fighting formations rarely had to relocate from the front lines to secure rear areas.

Much of the first "wave" of partisans were wiped out by the end of the winter of 1941 to 1942. On the flatlands of the Ukraine, they encountered a hostile civilian base and found few places in which to hide. Even in overrun areas further north with a Russian-ethnic population more sympathetic to resistance, most guerillas were forced deep into swamps and forests and were wiped out by German military patrols, starvation, and the bitter cold.[17] After the spring thaw, Stalin's government had to rebuild much of the partisan movement from scratch and dispatch thousands of agents to operate behind enemy lines. These efforts had some success in northern districts, but partisan activity was quite limited in 1942 in Ukraine through which the German supply lines stretched east to the momentous battles in the Caucasus and along the Volga. It was only later in the war with an increasing possibility of German defeat and withdrawal that partisan activity accelerated across occupied territory from the Black Sea to the Baltic. Even then, many of the rear areas that came under partisan control were wooded or swampy regions that had little value to the invaders.

Despite the partisans' best efforts, the Germans were able to control most of 850,000 square miles of occupied territory containing upward of 70 million Soviet citizens while utilizing only limited resources and fewer than 110,000 men.[17] Nine weak "security" divisions made up of older soldiers equipped with captured or obsolete weapons provided most rear-area security for the German conquerors in 1941. In addition, there were fewer than ten thousand men in the infamous and genocidal *Einsatzgruppen* of the SS, who spent most of their time slaughtering unarmed civilians. As partisan activity increased in later years, so did German recruitment of collaborators. These "former Russians" were given arms not needed by the *Wehrmacht*, organized into partisan-suppression units, and sent out to fight their countrymen. In light of the brutally harsh treatment meted out by the Germans, how is it that they were able to employ such small occupation forces to rule over such a large Soviet population for so long?

It is an unfortunate fact that despite the often-repeated modern commentary that winning hearts and minds is the way to conquer a nation, terror and genocide have historically been more likely to lead to victory for invaders. From the utter destruction of Carthage by Rome, to Tamerlane's pyramids of skulls, to the California state government's twenty-five-cent bounty for each Native American scalp received, murder, arson, and fear have proven to be the most effective strategies for subjugating a people defeated in arms. Hitler made it clear that he planned to proceed with just such a policy in the east when he declared, "There's only one duty: to Germanize this country [Russia] by the immigration of Germans, and to look upon the natives as Redskins."[18] In this comment, he explicitly linked his policies to those employed so successfully by the United States in the 1800s. The Axis lost the war and were ground to dust, but their strategy toward the people of the USSR was one practiced repeatedly with success by invaders since the dawn of civilization.

(4) Not only did local civilians celebrate the arrival of Nazi invaders as relief from the terror of Soviet rule, they often eagerly joined the invaders in rounding up and killing those targeted for death by the invaders. All across the western parts of the USSR, local residents assisted in pogroms against Jews, Communist Party members, and other "undesirables." The Germans had little difficulty in finding citizens willing to collaborate with the occupation regime. New mayors were installed, priests returned to churches closed under communist rule, and fighting-age men were recruited to take up arms in support of the German cause. After aiding the invaders, these men were marked for "liquidation" by Stalin's government and had little choice but to remain in the service of the Axis.

The numbers willing to work or fight for the Nazis were quite large. As already discussed, the *Waffen-SS* and the *Wehrmacht* had significant success recruiting in the east. The Rand Institute estimates that as many as two million Soviet citizens joined various German armed units, and that some ethnic groups of the USSR came to be better represented in the invader's military than in the Red Army.[19] Many more civilians who did not join the fight still sought out positions in the occupation administration, or otherwise assisted in its functioning. The Nazis recruited so many Soviet citizens into rear area security roles that in raw numbers the fighting against partisan units often took on the character of a civil war.

It is reprehensible but undeniable that the slaughter of Jews, communists, and others appealed to a segment of the population in occupied areas of the USSR and across the rest of Europe. Nazi ideology was revolting to many, but it inspired tens of thousands of others to take up arms to fight with the Axis. In a final analysis, Germany's brutal treatment of the occupied Soviet areas likely led to less collaboration, increased partisan activity, and greater disruption to supply lines. The Nazis would have benefited from imposing a more conciliatory program that offered self-rule to western areas of the USSR. However, a scenario including such "enlightened" policies would have been at odds with the base dogma of fascist National Socialism, and diluted the motivating factors that led the racist/anti-Semitic/intolerant German public and its European allies to fight so effectively for so long even after the likelihood of victory dimmed to an ember.

It is difficult to conclude with certainty that the Germans' evil practices led to a decisive skewing of the war in favor of the Red Army. The war was not won in skirmishes between small groups of lightly armed fighters in the swamps and forests of Belorussia. The conflict's decisive actions took place in the grinding toil of the two sides' massive arms factories and in the great set-piece battles that raged across the USSR, such as those for Moscow, Leningrad, Kiev, Stalingrad, Kursk, Smolensk, Vitebsk, Kharkov, and Minsk.

To conclude, we have now evaluated the prominent theories put forward to explain the failure of the German invasion of the USSR. A few of these arguments do not hold up under scrutiny. An earlier drive on Moscow would have been underpowered and is unlikely to have ended the war. Chances are high that such an attempt would have ended in disaster for the *Wehrmacht*. Similarly, complaints that the Barbarossa force was too small and unable to fight more than one six-month campaign seems to be contradicted in light of Germany's massive military victories in 1942 and its concurrent conquest of vast territories of the USSR. An invasion that started a few weeks earlier in the absence of both a Balkan campaign and a particularly wet spring would have delivered some advantage to the Germans. Yet an earlier launch date of Barbarossa at the start of June would have offered little comfort to Army Group Center fighting house to house in Moscow in the cold, autumn rain as the roads carrying its supplies turned to mud.

Other theories have more merit. A larger invasion force, more tanks, or more tracked supply vehicles certainly would have helped. However, logistical factors made it quite difficult to supply the German armies once they had penetrated hundreds of miles into Soviet territory. Had the *Ostheer* been larger, its supply problems would have been compounded. Similarly, of some advantage to the Germans would have been a focused advance into eastern Ukraine after the Battle of Kiev. Still, such a change in the axis of attack would have exposed Army Group South's long flanks to a winter counterattack, which might very well have been just as painful as the one experienced historically by Army Group Center.

A milder winter, paved roads, or better railways would each have allowed the Germans to push further east in less time. However, such scenarios did not characterize the physical realties of the USSR in 1941, and represent factors completely out of control of the invaders. Counterfactually tweak one, two, or all three of these points and there is still no clear evidence that the Germans would have been able to defeat the determined resistance of the Red Army supported by a patriotic Soviet population and Anglo-American supply deliveries. Had the invaders encountered better infrastructure and somewhat warmer temperatures, how would this have changed history? By late 1941 the *Wehrmacht* would still have found itself deep in enemy territory in subzero temperatures at the end of a very long logistical line fighting new conscript armies and fresh divisions shipped in from Siberia. Such a scenario would have advantaged the Germans but would not have guaranteed victory.

Finally, had the Nazis administered the western USSR less harshly, there would have been less partisan activity and more collaboration with the invaders. However, would the German rank and file have fought as hard if it had not been fighting for the warped ideological tenets of *Lebensraum* and a chance to rid the world of Jews and Bolshevism? Would Stalin's government have been any less effective in mobilizing the Soviet people to fight? In the end, none of the traditional reasons given for the Axis defeat by the USSR are individually satisfying. The change of one of the above-discussed factors or decisions and the German military may have been somewhat more successful. However, none of the points examined would necessarily have been decisive.

· *14* ·

A Japanese Attack on the USSR and the Key to German Victory

*H*itler was quite successful in his diplomatic efforts prior to the invasion of the USSR. As previously discussed, large numbers of Romanians, Italians, Finns, Hungarians, Croats, Spaniards, and Slovaks fought in national units side by side with the *Wehrmacht* as the invasion pushed east. In the Far East, Japan began to mass its military along the Soviet borders and prepared to invade as well. Far from its allies, surrounded by enemies and losing ground and armies at an astonishing rate, the Soviet Union appeared to be close to utter defeat at the end of July 1941.

This and the next four chapters will argue that the attack on the USSR would have resulted in a successful conquest if Nazi Germany had been able to convince its Japanese and Finnish allies to engage in courses of action that can be referred to respectively as "the Dagger in the Back" and "the Anaconda." The first plan would be to persuade the Japanese to invade the Soviet Union in the Far East in 1941 or 1942. The second was a less aggressive plan to cajole the Japanese and the Finns to cut the critical supply lines of Anglo-American aid arriving at the ports of Murmansk and Vladivostok.

To understand why either of these two options would have been decisive, we need to consider the strategic positioning of the Soviet Union, Japan, and Finland upon the launch of Barbarossa and the importance of matériel aid the USSR received from Britain and the United States. From 1938 to the middle of 1941, Hitler effectively executed his plan for an enlarged Germany with hegemonic status over northern Europe: he gained Austria, Czechoslovakia, eastern Poland, Denmark, Norway, Belgium, and the Netherlands along with portions of France, Poland, Greece, and Yugoslavia with a maximum of diplomacy and a minimum of fighting. Axis allies Italy, Hungary, and Bulgaria received parts of France, Greece, and Yugoslavia as war prizes and were tied into the new Nazi economic order for the continent. Hitler's diplomatic preparations before the launch of Barbarossa were also quite successful in isolating the Soviets and binding additional allies to the German cause. However, to defeat the USSR, geopolitical realities required specific efforts from Finland and Japan in the fighting to come.

Germany initially saw Finland and Japan take steps toward a coordinated conquest of the USSR, but the Nazi government was unable to convince its allies to harmonize their efforts and all three went down to defeat. After the start of Barbarossa, the Japanese began a rapid buildup of forces along the Soviet border in the Far East, and the Finnish army advanced both south and east into the USSR. However, later in 1941, the Japanese reversed their military buildup and the Finns abruptly ended offensive operations. These two events allowed the USSR to import many billions of pounds of matériel aid from its allies through Murmansk and Vladivostok. Immense shipments of guns, ammunition, tanks, trucks, petroleum, food, radios, and hundreds of other items were unloaded at these two ports and transported along rail lines running perilously close to the armed forces of Finland and Japan. Not only did these two intense enemies of the USSR not interdict this flow of supplies, but a cold peace prevailed along these fronts, allowing the Soviets to transfer more than a million trained soldiers west and south to fight the Germans in the battles for Moscow, Stalingrad, Leningrad, and Kursk.

While both Finland and Japan considered the USSR to be their most dangerous enemy with designs on their territories, these two German allies did little to weaken their Soviet nemesis in 1942 and 1943. They watched passively as the Red Army grew in power. Once out of mortal danger, the USSR launched overwhelming offensives against Finland (June 1944) and Japan (August 1945). Finland suffered terrible casualties in what it called the "Continuation War," and sued for peace, ceding large amounts of its territory, and agreeing to painful reparations payments. In 1945, the Red Army quickly overran the Japanese mainland empire in northern Asia that had been acquired at the expense of much blood and treasure over the previous half century. The Soviets advanced offshore to take the southern half of Sakhalin Island and the Kuriles, and were poised to invade Hokkaido, the northernmost of Japan's main home islands, when World War II ended. With all the advantages held by the Axis in the summer of 1941, and with the Finns and Japanese harboring historical animus toward the USSR, why did these German allies not assist in the dismantling of the Soviet nation? To understand the primary reasons why the USSR defeated the fascist invaders in the great battles of the Eastern Front, we need to delve into the diplomatic and military decisions made by the governments of Germany, Japan, and Finland.

HOKUSHIN-RON: THE STAB IN THE BACK

The most straightforward action that would have doomed the USSR to defeat in World War II was an attack by Japan on the Soviet Far East after the launch of Barbarossa in 1941. Hitler and his henchmen may have hoped that the Red Army would collapse under the initial blows of Barbarossa, but this was unlikely considering the history of Russian perseverance when invaded over the centuries. In the face of continued organized resistance, Germany would find it difficult to defeat the USSR militarily in one season of campaigning unless Soviet forces in Siberia were tied down along the Manchurian border. If the threat of war with Japan diminished, the bulk of the 1st and 2nd Red Banner armies stationed in the Far East would be available for redeployment to the European battlefields. While an initial German invasion in the west of the USSR might be quite successful, it would then have to fight these fresh "Siberian" formations, which could be quickly shipped by established rail lines to aid in the defense of major interior population, industrial, and transportation hubs of the Soviet state such as Moscow, Stalingrad, Kuybyshev, and Gorky.

The further east the Germans advanced the more compact the Red Army lines of communication and the shorter the distance the Siberian armies would need to be repositioned. As the great majority of the Barbarossa invasion force was composed of infantry that had to travel by foot, it was unlikely that the bulk of the *Ostheer* could fight its way across the more than one thousand miles from the western frontiers of the USSR to the planned Astrakhan-Arkhangelsk stop line in the second half of 1941. Such a goal became even more unlikely if the Red Army could deploy fresh troops along a defensive front stretching from Rostov-on-Don up the Volga and then to Moscow. Thus, to push east and achieve its territorial goals, Germany required Japanese aid to pin down the Red Army formations stationed in the Far East.

Militarist Japan emerged from its isolationism in the late nineteenth century as an expansionary, warlike empire with fantasies of racial superiority. The nation's ideology claimed its head of state to be godlike, infallible, and demanding of unquestioning obedience on the battlefield. The military came to dominate the government as the resignation of the ministers of either the army or navy departments triggered the dissolution of any cabinet. This meant that the civilian politicians generally took on caretaker and consensus-building roles. The emperor remained powerful, but in general only influenced policy on the margins.

Japan's great weakness was the impoverishment of its geography. Its islands possess almost none of the natural resources required for the industrial economy of the twentieth century world: little or no coal, petroleum, iron ore, aluminum, or copper and not even enough arable land to feed its growing population. This lack of self-sufficiency resulted in the great question in Japan being not if it should seize an overseas empire, but in which direction to conquer. In the decades before World War II, its military and civilian government ministers struggled to reconcile two expansionary urges. The first was *Hokushin-ron* or "Northern Road," which argued for a Japanese focus on the conquest and exploitation of Siberia, Korea, and Manchuria. The second was *Nanshin-ron* or "Southern Road," which called for expansion into Southeast Asia and the Pacific islands. The Imperial Japanese Army (IJA) was the primary champion of the former; the Imperial Japanese Navy (IJN) supported the latter.

In the first decades of the twentieth century, the Japanese Empire spread along both these northern and southern roads. On the mainland, Korea and Manchuria were conquered. Great expanses of the Pacific also came under Tokyo's control as Japan seized the Pescadores, Marianas, Caroline, and Marshall archipelagos along with Taiwan and the southern half of Sakhalin Island. Japan's control of Manchuria was a constant source of friction with the Nationalist Chinese Government (*Kuomintang* or KMT) of Chiang Kai-shek that claimed the territory as its own. Militaristic factions in the Japanese government agitated for a war to crush the KMT's power and impose Japanese hegemony over eastern China. Several senior Japanese officials, such as the influential General Kanji Ishiwara, then serving as vice chief of staff of the *Kwantung* army, warned against such a clash with China: "It will be what Spain was for Napoleon, an endless bog."[1] Nevertheless, a vicious war of conquest was launched against the Republic of China in July 1937. Despite great early victories, the "China Incident," as it was known in Tokyo, was a disaster for Japan as the fighting dragged on indefinitely, drained much of its army southward, and poisoned relations with the Western powers.

Even as the Japanese Empire pushed deeper into China, those in favor of *Hokushin-ron* wished to drive the Soviets out of the Far East. The Soviet fleet and army based at Vladivostok represented a threat to Japan's mainland empire and its internal sea lanes. Petroleum from the northern region of Sakhalin was a potential source of supply to offset dependence of shipments from the United States and other Western powers. Many agitating for an attack on the Soviet Far East believed eastern Siberia would yield great finds of natural resources to power Japanese industry. Russian-Japanese enmity was longstanding and took on a more ideological tone with the formation of the USSR as Tokyo feared a local communism rising as a threat to the Imperial System.

As already noted, the border between the USSR and the Japanese Empire was one of the most violent in the world in the second half of the 1930s. Tens of thousands of IJA soldiers were wounded or killed fighting the Red Army, and plans were well developed to attack and drive the Red Army out of the Far East. That Japan desired to conquer eastern Siberia was clear. The question was only a matter of timing. The pitched battles of Lake Khasan and Khalkhin Gol in 1938 and 1939 taught the Japanese that the Red Army had developed into a robust foe with a strong aviation arm and mechanized tank force. With that in mind, the Japanese military planned for a multistage operation, with an initial attack from both the sea and air on military installations around Vladivostok and the northern half of Sakhalin Island with its precious oil fields. This joint operation would destroy the Soviet Pacific Fleet, eliminate the threat of bomber attack on the Japanese home islands from long-range VVS aircraft, and take control of the USSR's Maritime Province. The second stage of the offensive would be an advance westward by the IJA out of its Manchurian puppet state of Manchukuo to the shores of Lake Baikal. Finally, Japanese units would push further west along the

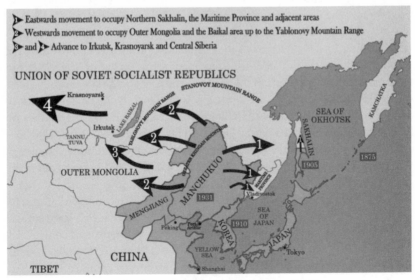

Hokushin-ron: **Japan's Plan for an Attack on the Soviet Far East**[2]

Soviet railways to capture the industrial cities of Irkutsk and Krasnoyarsk, and permanently detach eastern Siberia from the rest of the USSR.

Japan had already successfully defeated Moscow in 1905 in a full-scale war. By the end of the 1930s, the island nation's navy was dramatically larger than the maritime forces the USSR had stationed in the Far East, and its army was well positioned to envelop the strategic port city of Vladivostok and sever the Trans-Siberian Railroad. Chances of Japanese victory would soar if the USSR had to fight a war in Europe at the same time as it faced an invasion in the Far East.

Japan and Germany began negotiating an alliance against the USSR in 1935. In 1936, the two nations ratified the Anti-Comintern Pact. While the published text of the agreement only discussed efforts by the signatories to combat the activities of the Comintern, there were several secret addenda. In these, Germany and Japan both promised not to enter into separate political agreements with the USSR and to maintain benevolent neutrality if either became involved in a war with the Soviets. Germany also agreed to recognize the Japanese puppet state of Manchukuo and end arms shipments and military assistance to the KMT. In 1937, Italy and Spain also joined the pact. Japan's relations with the USSR deteriorated, and fighting flared along Manchukuo's borders.

While antipathy for the USSR brought the Japanese-German alliance into being, the relationship never became particularly strong. There was little coordination between the nations' senior military commanders, and Hitler did not share crucial aspects of his plans with his partner in the Far East. While the German dictator held several meetings with the leaders of allied European nations such as Mussolini, Franco, Antonescu, Tiso, Horthy, Quisling, and Ryti, he never met with those of Japan. Foreign Minister Yosuke Matsuoka did visit Berlin fatefully in the spring of 1941, but his counterpart, Ribbentrop, never made the return trip to Tokyo. This absence of high-level coordination took place despite Japan being by far the most militarily potent of Germany's allies in World War II. By the launch of Barbarossa, the IJA had a battle-hardened force in excess of 1,500,000 soldiers in fifty-one infantry divisions and ten armored regiments.[3] Another five hundred thousand sailors served in the world's third largest navy with one of the best air arms in the world.

It is likely that prior to December 7, 1941, a concerted German diplomatic effort could have convinced Japan to enter into a joint attack on the USSR. As early as 1933, the new Nazi government had considered a combined attack with Japan to carve up the Soviet Union, confident that the Western capitalist powers would hesitate to come to the aid of the communist state.[4] However, Hitler's immediate need in 1939 was to

Table 11.   The 1941 Naval Balance in the Pacific[5]

	Japanese Fleet	Soviet Pacific Fleet	US Pacific Fleet	US Asian Fleet	Britain and Commonwealth	Dutch East Indies
Battleships	10		9		3	
Aircraft Carriers	10		3			
Cruisers	38		20	2	8	3
Destroyers	112	9	50	13	5	7
Submarines	65	48	33	17		15
Totals	**235**	**57**	**115**	**32**	**16**	**25**

restrain Stalin in the east so that he could turn his military's full attention to defeating France, Poland, and Britain. This explains the German push for a nonaggression treaty with the USSR. However, Tokyo received little warning of these political maneuverings and the Molotov-Ribbentrop Pact was a great disappointment to the Japanese. It violated the Anti-Comintern Pact, undermined Japanese trust in German reliability, and reduced the need for the USSR to maintain forces in Europe as the *Wehrmacht* focused on France and Britain.

Hitler could have justified the pact with Stalin to his Japanese allies as part of a process leading to a joint attack on the Soviet Union. Under such an explanation, first would come the dismantlement of Poland, bringing German troops that much closer to Moscow, second the defeat of the French and the British, and then finally the combined might of the Axis powers would crush the isolated USSR in an enormous double envelopment from both east and west. Luckily for world civilization, such conversations did not take place.

Instead, reverberations of the Molotov-Ribbentrop Pact moved the Japanese government away from a war along the "northern road" and toward a southern strategy of expansion. While Hitler's diplomatic actions sowed distrust in Tokyo regarding joint action against the USSR, his military victories brought Japan that much closer to war with the United States and Britain. As the *Wehrmacht* rolled west across Europe, the Dutch, French, and British were critically weakened in their ability to defend their possessions in the Far East. Resource-poor Japan coveted French Indochina, British Malaya, and the Dutch East Indies for their wealth of petroleum, tin, rubber, copper, tungsten, chromium, iron ore, manganese, nickel, and rice. The defeat of France and the Battle of the Atlantic also forced the United States, just beginning to rearm, to focus its military efforts on supporting Britain rather than deterring Japanese aggression.

Large numbers of US destroyers sailed through the Panama Canal to operate as Atlantic convoy escorts. The dominance of the Japanese Fleet in the Pacific increased accordingly.

While the Germans and British traded blows in the west and Nazi-Soviet relations cooled, the Japanese war of aggression in China continued. The further the Japanese pushed into the country, the faster their casualties rose. Still, by 1940 the Japanese had achieved their goals in China: they had driven back the KMT, conquered the most economically productive regions of the nation, and set up a functioning puppet government in Nanking. However, Chiang Kai-shek spurned all peace feelers to end the war. While forced west to a new capital at Chungking, his government welcomed aid from Britain, the USSR, and the United States, raised new military formations, and launched several counteroffensives. The Japanese, increasingly desperate to end the "China Incident," began to look for ways to cut off foreign aid flowing to the *Kuomintang*.

After the ejection of the BEF from Continental Europe in June 1940, Hitler and Ribbentrop expressed confidence to Japanese ambassador Hiroshi Oshima that Britain would soon sue for peace. However, as

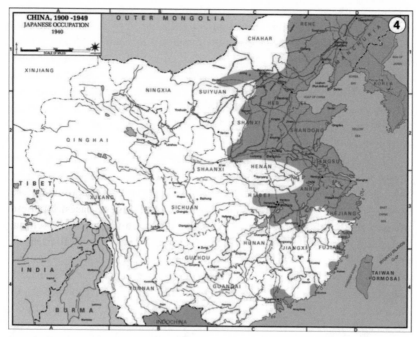

Japan's Conquests in China by 1940[6]

it became clear that Churchill's government was determined to fight on, the Germans began to change their thinking. Instead of using Tokyo as a counterweight against the USSR, they looked to their ally in the Far East to pressure the British and the United States. Many in the Japanese government concluded that the European colonies in the Pacific would never again have such weak defenses. The slogan, "Don't miss the bus!" became common among those promoting the "southern road" strategy to expand the empire in Southeast Asia.

The goals of ending the war in China, pushing southward at the expense of the European powers and gaining sources of critical natural resources were united in efforts to sever the flow of military supplies to the KMT's armies via the railway terminating at the French Indochinese port of Haiphong. At the same time that the French government was negotiating an armistice with Germany, the Japanese presented Governor Georges Catroux with demands that aid cease flowing to China from Indochina and that an IJA military inspection team enter the area to oversee compliance. After the French surrender and the internment of its fleet, the Japanese asked for more and insisted that it receive troop transit rights through northern Indochina as well as the use of several military airfields to better encircle and attack the embattled KMT forces. The French government dragged out the negotiations and unsuccessfully appealed to Germany for assistance in moderating its ally's demands. Eventually the Japanese invaded the northern portion of Indochina by land and sea in late September and, after brief fighting, the local French forces capitulated. The Japanese duly moved its aircraft to the demanded bases, and the colonial government was no longer in any position to turn down Japanese purchase requests for shipments of rubber or tin from Southern Indochinese plantations and mines.

The Japanese invasion of northern Indochina led to the first joint planning meeting in Singapore that November of British, Australian, and Dutch military commanders. US representatives soon joined these meetings as full participants. With its new Indochinese bases, Japanese forces were now that much closer to British Malaya and Dutch Indochina. However, Tokyo hesitated in going to war with Britain in 1940 as urged by Germany. Before launching an attack, it was hoped that a diplomatic agreement with the United States could be negotiated in which Washington would acquiesce to the formation of Japanese hegemony over a new "Greater East Asia Co-Prosperity Sphere," which included the former European colonies in Southeastern Asia.

· *15* ·

The Pursuit of Oil and
the Road to Global War

$\mathscr{P}$rior to World War II, Japan sourced the majority of its petroleum, scrap iron, and copper from the United States and was economically dependent on this bilateral trade relationship. However, aggression in China had strained relations with Washington and put the flow of natural resources at risk. Significant US economic investments in China had suffered in the fighting, and atrocities committed by the IJA had inflamed American public opinion. In retaliation, the United States terminated its commercial treaty of 1911 with Tokyo and used its influence in the global financial markets to keep Japan from borrowing overseas.[1] After Germany defeated France and the Netherlands, the Roosevelt administration warned Tokyo that it would oppose the seizure of any colonial territories in Southeast Asia. The Export Control Act of 1940 became law on July 5, which gave the president a flexible tool to cut off trade with Japan and possibly deter it from expanding southwards. When the Japanese strong-armed the French authorities in Indochina, the United States embargoed aviation fuel and scrap metal shipments. Tokyo feared that its flow of petroleum would cease completely without an overall political settlement with Washington.

The Japanese knew that its reliance on imported petroleum was the great weakness of its economy and its empire. The government took steps to prepare for an oil embargo: it increased its purchases from the United States and built up a stockpile of fifty-four million barrels of oil against annual imports of more than thirty million barrels.[2] The government imposed severe measures to curtail civilian consumption, going so far as to force the nation's commercial fishing fleet to forgo motors and return to the use of sails.[3] Finally, it cast about for an alternative source of petroleum to replace supplies from the United States. However, Japan's aggressive military actions in the late 1930s had left it with few alternatives.

Geographically the closest supply of foreign oil production was just outside Japanese control in the northern half of Sakhalin Island. Japan had occupied the area during the Russian Civil War and began drilling there in 1920. International pressure forced the Japanese to withdraw and cede the territory back to the USSR, though it secured a concession for a company based in Tokyo, JSOCNS (Joint Stock Oil Company of Northern Sakhalin), to drill for and export oil.

Exports of oil from Sakhalin began to ramp up in the early 1930s, and the Japanese prepared to drill many additional wells. The Soviets also started their own company in the area, Sakhalinneft Trust, which was soon producing three times the output of JSOCNS.[4] The island is also rich in coal, and millions of tons were exported to Japan through 1945. Politics and war then interfered with these rising trends in resource extraction. The fighting along the Far Eastern borders with the USSR in the second half of the 1930s, and the signing of the Anti-Comintern Pact, resulted in a predictable deterioration in Soviet-Japanese relations. JSOCNS was required as part of its concession agreement to have more than 50 percent of its employees be Soviet citizens. The company began to experience significant "labor relations" issues and work slowdowns. The NKVD arrested hundreds of Soviet employees of JSOCNS and accused them of espionage. Production declined significantly after 1934, and new exploration by the company was blocked.[5] Sakhalin clearly could yield more oil, potentially enough to supply all of Japan's needs (currently, with more advanced technology, northern Sakhalin's onshore and offshore fields produce more than 230 million barrels per year). However, any significant increase in JSOCNS output and exports was unlikely to take place as long as Japanese-Soviet relations remained strained.

Table 12.   JSOCNS Petroleum Exports to Japan in Barrels[6]

1926	1929	1932	1934	1938
210,000	1,050,000	1,298,045	1,680,000	1,128,400

Further afield were the oil fields of Malaya on the British-controlled island of Borneo. However, Britain was unwilling to sell Japan significant supplies and had raised the possibility of organizing an international petroleum embargo against it through the League of Nations as early as 1934.[7] Britain's General Hankey wrote,

> We have been warned again and again by our diplomatic representatives at Tokyo, that any sanctions against Japan, whether by the League or

unilaterally by ourselves will precipitate a war. For war, thanks to the domination of the pacifists, we are totally unprepared. We have only a few cruisers in the Far East, our bases at Hong Kong and Singapore are at the mercy of Japan, and would be captured or destroyed long before our main fleet could arrive from the Mediterranean. So the result of an embargo against Japan, whether by the League or by ourselves, would open the whole of the European possessions and trade in the Far East to Japanese depredations.[8]

The British supported the Nationalist Chinese government, feared Tokyo's territorial aspirations in the Far East, and came close to war with Japan in 1939 over the "Tientsin Incident," in which the Japanese military besieged British settlements in that northern Chinese coastal city.

Finally, the Japanese sent a large mission of diplomats and military officers to Batavia, capital of the Dutch East Indies, in September 1940 to negotiate greater oil exports from that colony. The Japanese asked for an increase in petroleum trade flows from 4,500,000 barrels annually to 22,000,000. Such an amount would have almost perfectly supplanted imports from the United States. The local Dutch administrators dragged out the negotiations over three months and eventually agreed, under certain conditions, to increase shipments to 14,500,000 barrels per year.[9] The problem with this settlement was that the companies operating most of the wells in the East Indies had already pledged to join any Anglo-American petroleum embargo and openly prepared to sabotage the local oil fields and refineries if the Japanese moved militarily against them.[10]

The government in Tokyo knew that without securing a sufficient ongoing supply of fuel, it would need either to come to an accommodation with the United States or militarily seize the oil fields it required with potential targets in Sakhalin, the Dutch East Indies, and/or British Malaya. President Roosevelt made it clear in a letter to his wife in November 1940 that an oil embargo was likely to force Japan to choose war: "The real answer which you cannot use is that if we forbid oil shipments to Japan, Japan will increase her purchases of Mexican oil and furthermore, may be driven by actual necessity to a descent on the Dutch East Indies. At this writing, we all regard such action on our part as an encouragement to the spread of war in the Far East."[11]

THE ROAD TO GLOBAL WAR

It was against this backdrop of deteriorating relations with the United States and the USSR that Japan, Germany, and Italy strengthened their alliance with the signing of the Tripartite Pact in September 1940. The agreement bound the Axis nations together and pledged the three signatories to a military alliance if one was attacked by a new belligerent. This gave both Germany and Japan protection against potential assaults by either the USSR or the United States. The Tripartite Pact also "granted" Japan the right to create a "new order" in Asia, while Germany and Italy "received" the same in Europe from its Far Eastern ally.

Such a reordering of national borders by the Axis nations was unlikely to be to the advantage of the USSR. While the Soviets were told that the Tripartite Pact's aim was ensuring US neutrality, the language of the document also meant that the USSR would find itself in a war on two fronts were it to attack either Japan or Germany. As already discussed, Molotov traveled to Berlin where he received an offer for his nation to join the Tripartite Pact and escape the geographic vice of a military alliance of the Japanese and Nazi empires. Of course, Stalin rejected this offer, and Hitler prepared for war.

While the Tripartite Pact improved Japan's positioning were it to become engaged in a conflict with the USSR and a *Hokushin-ron* strategy, it also helped to ensure Soviet neutrality if Tokyo sent its forces south to seize Southeast Asia. The *Kriegsmarine* further raised Japanese hopes for success of such a *Nanshin-ron* venture due to the actions of an obscure commerce raider. In the same week of November 1940 that Molotov and Hitler held their contentious meetings in Berlin, the German auxiliary cruiser, *Atlantis*, shelled and boarded the British cargo ship SS *Automedon* off the coast of Sumatra. Before sinking, the captured ship yielded fifteen bags of top-secret mail, decoding tablets, fleet orders, and naval intelligence reports addressed to Britain's Far Eastern Command. This correspondence revealed current assessments and disposition of military forces in the Pacific, detailed notes on Singapore's fortifications, and the British War Cabinet's conclusion that it was far too weak in the Pacific to prevail in a war against the Japanese. The documents were loaded onto a German prize ship, the *Ole Jacob*, which steamed at best possible speed for Yokohama.[12] A day after its arrival, December 5, the Germans turned over the mail to the Japanese. This intelligence coup elated the Japanese military and played a role in the decision to "go south."

While German preparations for Barbarossa were underway in early 1941, its diplomacy with Japan continued to focus on bringing its Asian ally into the war against Britain. Ribbentrop met with Ambassador Oshima multiple times in February 1941 and argued for a Japanese attack on British Malaya and its main military base at Singapore.[13] In an attempt to ensure peace along the Soviet border and coordinate his nation's efforts against the British, Foreign Minister Matsuoka of Japan visited Moscow and Berlin in March 1941. It was a fateful trip.

When Matsuoka arrived in Germany, he immediately discerned the significant deterioration in relations between the Nazis and the USSR. However, while planning for Barbarossa was well advanced, and allies such as Finland and Romania were told of the coming attack, Hitler decided not to trust the Japanese with this crucial information. In fact, he issued orders that nothing be said about Barbarossa to his Far Eastern partner.[14] It was an error of far-reaching consequences. While not mentioning details of the invasion, Ribbentrop did tell Matsuoka that German-Soviet relations could spiral into war in the future: "In order to eradicate our European problems, we may need to confront the Soviet Union militarily."[15] However, the Japanese visitor was not told such an armed conflict was imminent. When Hitler and Ribbentrop met jointly with the visiting foreign minister, they argued for a Japanese strike on the British in Asia.

With Japan already leaning toward an attack on the European colonies in Southeast Asia, and kept unaware of the imminence of the German invasion of the USSR, Matsuoka headed east to Moscow hoping to secure his nation's northern flank and give it strategic flexibility. His meetings with Stalin resulted in a treaty specifying that for five years if either Japan or the Soviet Union entered into a new military conflict, the other would remain neutral for its duration. In addition, the two nations signed a declaration to respect the existing borders of Manchukuo, the USSR, and the Soviet client state of Mongolia.[16] Japan agreed to relinquish its petroleum concession in northern Sakhalin and in return, the USSR would cease sending military aid to the Nationalist Chinese government. With the risk of attack from the Soviets reduced, the southern road for conquest became that much more appealing to the government in Tokyo.

Immediately after the signing of the formal documents in Moscow, the Japanese foreign minister talked of a lasting peace and proclaimed to Stalin over toasts of vodka that, "I'm a man of my words. If I ever lie to you, I will commit *seppuku* in the Japanese fashion, and present my head to you."[17] Despite his words, Matsuoka, like any good diplomat, was an expert liar. He considered the new agreements temporary at best, to be discarded at the first opportunity. On the day of his arrival back in Tokyo, April 22, he stated to the assembled senior staff of the foreign ministry that Japan should attack the USSR as soon as possible. An hour later, he was granted an audience with the emperor, where Matsuoka urged Japan to prepare for an offensive war against the Soviets and conquer as far west as Irkutsk.[19] However, with the USSR, having pledged to remain neutral, the IJN and those in favor of *Nanshin-ron* were encouraged to push for a military campaign into Southeast Asia.

Matsuoka's diplomatic success in Moscow caused annoyance in Berlin at a time that the *Wehrmacht* was assembling the bulk of its forces for Barbarossa and wished to see the USSR diplomatically isolated. However, the Soviet-Japanese Neutrality Pact was not entirely negative for the Nazis. It helped convince Stalin that no German attack was forthcoming. Moreover, it increased the chances of a strike on the British Empire in Asia. Finally, it forced the United States to consider a Pacific war against a Japanese military unburdened from the risk of conflict with the USSR.

At the same time that the Japanese government of Prime Minister Fumimaro Konoe negotiated with the United States, it also assigned the commander of the Combined Fleet, Admiral Yamamoto, to begin planning an attack on Pearl Harbor. As the dual diplomatic/military tracks progressed, the date for the launch of Barbarossa drew near and rumors of the German offensive spread to Tokyo. Contemplating a conflict with Britain and the United States, the Konoe government opposed its Axis allies entering into a massive new land war in Europe with a new enemy. Konoe had Matsuoka cable Ribbentrop urging against a war with the USSR. The German's reply was, "Today it is impossible to avoid a war against the Soviet Union. If the war really comes, however, I am convinced that it will be over within a few months. Please trust me on this. In this war Germany does not need any help from Japan. Moreover, the outcome of the war will favor Japan."[19] Such frank language from Ribbentrop made it clear to the government in Tokyo that the fraying peace between Germany and the USSR would not last much longer. It also highlights the shortsightedness of Nazi diplomacy to not consider attempts to coordinate Japan's entry into such a conflict with the USSR.

Ambassador Oshima in Berlin communicated in a stream of increasingly specific cables to his superiors in Tokyo that the Nazis would soon invade the Soviet Union. On April 16, 1941, he wrote, "In case Germany and Russia go to war, of course we might revive our one time anti-Communistic national policy, but now that we have concluded a neutrality treaty with Moscow and inasmuch as Germany is confident that she can whip the Russians, I do not think that she expects us to make a simultaneous attack on them. I think that all Germany would desire would be that we keep our soldiers and military establishments intact in Northern Manchukuo to prevent Russian soldiers in that area from being transferred to the scene of the conflict."[20]

Then on April 24, 1941, he sent: "Germany is fairly confident that she can defeat the Soviet and she is preparing to fight the Soviet at any moment. . . . it is up to us to get ready and lay our plans for whatever takes place. Will you please prepare a counter policy?"[21] On May 6, Oshima followed this up with, "However Germany is gradually stepping up her preparations for war against the Soviet and this will be completed during May."[22] The Japanese ambassador in Bulgaria, Yamaji Akira, also sent the following on May 9: "Summary of reports indicate that: In preparation for a long drawn out war and successful termination of her Near Eastern campaign, Germany will take over the grain fields of Ukraine and Caucasus as soon as the harvest is ready. This means war with the U.S.S.R. about June."[23]

Lastly, in early June, Oshima met in person with Hitler and Ribbentrop, who told him that war with the Soviet Union was very likely in the near future and that the *Wehrmacht* would crush the Red Army in a series of rapid campaigns. They urged Japan to join the war with its Axis partners. The ambassador cabled home that the German invasion was imminent and the Japanese government's Liaison Conference (composed of government ministers, representatives of the emperor, the IJA, and the IJN) discussed their nation's options. The conference concluded that the primary Japanese course of action would remain a thrust to the south, but that preparations would also take place to invade Siberia if the USSR looked close to collapse.[24]

· *16* ·

The Critical Summer
and the Road South

*O*nly ninety minutes after receiving news that the German invasion had commenced, Matsuoka arrived at the Imperial Palace to meet with the emperor and urge that Japan also attack the USSR. The foreign minister then began an effort to convince other high-ranking members of the government to agree to his advised course of action.[1] Thus began an extremely important period in the history of the world. A Japanese decision to "take the northern road" and invade would have doomed the USSR. The Soviet Far East armies would have fought in place rather than deploying west to defend Moscow, Leningrad, and later, Stalingrad. War with Japan would have also closed off the port of Vladivostok to the massive flow of aid from the United States that did so much to keep the Red Army fed, fueled, and armed over the course of World War II.

After a Soviet defeat in the vice of the Nazi and Japanese militaries, Germany's enhanced economy would have been free to shift from production of army equipment to that of increased aircraft and naval vessel output to confront Britain and United States. Japan would have been able to source its requirements of metals and petroleum from across the Trans-Siberian Railway and redeploy the divisions of the *Kwantung* army south to continue its aggression in China. It is little exaggeration to say that the fate of the world hung in the balance while the major power groups in the Japanese government deliberated the empire's course of action. Thus, a deeper examination is warranted here into the arguments that raged in the halls of power in Tokyo over the summer of 1941.

Senior officials in Tokyo had for years regarded the USSR as their most dangerous enemy.[2] Joining the Germans in a war on the Soviet Union represented a golden opportunity for Japan to secure its mainland empire in northern Asia. In addition, northern Sakhalin Island could also be a potential solution to Japan's need for a secure source of petroleum. However, there was also the attraction of moving south, displacing the European colonial powers from Southeast Asia, and securing the proven output of oil and other commodities from that region. The IJN wanted to "go south" to improve its prestige, financial allocations, and power versus the IJA, which would gain from a land campaign in Siberia. The navy was desperate to find a proven source of oil without which its modern fleet would be stranded at anchor. The army's freedom of action was constrained by the ongoing fighting in the heartland of China, which tied down more than half of the IJA's formations. Matsuoka and his allies argued for a decision to go north, while other senior officials (especially those from the navy) pushed to head south. Discussions became quite heated in the "Liaison" and "Imperial" conferences as well as the "Supreme War Council" meetings of senior government officials. The foreign minister forcefully argued his case in one of these formal settings on June 25:

MATSUOKA: I have not said anything official to Ott [Eugen Ott, the German ambassador to Japan]. I would like to have an early decision on our national policy. Ott keeps talking about the movement of the Soviet Far Eastern troops to the West.

WAR MINISTER TOJO: The dispatch of the Far Eastern troops to the West no doubt affects the Germans greatly, but it is natural that Japan should not feel strongly about it. We shouldn't put our complete faith in Germany.

NAVY MINISTER OIKAWA: On behalf of the navy I want to say something about diplomacy in the future. . . . The navy is confident about a war against the United States, and Britain, but not confident about a war against the United States, Britain, and the Soviet Union. . . . This would make it very difficult for naval operations. In order to avoid a situation of this kind, don't tell us to strike at Soviet Russia and also tell us to go south. The navy doesn't want the Soviet Union stirred up.

MATSUOKA: You say you are not afraid of a war with the United States and Britain, so why is it that you do not wish to see the Soviets enter the war?

OIKAWA: If the Soviets come in, it means fighting an additional country, doesn't it? At any rate, don't talk too much about the future.

MATSUOKA: Have I ever talked that way? This is why I say we should hurry up and make a decision on the basic principles of our national policy. . . . When Germany wins and disposes of the Soviet Union we can't take the fruits of victory without having done something. We have to either shed blood or engage in diplomacy. It's best to shed blood.[3]

On June 27 the Liaison Conference reconvened and the military agreed to begin preparations to build up forces along the Soviet border:

MATSUOKA: I would like a decision to strike north first, and would like to communicate this intention to Germany.
ARMY CHIEF OF STAFF SUGIYAMA: A moral and honorable diplomacy is fine, but at present we have a large force stationed in China. ... The Supreme Command must get ready; we cannot decide now whether or not we will strike. It will take forty to fifty days to get the *Kwantung* army ready. It will take additional time to organize our present forces for war and get them ready to take the offensive. The German-Soviet situation should be clarified by then. If conditions are good, we will fight.

On June 28, Ribbentrop cabled an official request for Japan to join its Axis allies and enter the war against the USSR. Matsuoka duly brought this information to the Liaison Conference on June 30:

Until today Germany had asked us for no more than cooperation in the German-Soviet war; but today Ott showed me instructions he had received from his government and asked that we enter the war. Of course, the request to enter the war was appended to his instructions and was expressed as his personal opinion and wish. In any case, the empire must decide to enter the war. Why don't we stop building a fire in the South? Why not postpone occupying French Indochina, and instead proceed northward? How about postponing the occupation for six months? ...

I have never made a mistake in predicting what would happen in the next few years. I predict that if we get involved in the south, it will become a serious matter. Can the Army Chief of Staff guarantee that it won't? Furthermore, if we occupy southern Indochina it will become difficult to secure oil, rubber, tin, rice, and more. Great men will change their minds. Previously I advocated going south, but now favor the north.
CHIEF OF THE BUREAU OF MILITARY AFFAIRS MUTO: It is by occupying southern Indochina that we can acquire rubber and tin.
MINISTER OF HOME AFFAIRS HIRANUMA: I think we should go north. The question is whether we can. Here we must follow the thinking of the military.

NAVY CHIEF OF STAFF NAGANO: So far as the navy is concerned, if we get involved in the north, it will be necessary to switch all preparations now being made in the south to the north; this will require fifty days.[5]

The discussion continued later that day in the Supreme War Council:

PRINCE HIGASHIKUNI: What about plans to solve the Northern Question?

PRIME MINISTER KONOYE AND ARMY CHIEF OF STAFF SUGIYAMA: In concrete terms, it will be necessary to make a decision after further study of the strategic situation, both political and military. We have already studied this problem from the viewpoint of military strategy; but it will be necessary to decide on plans for the north only after we consider the demands of political strategy and assess the state of our preparations and the world situation.

PRINCE ASAKA: It looks like we are sitting on the fence; which is first, north or south? I think it would be better to go north first . . .

WAR MINISTER TOJO: Anybody can easily make a decision in the abstract. The difficulty comes from doing this while we are still engaged in the China Incident; if it weren't for the China Incident, it would be easy.[6]

Momentum toward a strike on the USSSR built in the "Imperial Conference," which took place at the emperor's palace in Tokyo on July 1 and 2:

MINISTER OF FINANCE KAWADA: Is the army making war preparations?

SUGIYAMA: Yes we are. First we are putting our troops in Manchuria on a war footing. Next we will prepare them for offensive action. We must exercise great care while doing this, so that they do not get out of hand. . . . On the solution of the Northern Question: It goes without saying that we should act in accordance with the spirit of the Tripartite Pact with reference to the German-Soviet war; but it seems appropriate for us not to participate in that war for the time being, since we are presently acting to settle the China Incident, and since our relations with Great Britain and the United States are in a delicate state. Nevertheless, if the development of the German-Soviet war should turn out to be favorable to our empire, I believe that we will have to decide on using force to settle the Northern Problem and assure the security of our northern borders. Therefore, it is vitally important for us to make in secret the necessary preparations for military operations, and to be in a position to act independently. . . .

Statement by the Navy Chief of Staff Nagano:

HARA [Yoshimichi, president of the Privy Council. He often asked questions or made statements on behalf of the emperor]: I agree that it will be difficult if we rely only on diplomatic negotiations. But military action is a serious matter. I regard a war against Great Britain and the United States which is mentioned in Section 2 of the Summary as a very serious matter. . . . Next, I believe all of you would agree that the war between Germany and the Soviet Union really represents the chance of a lifetime for Japan. Since the Soviet Union is promoting communism all over the world, we will have to attack her sooner or later. Since we are now engaged in the China Incident, I feel that we cannot attack the Soviet Union as easily as we would wish. Nevertheless, I believe that we should attack the Soviet Union when it seems opportune to do so. Our empire wants to avoid going to war with Great Britain and the United States while we are engaged in a war with the Soviet Union. The people are eager for a war against her. I want to see the Soviet Union attacked on this occasion. . . . Some people say that it would be improper for Japan to attack the Soviet Union in view of the Neutrality Pact; but the Soviet Union is notorious for her habitual acts of betrayal. If we were to attack the Soviet Union, no one would regard it as treachery. I am eagerly waiting for the opportunity to attack the Soviet Union. . . . I believe that Japan should avoid taking belligerent action against the United States, at least on this occasion. Also I would ask the government and the Supreme Command to attack the Soviet Union as soon as possible. The Soviet Union must be destroyed, so I hope that you will make preparations to hasten the commencement of hostilities. I cannot help but hope that this policy will be put into effect as soon as it is decided.

For the reasons I have already given, I am in complete agreement with the proposal put before us today.

TOJO: I am of the same opinion as Mr. Hara, president of the Privy Council. However, our empire is now engaged in the China Incident, and I hope the president of the Privy Council understands this.

SUGIYAMA: I completely agree with the war minister. We will exercise strict supervision to prevent misconduct, so set your mind at ease. I will take this opportunity to describe the situation with respect to the *Kwantung* army. Of the Soviet Union's thirty divisions [in the Far East], four divisions have already been sent to the West. . . . I want to reinforce the *Kwantung* army, so that it can defend itself, can provide backing for diplomatic negotiations, can be prepared for offense, and can take the offensive when the opportunity comes. I think that the outcome of the war between Germany and the Soviet Union will become clear in fifty or sixty days. Until then we will have to mark time in the settlement of the China Incident and the negotiations with Great Britain and the United States.[7]

The document to emerge from the Imperial Conference designed to guide Japanese foreign policy contained the following: "Our attitude with reference to the German-Soviet war will be based on the spirit of the Tripartite Pact. However, we will not enter the conflict for some time but will steadily proceed with military preparations against the Soviets and decide our final attitude independently. . . . In case the German-Soviet war develops to our advantage, we will settle the Soviet question and guarantee our northern border militarily.[8]

Thus, Japan readied itself to go to war with the USSR, and preparations were to be complete by the start of September. More than five hundred thousand additional troops were massed along the Soviet border under an operation designated *Kantokuen*, or "*Kwantung* Army Special Grand Maneuvers."[9] The entire Japanese army was placed on a war footing, and more than three hundred independent units were transported to Manchukuo and Northern Korea. Operational attack plans called for special deep penetration units of "White" Russians and Mongolians to cross the border and engage in acts of sabotage. Their primary mission was to cut the Trans-Siberian Railway network in several places as it ran its lengthy course along Japanese-controlled territory.

The IJA soon had more than 800,000 soldiers, 250,000 horses, 30,000 vehicles, and 700 aircraft positioned in northern Manchukuo and Korea. This concentration of men and equipment was approximately the same size as Soviet military forces in the Far East at the start of Barbarossa.[10] When adding in the striking power of the IJN and its Special Naval Landing Forces, Japan would have had several advantages in a war with the Soviet Union in the second half of 1941. First, it would hold the initiative in choosing the time and location of attack. Second, it could engage in land operations on interior lines and receive supplies by sea as well as via a dense railway network. It would have a significant preponderance in the areas of naval power and combat aviation and could launch amphibious assaults along the Soviet coastline. Finally, Red Army units in the Far East could not count on reinforcements or resupply from Europe in the face of the ongoing German attack.

The Japanese military promised in the Imperial Conference that it would be ready to strike in Siberia by early September 1941. An attack in the Far East at that time would have been devastating to the USSR just as it was suffering the crushing defeat of its armies around Kiev, and only a few weeks before the Germans launched Operation Tyfun. Had the Japanese invaded, it is quite likely that the Trans-Siberian Railway would have been cut at several points along the Manchurian border. This would have made it impossible for Stalin to redeploy many of his Far Eastern divisions to Europe even if he took the drastic step of ordering a wholesale retreat and the abandonment of the eastern half of his country.

Had the Japanese waited several additional weeks to launch an offensive, the onset of winter would not necessarily have been to the attacker's disadvantage. An IJA thrust east from the railhead at Heihe in northern Manchukuo would have only needed to advance a short distance to cut the Trans-Siberian lifeline to Soviet Pacific coast. The Japanese military was used to the region's harsh cold and would have operated on interior lines, with larger forces and command of the sea. There is no reason to expect that Tokyo's forces would not have been able to besiege Vladivostok and capture its airfields, port, and army bases at leisure. At the same time, local IJA units supported by the might of the Japanese navy would have easily overwhelmed the small number of Red Army soldiers based in northern Sakhalin Island and seized the area's oil fields for the emperor. The spring thaw of 1942 would then have afforded the Japanese the opportunity to launch the second phase of their invasion plan, with an offensive west toward Lake Baikal.

Kantokuen was the high point for Japan's proponents of a *Hokushin-ron* offensive and an attack on the Soviet Union. The IJA was a few weeks away from finalizing the positioning of men and equipment to attack over the USSR's borders. With each German victory, the proponents of taking the northern road would have gained in confidence, and momentum would have increased for Japan to join the war. Had the Japanese invaded, many

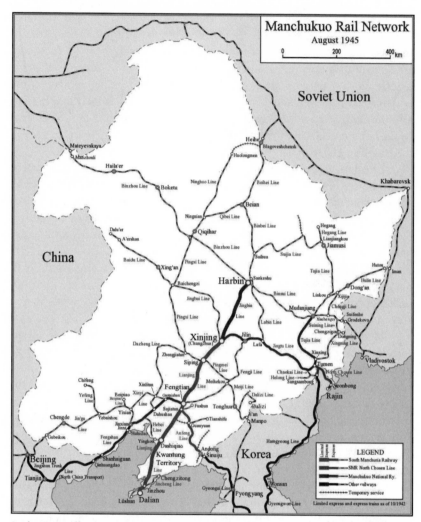

Soviet Trans-Siberian and Japanese Manchurian Railway Lines[11]

Red Army divisions in the Far East would have been cut off and forced to fight in Siberia in late 1941 rather than redeploying to Moscow. It was at this critical moment that actions in Washington, and the Imperial Palace in Tokyo, tilted history and steered Japan back onto the southern road, which led to ruin and defeat.

First came intervention from the United States. The US Diplomatic Corps had become increasingly alarmed by Matsuoka's outspoken pro-Nazi stance as gleaned from intercepts of the broken Japanese consular code, as well as discussions the foreign minister had with US press correspondents and Ambassador Joseph Grew in Tokyo. This came to a head with a harsh diplomatic note that arrived from US Secretary of State Cordell Hull in late June, in which he complained "that some Japanese leaders in influential official positions are definitely committed to a course which calls for support of Nazi Germany and its policies of conquest, and that the only kind of understanding with the United States which they would endorse is one that would envisage Japan's fighting on the side of Hitler should the United States become involved in the European hostilities though carrying out its present policies of self defense. The tenor of recent public statements gratuitously made by spokesmen of the Japanese Government emphasizing Japan's commitments and intentions under the Tripartite Alliance exemplify an attitude which cannot be ignored."[12] The note made clear that relations with the United States would deteriorate if stridently pro-Nazi ministers remained in the Japanese cabinet. In other words, the United States wanted to see Matsuoka removed from office.[13]

Then on July 6, President Roosevelt sent a telegram to Prime Minister Konoe which read, "We have information that Japan is going to take military action against the Soviet Union. We would like to have an assurance from Japan that such information is not based on fact." Not only was this a warning that the United States opposed a Japanese attack on the USSR, but the cable also broke protocol as it was strictly addressed to Konoe rather than the foreign minister.[14] Once again, the United States had shown its antipathy to dealing with Matsuoka in the future.

The result of these diplomatic missives was to harden an insulted Matsuoka's stance in terms of negotiating with the United States, and it increased the worries of other senior Japanese officials that their nation was about to lose its critical stream of imports from points across the Pacific. Konoe met with the cabinet on July 15 and then separately with Navy Minister Oikawa, Army Minister Tojo, and Home Minister Hiranuma. Konoe and the military heads decided that the prime minister would order the entire cabinet to resign and then an identical government would be formed, except with a new foreign minister more amenable to Washington.[15] This took place on July 16, and Admiral Toyoda Teijiro, an advocate for maintaining peace with the United States, took over the foreign ministry. With the fall of Matsuoka from power, the *Hokushin-ron* faction lost its strongest voice.

Konoe's hopes that diplomacy with the United States would lead to an acceptance by Washington of a Greater East Asia Co-Prosperity Sphere did not last long. The Vichy France government relented to pressure and allowed Japanese troops to occupy southern Indochina on July 26. The United States immediately responded with a freeze on Japanese assets and bank transfers, and then on August 1, it embargoed the export of all petroleum. The British and Dutch followed suit and imposed similar sanctions. With its limited reserve of fuel stocks set to dwindle, a Japanese military move to obtain a secure source of petroleum became all but a certainty.

Another critical intervention to turn away from *Hokushin-ron* then came from the emperor:

> On July 30 Hirohito made a major operational intervention by suggesting to General Sugiyama that the buildup in Manchukuo stop as it was probably preventing the Soviet Far Eastern Army from redeploying to fight in the West. No thought was given to aiding his ally Hitler. At this time the emperor did not desire a full-scale war with either the Soviet Union or the United States; but if war had to be, he was more inclined to risk it southward into the Anglo-American sphere of interest than fight the Russians; and if the Soviet Far Eastern Army departed westbound, in relative terms Japan war-power in the North would immediately improve. . . . So, though for a short period of time in early July, the "peace-loving" emperor had contemplated a military invasion of the Soviet Union even though he had ratified the Neutrality Pact with Russia a mere three months earlier, he changed his mind, gave an operational command, and as a result the liaison conference on August 9 cancelled for that year the "planned" invasion of the Soviet Union. Hirohito's intervention thus prevented Japan from going to war with the Soviet Union as the army high command wanted.[16]

As Japan shifted its forces away from the Manchurian border and the USSR moved its Far Eastern divisions west, Hitler's best chance for defeating the Soviet Union slipped away. It is ironic that German victories in Europe created the very conditions that led Japan to favor an advance to the south and away from an attack on the USSR. The armed power of France and the Netherlands had been smashed, the British Empire was under siege and had shifted the bulk of its military assets to Europe, and even the United States had moved significant naval forces to the Atlantic. Soviet forces stationed in the Far East remained powerful throughout 1941, while the defenses of French Indochina, British Malaya, America's Philippines, and the Dutch East Indies appeared weak. Frontal attacks on KMT forces in the Chinese interior had failed to bring Chang Kai-shek to the negotiating table, and a descent on Southeast Asia offered a way to isolate the Chungking government and cut its sources of military supply. Hitler chose to exclude the Japanese from planning for the invasion of the

USSR, while urging instead an attack on Singapore and delivering intelligence that the British were unprepared for war in the Far East.

In retrospect, Japan was primed to join a war of aggression against the Soviet Union in 1941, and had it done so, the USSR would have been doomed to defeat. Unable to redeploy its Far Eastern armies to check the German advance in its west, the Red Army's defense of Moscow and Stalingrad would have been critically weakened. Allied aid to the USSR would have arrived in smaller quantities. In such a scenario, the Soviets may have continued to resist after 1941, but a USSR forced to fight in both the west and the east and shorn of so much of its population, industry, and natural resources would not have been able to push back the *Wehrmacht*.

Had the Nazis coordinated with Tokyo and promised to share the natural resources of a defeated USSR, it is quite possible that the "northern road" of conquest would have been taken in the Far East. Control of Siberia, steady supplies of oil, iron ore, and coal, and destruction of its most powerful regional enemy would have represented a prize too valuable for Japan to ignore. However, Hitler chose not to include his strongest ally in planning for the dismemberment and despoilation of the USSR. Thus, Germany did not follow up with Japan on the military partnership implied in the terms of the Tripartite Pact. As history played out, a Japanese invasion of the USSR in late 1941 still came close to taking place. The IJA did mass its armies along the Siberian borders, and high-ranking members of the government in Tokyo argued for an attack knowing that Red Army forces in the Far East would have been deprived of reinforcement and resupply from European Russia in the face of the ongoing German invasion. While of little comfort to the populations of Southeast Asia at the time, world civilization received a lucky break when the Japanese decided upon *Nanshin-ran*.

• *17* •

The Anaconda Option

$\mathcal{E}$ven after Japan chose not to attack in Siberia and launched its offensive across the Pacific on December 7, 1941, there was still an opportunity for Hitler to use diplomacy to defeat the Soviet Union by squeezing it from all sides. The USSR had lost much of its most productive agricultural lands, many of its most important industrial centers, and its military had suffered millions of casualties. If the Soviet state had its supply lines cut off and was forced to retain larger numbers of its army units in the Far North and Far East, a conflict balanced between victory and defeat could tilt in the Axis's favor.

As the advance on Moscow slowed in the winter cold, Germany's military and political leaders realized that they faced a desperate war for survival. The *Wehrmacht* was doing all it could do. Germany's allies were not. In the north, the Finns had decided to halt their armies' advances tantalizingly close to both Leningrad and the Kirov Railway. In the Far East, the Japanese navy dominated the approaches to the Soviet Pacific coastline, and the *Kwantung* army was positioned along the Soviet border. If these two allies of Germany could be convinced to sever the flow of the USSR's supplies arriving at Murmansk and Vladivostok and tie down significant Red Army formations, a German victory was still likely. What was needed in the Far East was little more than the Japanese government announcing it would quarantine shipments to Vladivostok and have its military in Manchuria engage in aggressive military maneuvers designed to keep the Soviet forces in the region on edge. In the Far North, Germany needed the Finns to move to the offensive, cut the rail link to Murmansk, and assist in the siege of Leningrad. Such a constriction or "anaconda" strategy would have crippled the USSR when it was most vulnerable. Before delving into

German efforts to interdict the flow of aid to the Soviet Union, we need to explore how large were these aid shipments and their significance to the defeat of the *Wehrmacht*.

FEEDING THE BEAR

Immediately after the launch of Barbarossa, both Britain and the United States pledged to send significant matériel aid to the USSR. This stream of aid became a massive flow of just about everything Stalin requested. While "only" eight hundred million pounds of aid arrived in 1941, the arrival of items such as British tanks were exceedingly helpful in the Battle of Moscow. Deliveries rose more than 600 percent in 1942, almost doubled again in 1943, and peaked at fourteen billion pounds in 1944.

There has been a great deal of debate regarding the importance of this matériel aid to the German defeat in World War II. For obvious reasons, the rulers of the USSR wished to minimize the impact of assistance from the capitalist nations during the decades of the Cold War while emphasizing the undeniably heroic efforts of the Soviet citizenry. With the collapse of the Iron Curtain, this version of the truth has been increasingly questioned in recent years. An example that reflects this change of opinion is the article "Lifesaver Lend-Lease. It is Not Necessary to Minimize Its Importance in Our Victory in the Great Patriotic War," by Russian historian Aleksandr Vislyk, published in Moscow in 2001.[1] An interview Marshal Zhukov gave to journalist Konstantin Simonov in the 1960s was suppressed for more than forty years. In that now declassified recording, "Zhukov frankly and confidentially lamented the fact that Soviet propaganda had systematically demeaned the importance of this American aid to the Soviet war effort. He noted that the rationale for this Soviet propaganda line was to counter what the Soviet authorities considered to be—unwarrantedly—a detraction from the heroism of Soviet soldiers and civilians in the war."[2]

The consensus had been that Lend-Lease Aid never amounted to more than a few percent of Soviet military output during the war years. With the dissolution of the communist government and access to previously classified archives, Russian historians have documented that previously published Soviet production figures for 1941 to 1945 were significantly inflated. Historian Boris Sokolov's calculations are that

Lend-Lease shipments made up 15 to 25 percent of military goods as a percentage of Soviet output in the war years. For some items such as aircraft, aviation fuel, trucks, and ordinance, the share was in the range of 30 to 60 percent.[3] These conclusions are more in line with "a 1945 German army study conceded that Allied aid 'amounted to only 15% of the total Russian production,' but argued that the deliveries of food, machine tools and motor vehicles 'constitute one of the principal explanations for the strengthened resistance shown by the Russians during the critical period.'"[4] Sokolov agreed with this conclusion when interviewed in 2017: "To end this discussion the most vital is the fact, that the Lend-Lease shipments helped greatly to support the resistance in the hardest year—1942, when the whole technical potential of the Red Army from before 22nd of June 1941 ceased to exist and the evacuated factories were just beginning to return to the full capacity or were only now starting to produce new types of equipment. Without a shadow of a doubt, the USSR would have collapsed had it not been for the Lend-Lease."[5]

The aid from the United States and Britain that the USSR so desperately needed arrived via three major routes: the Far East (primarily to Vladivostok), the White Sea (primarily to Murmansk), and overland through Iran after being unloaded in Persian Gulf ports. Smaller amounts of aid arrived in the form of military aircraft flown in across Alaska to the Soviet Arctic and, after 1944, via the Black Sea. Each of the three main routes had their own complications. After the attack on Pearl Harbor, Japan declared it would still allow passage of nonmilitary American goods to Vladivostok, but only in neutral or Soviet-flagged ships. The Japanese routinely boarded and inspected inbound ships for compliance with these terms. The transit of military hardware to the White Sea ports of Murmansk and Arkhangelsk was shorter but subject to interdiction by German aircraft, U-boats, and surface ships. While both arctic ports were open to receive convoys in the summer, this was the most dangerous time for passage due to the long arctic days providing light for aircraft attack and U-boat operations. The water route to the Persia Gulf was generally free of Axis interference but was significantly longer, and the United States had to bring in engineers, equipment, and thousands of men to improve the Iranian rail system so that it could transport a greater volume of the Lend-Lease aid overland to the Soviet border.

As can be seen from the accompanying table, the most important supply route was across the Pacific to the Soviet Far Eastern port of Vladivostok. This is where the bulk of nonmilitary items requested by Stalin

Table 13.   North American Aid Shipments to the USSR in Millions of Tons[6]

Year	Far East Tons (M)	%	White Sea Tons (M)	%	Persia Tons (M)	%	Black Sea Tons (M)	%	Arctic Tons (M)	%	Total Tons (M)
1941	0.2	54	0.2	43	0.0	4	0.0	0	0.0	0	0.4
1942	0.8	30	1.1	39	0.8	29	0.0	0	0.1	3	2.7
1943	2.7	50	0.8	14	1.8	34	0.0	0	0.1	3	5.4
1944	3.2	46	1.6	23	2.0	29	0.0	0	0.1	2	7.0
1945	2.3	57	0.8	20	0.1	1	0.8	19	0.2	4	4.1
Total	**9.2**	**47**	**4.4**	**23**	**4.7**	**24**	**0.8**	**4**	**0.5**	**3**	**19.6**

Note: 1.1M tons of this aid was from Canada.

arrived. This aid was critical: it allowed the USSR to transport its men to the front, feed them while there, and produce the armaments to beat back the Germans over four long years of war.

Table 14.   Composition of North American Aid to the USSR by Weight[7]

Item	Tons	%
US Aid:		
Food	5,000,774	26
Metals	4,004,094	20
Trucks & other vehicles	2,565,730	13
Petroleum Products	2,367,063	12
Machinery & equipment	1,397,590	7
Chemicals & explosives	1,258,496	6
Other	1,919,620	10
Canadian/British Aid	1,084,886	6
Totals	19,601,046	100

More than twenty million tons (forty billion pounds!) of aid arrived by September of 1945. In excess of 70 percent of all Lend-Lease shipments by weight were food, vehicles (primarily trucks), metals, and processed petroleum products (especially aviation fuel). Food was the largest category of aid with more than five million tons delivered. Most of this edible aid was in the form of calorie-dense shelf-stable proteins and fats that the Soviet agriculture system could not produce due to agricultural labor shortages and German control of territory in the Ukraine. For millions of Soviet soldiers and laborers, this food was the difference between a calorie-deficient diet and outright starvation.

Table 15.   **Aid Shipments of Selected Items in Units to the USSR**[8]

Aircraft	21,203
Tanks	11,196
Other Armored Vehicles	4,158
Locomotives	1,966
Railroad Cars	11,075
Jeeps	47,238
Trucks	363,080
Tractors	7,570
Motorcycles	32,200
Radio Stations	35,089
Radio Receivers	5,899
Field Telephones	380,135
Airfield Landing Mats (sq. meters)	55,200,000
Boots (pairs)	14,793,000
Camouflage Net (meters)	2,000,000

While military items shipped to the USSR such as tanks and aircraft were significant, it may be the nonmilitary supplies delivered that made the largest difference between victory and defeat. In retirement, Khrushchev was more honest than most communist leaders regarding the importance of Western aid to the Soviet military victory. He singled out the significance of nonmilitary aid items that allowed the Red Army to transport and feed its soldiers in the long years required to defeat the *Wehrmacht*:

> To acknowledge the material aid which we received in the past from our adversaries of the present doesn't have any bearing on the situation of today. We shouldn't boast that we vanquished the Germans all by ourselves. . . . I wanted only to stress how many of our cars and trucks we had received from the Americans. Just imagine how we would have advanced from Stalingrad to Berlin without them! Our losses would have been colossal because we would have had no maneuverability. In addition we received steel and aluminum from which we made guns, airplanes, and so on. Our own industry was shattered and partly abandoned to the enemy. We also received food products in great quantities. . . . Without Spam we wouldn't have been able to feed our army. We had lost our most fertile lands—the Ukraine and the northern Caucasus.[9]

In light of recent historical research, the weight of data, and simple common sense, it is difficult to deny that Lend-Lease aid was a prime factor in the USSR's victory over Germany. To summarize, this aid was critical in the following primary areas:

1. Food aid supplied the calories needed by millions of Soviet soldiers and workers to perform their roles in the wartime years.
2. Donated trucks and jeeps gave the Red Army dramatically more mobility to get its troops and their equipment to the front, and exploit victories against the Germans as the fighting moved steadily west.
3. Lend Lease planes and aviation fuel gave the VVS the necessary airpower to gain air superiority over the *Luftwaffe*.
4. Deliveries of metals, machine tools, explosives, and chemicals to Soviet industry supercharged its production of tanks, artillery, and ammunition.

Could the USSR have defeated the *Wehrmacht* in World War II without this massive volume of Western aid? Perhaps, but without it, the fighting would have gone on much longer. German losses would have been less severe, while those of the Red Army would have been greater. The retreat of the Axis armies would have been slower if it took place at all. In addition, as has been discussed previously, the Russian military effort collapsed in 1917 after three long years of war. The Russian people were incredibly tough and patriotic in both the 1914 and 1941 conflicts, but all national populations have a breaking point. In the absence of Lend-Lease, it is easy to envision a flagging of Soviet resistance in 1945 or 1946 after suffering millions of additional casualties and the Red Army still fighting to regain Ukraine and Belorussia.

The rising flow of Western aid was likely the difference between a successful defense of Moscow, Leningrad, and Stalingrad . . . and defeat. While impossible to prove a counterfactual with finality, the massive deliveries of Western supplies mightily strengthened the Soviet state and its ability to fight the invaders in the titanic battles that raged from the Baltic to the Black Sea. So even had Japan not attacked in Siberia, the USSR could have been defeated had it lost access to the aid that flowed in to Vladivostok and Murmansk. Such a conclusion requires us to investigate why Finland and Japan did not act to close down these ports.

THE JAPANESE FAIL TO BLOCKADE VLADIVOSTOK

While the Nazis planned to cut the Soviet supply lines from Murmansk in 1941, they also needed to be concerned that the massive economy of the United States could send great quantities of supplies to the USSR via the port of Vladivostok. Such worries would be moot if the Japanese attacked the Soviets in the Far East. However, even if Japan did not formally go to war with the USSR, it could easily impose a blockade of its Pacific coast.

As already discussed, Germany began an effort to convince the Japanese to attack the USSR immediately after the launch of Barbarossa. On July 10, 1941, Ribbentrop cabled Tokyo that since Russia was about to collapse, it was "simply impossible that Japan does not solve the question of Vladivostok and the Siberian areas as soon as her military preparations are completed. . . . The natural objective still remains that we and Japan join hands on the Trans-Siberian railroad before winter starts."[10] Of course, the government in Tokyo decided against an invasion of the USSR and chose to allow the passage of nonmilitary supplies through to Vladivostok. The first aid shipments for the Soviet Far East departed the United States in October 1941, and by the end of the war total deliveries from North America to this one Pacific port filled almost four hundred thousand railroad cars that were then transported west across the Trans-Siberian railroad.[11]

Hitler was impressed with the audacity of Japan's attacks on Pearl Harbor and was inclined to join his Axis ally in the conflict. The wording of the Tripartite Pact did not require Germany to declare war on the United States, just as it did not demand that Japan go to war with the USSR. The treaty only specified such an act in the event one of the signatories had itself been attacked. Ribbentrop advised Hitler against declaring war, but the Führer believed the alliance would be "dead" if he did not do so. Both of the Axis powers knew that a German declaration of war on the United States would be a major positive for Japan. Only a few days before the attack on Pearl Harbor, the American war plan had been leaked to the world and published under banner headlines by the isolationist *Chicago Tribune* and its affiliated newspaper, the *Times Herald* in Washington.[12] The "Victory Program" called for the United States to remain on the defensive in the Pacific while spending two years raising a massive army and then landing it in Europe to crush the Third Reich.

The Japanese certainly wanted Germany to join their war against the United States. The question was only what Hitler would get in return for complying with his ally's desire. This was an opportune moment to negotiate Japanese action against the USSR in return for a German declaration of war against the United States. If Japan would not go to war with the Soviets, at least it could agree to blockade supplies of American aid sailing to the port of Vladivostok. However, all Hitler received was an agreement from Tokyo not to enter into a separate peace with the Western powers. On December 11, as the *Ostheer*'s offensive was grinding to a halt, Germany declared war on the United States. This was the moment Hitler needed action by the Japanese against the USSR rather than the flimsy diplomatic "No Separate Peace" promise he received.

Ribbentrop claimed in his memoirs that he saw the danger clearly, "When after Pearl Harbour war was declared on the U.S.A., despite my advice to the contrary, I said to the *Führer*: 'We have one year to cut off Russia from American supplies via Murmansk and the Persian Gulf; Japan will have to look after Vladivostok. If this does not succeed, and if America's industrial potential combines with Russia's manpower potential, then the war will enter a phase in which it will be very difficult for us to be victorious.' The *Führer* remained silent."[13] The German foreign minister was correct—it was imperative for his nation that Japan cut of the flow of aid to the Soviet Far East. The Nazis did not need Japan to invade Siberia at this point to have a major impact on the war in Europe. All that was required was for the Japanese navy to blockade the port of Vladivostok and interdict Lend-Lease shipping heading there. To accomplish this mission, the IJN had a huge superiority over Soviet naval forces in the region. This imbalance in force became even larger after the launch of Barbarossa, as tens of thousands of sailors from the Soviet Pacific Fleet transferred into infantry brigades fighting on the European front lines. While such a Japanese blockade could have been interpreted as an act of war, the USSR would have been loath to escalate such a dispute when it needed to strip its military strength from the Far East and deploy it in Europe for its desperate fight against the Germans.

The Japanese failed to grasp that an overall German victory was essential to its own military success. If Hitler declared war on the United States, then the Americans would become allied with Britain and the Soviets by default. A stronger Soviet Union supported by allied aid could only result in the United States and Britain being able to deploy more of their military resources to the Pacific. Cutting off the port through which the majority of American aid entered the USSR would not only weaken the Soviets, it would have a direct impact on the odds of a sustainable Japanese victory. Thus, by not blockading Vladivostok, Japan missed an opportunity to injure its traditional enemy, gain favor with its allies, and improve its chances of defeating the combined forces of the Anglo-American empires.

Ribbentrop was also correct about the three major routes by which foreign aid could reach the USSR. However, Murmansk and Vladivostok were by far the most important. The Persian Gulf route required a much longer voyage, forcing an individual ship to make fewer round trips per year. In addition, the railway system through Iran underwent significant expansion in 1942 and 1943 by British and US military engineer forces, allowing it to transport significantly greater tonnages.

Table 16.   Sailing Distance and Travel Time to Lend-Lease Unloading Ports[14]

	Nautical Miles	Days
Seattle to Vladivostok	4,246	16
Boston to Murmansk	4,022	15
Newcastle, UK to Murmansk	1,468	6
New York to Persian Gulf (Abadan)*	11,985	45
New York to Persian Gulf (Abadan)**	8,445	32

*Via the Cape of Good Hope, ** Via the Suez Canal

With the attack on Pearl Harbor, the passage to Vladivostok became more complicated. The success of the initial Japanese offensives meant that US merchant ships had little chance of successfully navigating the North Pacific. However, the Japanese decision to allow Soviet ships through to Vladivostok with nonmilitary goods gave the United States a way to transport millions of tons of trucks, food, aviation fuel, and more across the Pacific in relative safety. Liberty ships, newly constructed along San Francisco Bay, became the property of the USSR, and appropriate Russian names were painted on their hulls in Cyrillic lettering. The freighters were then loaded to capacity and set sail with Soviet crews. The Japanese coast guard and IJN boarded and inspected these ships for contraband military equipment more than 175 times over the course of 1941 to 1945. Ironically the major military threat to these US aid shipments was the US Navy's own submarine force, which torpedoed six Soviet freighters as they passed the Japanese home islands.

Had Murmansk and Vladivostok been closed to Lend-Lease shipments in late 1941, the Persian Gulf corridor and the port of Arkhangelsk would have been hard-pressed to handle the volume of aid flowing to the USSR. At the very least, smaller amounts of aid would have arrived in each year of the war. Under such changed circumstances, a Red Army victory over the *Wehrmacht* might still have been possible, but it would have been harder fought and taken longer to achieve, Soviet casualties would have been greater, and Germany would have had more time to field new weapons and replace lost manpower. It is also possible that Stalin's forces, hungry, bled white, and poorly equipped, would have mutinied under the strain in a manner similar to what occurred in the Imperial Russian military in 1917.

While Lend-Lease aid flowed into Vladivostok to strengthen the USSR, the best units of the *Kwantung* army shipped out of Manchuria to slow the island-hopping US advance. One by one, the Axis nations surrendered until, after the fall of Berlin, Japan was the only one remaining in the fight. In an amazing effort of self-delusion, the Japanese convinced themselves that Soviet diplomatic intervention was the key to negotiating an advantageous peace with the United States. It is difficult to see how the USSR could have convinced the Americans to lay down their arms prior to the occupation of the Japanese home islands. In any event, Stalin had other plans. On August 8, 1945, two days after the atomic bomb detonation at Hiroshima, the USSR violated the neutrality agreement it had solemnly signed in 1941 and declared war on Japan. More than one and a half million Soviets poured over the borders into Manchuria, sweeping aside the much-diminished *Kwantung* army. Within two weeks, the Red Army had seized Port Arthur, lost by the Russian Empire to the Japanese in 1905. The Soviets soon occupied the rest of Manchuria, the northern half of Korea, the southern half of Sakhalin, and the Kuriles.

· *18* ·

Finland Fails Germany and Itself

$\mathcal{D}$id Hitler, his generals, and his advisors understand the importance of minimizing the USSR's lines of supply to the rest of the world? The record indicates that they did. History had taught Germany the importance of cutting off Moscow's shipments of foreign aid. The Russian Empire had more than enough manpower in World War I, but desperately required additional modern arms and ammunition to fight the Central Powers. The British provided massive shipments to the tsar's army in return for the gold in the Russian treasury and knowledge that this aid would lead to tens of thousands of dead German soldiers. As the Central Powers controlled the water approaches to Russia's major ports on the Black and Baltic seas, a new route was required. In 1915, the tsar's government began building the Kirov Railway running northward to a fishing village on an inlet on the Barents Sea that remains ice-free all year. That village, Murmansk, is now the world's largest city north of the Arctic Circle. More than seventy thousand German and Austrian POWs were forced into service laying the track, and twenty-five thousand died under appalling conditions.[1]

Once the new rail link to the Murman coast was operational, the British flooded the newly enlarged port with war supplies for the tsar's army. Additional shipments arrived in nearby Arkhangelsk, though this latter harbor was less useful because it was further from England and icebound several months of the year. More than ten billion pounds of equipment including rifles, bullets, artillery guns, shells, and even locomotives to haul the vast bounty were unloaded at these two White Sea ports. Utilization of these supplies was a factor in Russia remaining in the war as long as it did. So much was unloaded at Murmansk that more than one billion pounds of imported war matériel remained stockpiled at the port when the British landed an intervention force there during the Russian Civil War.[2]

Hitler made plans to block aid from flowing to the USSR via Murmansk from the very launch of Barbarossa. As in World War I, Germany and its allies could interdict shipping through the Baltic and the Black seas. Thus, the White Sea ports would be the obvious destination of military aid sent to the USSR. As an indication of Hitler's true trepidation that an attack on the Soviet Union could lead to a long conflict, he ordered that Murmansk be cut off from the rest of the USSR immediately upon the launch of the invasion. OKW, in charge of German military units in occupied Norway, planned to send a strike force led by General Eduard Dietl along the northern rim of Scandinavia to take the Soviet arctic port in Operation Platinfuchs (Platinum Fox). In case that effort did not succeed, a joint German-Finnish attack further south would interdict the Kirov Railway (also known as the Murman Railway) in Operation Polarfuchs (Arctic Fox) led by German General Hans Feige and his counterpart, Hjalmar Siilasvuo, the commander of the Finnish III Corps. Finally, in a third offensive to cut the railway, the Finnish VII Corps would push east toward Lake Onega and Belomorsk. With the Red Army focused on the massive Barbarossa invasion, stopping the main Finnish offensive north of Leningrad and guarding the Far Eastern borders, it was reasonable to expect that few Soviet forces would be available to protect Murmansk and its exposed rail line.

Germany invited Finland to join in a war of aggression against the USSR, and significant joint planning took place between the two nations' senior military staffs prior to the start of hostilities. With a burning desire to avenge the losses of the Winter War and some politicians dreaming of a "Greater Finland," the Nordic nation had enlarged its military to a total strength of 475,000 equipped with modern German and British arms.[3] A partial call up of reserves began on June 9, and a full mobilization was ordered eight days later.[4] Including female auxiliary units, more than six hundred thousand Finns were called to duty out of a population of less than four million.[5] On the 21st, Finland's president, Risto Ryti, told members of Parliament, "If a war breaks out now between Germany and Russia, it could be to the advantage of the whole world. Germany is the only state today that can defeat Russia. . . . this war is Finland's only salvation. The Soviet Union will never give up its attempt to conquer Finland. . . . if Germany now crushes the Soviet army, we may perhaps enjoy a century of peace."[6]

On June 22, the day of the launch of Barbarossa, German forces crossed into far northern Finland from Norway to secure Petsamo and advanced to positions along the Soviet border in preparation for a strike at Murmansk. Simultaneously, German and Finnish naval units laid mine-fields in the waters west of Leningrad to pen in the bulk of the Soviet Baltic Fleet. The *Luftwaffe* also utilized Finnish airstrips to attack targets in the USSR. While Finland's government declared it was not at war, its actions were clearly not those of a neutral nation. In retaliation, the USSR launched several air attacks to bomb Finnish military installations and cit-ies.[7] This gave the government in Helsinki the provocation it needed. The Parliament approved a "defensive war," and an offensive was immediately launched to recapture the lands lost in the Winter War of 1939.

The slogan used by the Ryti administration to rally the population was "A short border—a long peace." This shorter border would come into existence with the formation of a Greater Finland that would effectively double the size of the nation. These new frontiers would incorporate the Kola Peninsula, East Karelia from the White Sea to the southern ends of Lake Ladoga and Lake Onega, and all of the Karelian Isthmus (the strip of land between the Gulf of Finland and Lake Ladoga) north of the Neva River. President Ryti told his Nazi allies that he wished to see Leningrad destroyed, its population scattered, and the port turned into a German trading post. He indicated a desire that his nation no longer share a border with the USSR after the war and asked that Germany annex all Soviet lands south of the new Greater Finland. The Nazis gladly agreed to these terms.[8]

Over the last seventy years, the Finns have tried to downplay their contribution to Hitler's aggression in the east. They refer to the 1941 to 1944 conflict as the "Continuation War" to emphasize a link with the earlier unprovoked Soviet attack in the Winter War of 1939 to 1940. However, Finnish complicity in the German attempt to conquer the Soviet Union is clear. A military delegation traveled to Germany in May 1941 to discuss the impending invasion. It was led by General Axel Heinrichs, the Finnish army's chief of staff, and included the heads of operations, mobi-lization, and supply as well as the navy's Chief of Staff.[9] More than two hundred thousand *Wehrmacht* troops served in Finland, where they fought side by side with their local allies. As already mentioned, the *Luftwaffe* and *Kriegsmarine* utilized Finnish territory for air and naval strikes on the USSR. Collaboration extended to the political sphere as well. Finland be-came a signatory to the Anti-Comintern Pact, the Finnish Defense Force proudly displayed the swastika on their tanks, planes, and uniforms, and several senior German officials, including Hitler, flew north to meet in person with President Ryti and Marshall Mannerheim.

As in 1939, the Finns proved their prowess on the battlefield. Over the course of the Continuation War, the Red Army suffered more than

270,000 men killed in this northern theater compared to figures of 52,500 and 16,400 respectively for the Finnish military and the German units who fought alongside them.[10] It is quite possible these numbers would have become even more lopsided had Finland's armies remained on the offensive after the first six months of fighting instead of digging in along static front lines and waiting for the USSR to collapse.

In the opening months of the invasion, the combined German and Finnish armies were most successful in the southern portion of the theater and less so further north. Finnish forces advanced quickly down the Karelian Isthmus. Red Army formations either retreated under pressure or were surrounded and wiped out. Mannerheim ordered a halt south of the old 1939 border within fifteen miles of Leningrad. In East Karelia, the Finns, aided by the German 163rd Infantry Division, pushed much further into Soviet territory. The offensive captured all the land north of the River Svir, which connects the southern ends of Lake Onega and Lake Ladoga. The main line of the Kirov Railway was cut with the capture of Petrozavodsk, and the Finns continued to advance north towards Medvezhyegorsk.

Despite the success of Finnish advances in the south, the rail link between Murmansk and the rest of the USSR was still viable: the Soviets had recently completed a branch line at Belomorsk running along the southern end of the White Sea and from there linking into the nation's central rail network. The German effort in the far north bogged down quickly in the arctic tundra west of Murmansk. While they were more successful pushing east from Salla in a drive to take Kandalasksha, that offensive also stalled west of the Kirov Railroad. Finnish attacks further south advanced to take Kalevala and Rugozero, but then Marshal Mannerheim called off the advance before it pushed far enough east to cut the branch rail line.

As 1941 drew to a close, the Finns had achieved a great deal of their territorial goals and chose to halt their offensives under increasing diplomatic pressure from the United States and Britain. While not all of "Greater Finland" had been conquered, the Finns now controlled significantly more territory than it had prior to the start of the Winter War. Moreover, the lands in the south coveted by the Finns had been seized, which markedly improved the nation's industrial, population, and agricultural potential. Germany certainly might win the war, but Finland wanted to hedge its bets and maintain good relations with Britain and the United States in case the Western alliance defeated the Axis after the fall of the USSR. When Great Britain entered into a military alliance with the USSR in July 1941, it demanded that Finland halt its offensive at the old 1939

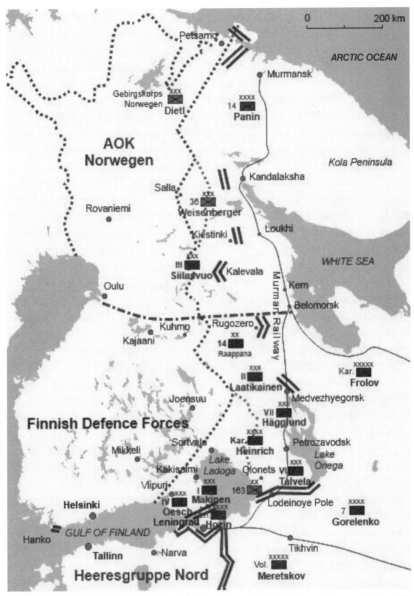

0   200 km

ARCTIC OCEAN

Petsamo

Murmansk

Gebirgskorps
Norwegen   Dietl

14   Panin

Kola Peninsula

AOK
Norwegen

Salla

Rovaniemi

36
Weisenberger

Kandalaksha

Kiestinki

Loukhi

WHITE SEA

Siilasvuo   Kalevala

Kem

Oulu

Belomorsk

Kuhmo   Rugozero

Kajaani

14
Raappana

Kar.   Frolov

II
Laatikainen

Joensuu

Medvezhyegorsk

VII
Hägglund

Finnish Defence Forces

Sortvala   Kar.
Heinrich

Petrozavodsk

Mikkeli

Lake
Ladoga

Lake
Onega

Käkisalmi

Olonets VI
Talvela

Viipuri

I
Mäkipen

163

Helsinki

IV
Oesch

Hanko   GULF OF FINLAND

Leningrad   Horn

Lodeinoye Pole

7
Gorelenko

Tallinn   Narva

Tikhvin

Heeresgruppe Nord

Vol.
Meretskov

German/Finnish Advances and the Front Lines in December 1941.[11] Note: *Wehrmacht* operational army group areas AOK Norwegen and Heersgruppe Nord are listed in this map in the original German.

Soviet borders. The Finns continued their advance, and Britain severed formal diplomatic relations on August 1. Washington also began to exert diplomatic pressure in October when it demanded that Finland withdraw its troops to the 1939 borders if it wished to maintain good relations with the United States. When this warning had no effect, a more specific threat was made: "Should material of war sent from the United States to Soviet territory in the north by way of the Arctic Ocean be attacked en route either presumably or even allegedly from territory under Finnish control . . . such an incident must be expected to bring about an instant crisis in the relations between Finland and the United States."[12]

Continued advances by the Finns resulted in a British ultimatum to Helsinki in November demanding that "unless by December 5th the Finnish Government ceases military operations and further withdraws from all active participation in hostilities, His Majesty's Government in the United Kingdom will have no choice but to declare the existence of a state of war between the two countries."[13] The Finnish government made no official reply to London or Washington, but the warnings certainly had an effect. Ryti convinced Mannerheim to halt all offensives after the capture of Medvezhyegorsk on December 5. Despite General Siilasvuo and his III Corp being nominally under German command, Mannerheim quietly transmitted orders to end the drive designed to take the town of Loukhi and cut the northern section of the Kirov Railway.[14] At the time, Siilasvuo's forces had recently taken the town of Kestenga, and the front lines were less than twenty miles away from Loukhi. The officers commanding the leading units at this front were optimistic and believed that prospects were good for a continued advance.[15] Nevertheless, the Finnish offensive halted.

While the Finns technically complied with the British ultimatum, the Churchill government was under pressure to show solidarity with its new military ally in Moscow. On December 6, 1941, Britain formally declared war on Finland, but a tacit understanding came into effect: the Finns did not push further into Soviet territory, and no direct British military actions took place against Finland. In addition, as the rail line to Murmansk was never severed, the United States maintained cool but peaceful relations with Finland for the duration of the war.

The increasing hesitancy of Finland's military stance was a major blow to the German war effort. Most immediately, it aided the defenders of Leningrad. Army Group North had reached the southern side of the city in August and requested that their ally in the north join in the assault on the metropolis. Mannerheim, after consulting with Ryti, refused. In his memoirs he explained, "It was for political reasons, which in my opinion outweighed military ones, that I opposed participating in an attack on

Leningrad.... The Russians' standing argument in their effort to conquer Finnish territory was that an independent Finland was a threat to the second capital of the Soviet Union. We should do best, therefore, not to put weapons into the hands of our adversaries in a controversy that was not to be resolved before the end of the war."[16]

Not only did the Finns hold their lines in front of Leningrad, they refused to participate actively in the siege, neither shelling the city from their positions nor allowing bombing missions against it from Finnish airfields. The Soviets quickly detected the halt of the Finnish offensive, which allowed them to transfer several units from the northern to the southern defenses of the city.

Similarly, by the end of the year, Mannerheim turned down all requests to advance along the Western Front to sever the Kirov Railway and stated simply, "I shall attack no more. I have already lost too many men."[17] Several German military and diplomatic officials traveled to Finland to plead for a resumption of offensive actions culminating in Hitler's visit in June of 1942 to meet with Ryti and Mannerheim. These efforts were in vain. The Finns took the position that they would resume the offensive as soon as Leningrad had fallen, arguing that only then could they safely redeploy forces from their southern front eastward to sever the railway to Murmansk.

Finland's decision to shift its forces to a defensive stance was a negative to Germany's struggle with the USSR in three major ways. First, Leningrad did not fall despite a siege that lasted almost three years and led to the death of up to a million civilians. Had the Finns assisted in the attack by bombarding the city and advancing south to cut its one remaining supply line across Lake Ladoga, Leningrad's defenders would have found themselves in a crisis. Without being able to access the so-called Road of Life across the lake's winter ice, the city's defenders would have run out of both food and ammunition. Instead, the siege continued. The result was that much of the *Ostheer*'s Army Group North remained tied down in positions around the city, unable to redeploy to participate in the battles to the south in 1942 and 1943 such as at Stalingrad and Kursk.

Second, four hundred thousand Finnish and two hundred thousand German soldiers remained positioned along an immobile front until 1944, which allowed hundreds of thousands of Red Army troops to redeploy to lend their weight to the great battles further south. Instead of being outnumbered as in the summer of 1941, by the autumn of 1943, the Finnish High Command estimated that only 250,000 to 270,000 soldiers of the Red Army confronted the 600,000 Finnish and German troops.[18] However, the Red Army could utilize the Kirov Railway to shift its forces to reinforce defenders under attack. The *Wehrmacht*'s divisions in the far north were not strong enough on their own to break through the Soviet lines without the assistance of their Finnish allies, who refused to advance. This more than 2:1 superiority in manpower, especially considering the previous success of Mannerheim's forces against the Red Army, makes it highly likely that the Finns could have successfully gone on the offensive had they chosen to do so.

Finally, the failure to cut the rail link and flow of supplies arriving in Murmansk was likely the biggest negative impact the Finnish change of heart had on the German war effort. Had the rail line to Murmansk been cut, the port of Arkhangelsk would still have been available. However, the amount of supplies delivered to this latter harbor would have been smaller as it was both ice bound through the long Arctic winter, and a longer sail from Britain. While the flow of assistance to the USSR grew dramatically from late 1941 to 1945, its impact was possibly most crucial early in the conflict. In just the first year of aid deliveries, nineteen convoys arrived at the White Sea ports, and the Soviets unloaded a bounty that included 3,052 aircraft and 4,048 tanks.[19] Considering that the Germans committed a total of 3,277 combat aircraft and 4,445 tanks to the launch of Barbarossa, this aid was of immense importance to the ability of the USSR to slow and then stop the invaders' advance. These supplies could not have been sent to Vladivostok as the Japanese only allowed nonmilitary cargos to pass their blockade and the transit lines from the Persian Gulf ports were not ready for large shipments so early in the conflict.

Regarding this period ending in June 1942, German historian Paul Carell wrote, "Day after day Murmansk was increasingly revealing its true significance. The cranes were busy on the piers. In all corners of the fjords lay ships with British and American names. The great stream of Western aid had begun to flow. And since Archangel was frozen up from November onward, supplies for the desperately fighting forces outside Moscow and Leningrad had to come via Murmansk. It was an endless stream, a stream which was not to cease again, but to grow in volume, a stream which ultimately decided the German-Russian war."[20]

The folly of the Finnish attack on the USSR was the failure of the Nordic nation's leaders to discern that their gains would be illusory if the USSR survived. The Finns did not appreciate that they had entwined themselves in a genocidal death struggle between communism and fascism, and half-measures on their part would only result in defeat. As historian Henrik Lunde concludes,

It is rather amazing that the Finns appear not to have realized—by their refusal to participate in operations against the Soviet Union after they had secured the lost territories and East Karelia—that the achievement of their own goals was totally dependent on Germany achieving its goal of destroying the Soviet Union. Germany's failure to do so either because of a military defeat or because of a negotiated settlement would jeopardize Finland's position. If Germany lost the war the very existence of Finland came into question. It therefore made virtually no difference what the Finnish war aims were as they were intrinsically linked to those of Germany.[21]

Germany's error of diplomacy in the north was that although it successfully enticed Finland into the Barbarossa effort, it failed to convince its ally that a lasting victory required the complete defeat of the USSR. By the end of 1941 it was clear that assaulting Leningrad, severing the flow of supplies arriving via Murmansk, and tying down the maximum number of Red Army troops in the far north were of great importance in the war effort. Once Finland joined Germany's assault on the USSR, total victory was the only option. If an undefeated USSR could recover, then it surely would visit its wrath on Finland. However, Hitler and his envoys were unable to persuade the Finns to be ruthless, and in the end it was the Soviets who emerged victorious. Germany found itself in a trap of its own making in the far north. The two hundred thousand German troops stationed there could not be removed as Hitler's war machine needed to protect the flow of nickel from Petsamo and the approaches to the Swedish iron mines. However, without the active assistance of the Finns, these German divisions sat idly by as the *Wehrmacht* slowly lost the war.

The Finns remained on the defensive and watched with growing alarm the defeats of the *Wehrmacht* and the surging power of the Red Army. The Germans continued to agitate for a Finnish offensive, but Mannerheim and Ryti demurred. In early 1943, the United States offered to broker a peace between Finland and the USSR. Stalin's terms were harsh and demanded that Finnish troops withdraw to the 1940 borders, a permanent cession of the Petsamo region, and payments of more than half a billion US dollars in reparations.[22] The Finnish government wished to negotiate an exit from the war, but Germany's Ribbentrop threatened severe repercussions in the event of the signing of a separate peace. With *Wehrmacht* troops controlling the northern half of the country and Finland receiving the bulk of its imports of food, fuel, and weapons from Germany, the small Nordic nation had placed itself in an untenable situation. Finland had entered the war without being willing to do everything in its power to ensure a German victory while failing to consider the possibility of a German defeat.

After the Red Army grew in strength and lifted the seige of Leningrad, Stalin decided it was time to organize a major offensive to knock Finland out of the war and secure the USSR's northern flank. The only good luck the Finns had in this regard was that the road to Berlin did not run through Helsinki. A significant reservoir of good will remained in the United States and Britain toward Finland from its intrepid defense in the Winter War. This led to a desire in Washington and London for the USSR to treat Finland leniently. Nevertheless, Stalin told US ambassador W. Averell Harriman, "They [The Finns] are a serious, stubborn, blunt people and a sense must be hammered into them."[23]

The Red Army committed almost half a million men into the Vyborg-Petrozavodsk Offensive which began on June 9, 1944. The Soviets brought to bear more than ten thousand artillery pieces (compared to fewer than two thousand for the Finns), 1,500 aircraft (250 for the Finns), and 800 tanks (110 for the Finns). While Mannerheim's men remained stout in battle, they were no longer fighting the Red Army of 1939 to 1941: Soviet weapons were much improved, its ranks were supplied by the bounty of the west, and its officers were battle-tested after three years of pitiless war. The Finns abandoned East Karelia and shifted troops to the western side of Lake Ladoga where the Red Army broke through multiple fortified lines that had been prepared across the Karelian Isthmus.

The Germans rushed an infantry division, an assault gun brigade, and several *Luftwaffe* squadrons to this northern front. In addition, significant military supplies such as new antitank weapons were airlifted to the defenders. Eventually, after a significant retreat, the Finns were able to stabilize their lines slightly south and east of the 1940 borders. Mannerheim's overall casualties were severe in the context of the nation's total population, with more than forty-five thousand killed or wounded in the five weeks ending July 15 compared to 176,000 suffered in the previous three years of war. Finland's limited manpower reserves were exhausted, and large Soviet forces were on the cusp of the industrial and population heartland of the Nordic nation. However, rather than push north and suffer more losses, Stalin was willing to negotiate as he wished to turn his troops west toward Germany. He had indeed hammered sense into the Finns, who sued for peace and accepted Soviet demands on September 19, 1944.

In the final agreement ending the Continuation War, Finland once again lost the lands in the south and east previously ceded in 1940 and had to give up Petsamo with its access to the Arctic Ocean. Reparation payments were set at $300 million, or half of Finland's 1939 GDP. The USSR also took possession of a forty-year lease on the Porkkala peninsula. The military base they built there dominated nearby Helsinki. The Finns were to demilitarize several islands in the Gulf of Finland and remove all minefields. The Red Army received the right to utilize Finnish railroads, roads, and air bases. Finally, the Finns agreed to a drastic reduction in the size of their armed forces once they had ejected all *Wehrmacht* divisions from the country. This took place in the short Lapland War, in which the Germans retreated into Norway but only after destroying almost every structure in the northern districts of their former ally. Finland was able to exit the Continuation War without a Soviet occupation, but a significant percentage of its young men lay dead, its territory shrank, and its sovereignty was curtailed.

Conclusion

$\mathcal{B}$y the end of 1940, Hitler had successfully achieved most of his war aims for Germany. His nation was now the master of former Northern Europe from the French city of Brest on the Celtic Sea to the Polish city of Brest on the Soviet border almost 1,500 miles away. While still opposed by a weakened Britain, Germany had the initiative, the allies, and the forces to consolidate its new empire. To finish off the British, Hitler was confronted with a problem primarily of geography and logistics: he did not possess the navy and air force required to breach England's moat, starve her out, or strike across the Mediterranean and the Levant to take her oil fields. However, the USSR represented a growing threat to his reign; it controlled flows of resources critical to the German economy and was building an enormous military with great potential offensive power. Communist doctrine was inimical to fascist National Socialism, and the Soviet Union represented Britain's last hope for a significant continental European ally.

Hitler explored options to defeat Britain in peripheral attacks and keep the United States out of the conflict while he watched in alarm as the USSR advanced west to occupy territories he also coveted. An attempt to redirect Stalin's expansionist aims to British territories in the Middle East was unsuccessful. Hitler could see that, unless he acted, the most likely path of history was a grand alliance of the British, Americans, and Soviets arrayed against him in 1942 or 1943 with sufficient economic power to crush the Axis. To preclude such an outcome, he convinced himself that the best option was an attack on the USSR before his enemies united diplomatically and completed their military buildups. While achieving success in such an attack was a gamble, the odds were in Germany's favor. In addition, of Hitler's three major likely opponents,

211

the Soviet Union was the only one that could be overpowered quickly by the forces the *Wehrmacht* had at hand. Hitler's fatal mistake was not thinking that the USSR could be defeated, but rather failing to realize that to achieve victory, Germany would require the active assistance of its two most militarily potent allies, Finland and Japan.

The Finns and the Japanese had the means at their disposal to fatally injure the USSR in the summer of 1941 concurrent with the initial months of the German invasion. What would have happened had Hitler been able to convince his two allies to engage in such an effort? If the Japanese had attacked in the Far East, the critical Red Army divisions, tanks, and air-craft from Siberia would not have been available to aid in the defense of Moscow and Leningrad. If the Finns had pushed south from Lake Ladoga, they would have completed the encirclement of the USSR's second city. Cut off from flows of supplies and attacked by both the Germans and Finns over the brutal winter of 1941 to 1942, it is likely that Leningrad would have fallen within six months.

Opposed by fewer Soviet divisions, Army Group Center would have made faster progress in Operation Tyfun as it pushed east. A bloody urban battle would have raged in the capital city, depriving Stalin's regime of Moscow's transportation hub and its manufacturing output. Under such a scenario, any Red Army winter counteroffensive would have packed less punch as it would have been mounted with fewer troops while opposed by additional *Wehrmacht* units freed to deploy southward from the shorter front held by Army Group North. At the same time, the Finns, in con-junction with the two hundred thousand German troops in the Far North, could have pushed east and severed the supply line from Murmansk.

By the spring of 1942, the Axis would control Vladivostok, Lenin-grad, and likely, Moscow. Hitler's attack toward the Volga and the Caucus-sus would have launched with an even larger force than occurred histori-cally. Conversely, Red Army forces opposing the Germans in Ukraine in 1942 would have been smaller and less well supplied. Even a slightly more successful Axis offensive would have resulted in the fall of Stalingrad, the seizure of the northern Soviet oil fields along the Caspian Sea, and an interdiction of the flow of US aid supplies up the Volga as they traveled northward from the Persian Gulf ports. In such changed circumstances, if the Soviet state did not collapse, it would have controlled a reduced geog-raphy, its remaining armies would have been smaller, and only a trickle of aid would have made it to the front lines.

In such a scenario with a Japanese attack on Siberia in 1941 and a more forceful Finnish war effort, it is difficult to see how the Germans would have failed to reach their planned Arkhangelsk-Astrakhan stop line by the end of 1942. While fighting may have continued deep in the USSR to the east of the Volga, the bulk of the *Wehrmacht* would have been free to return to Western Europe. More than a million of its battle-hardened soldiers would have redeployed westward to oppose any Anglo-American landings in North Africa, Sicily, Italy, or along the northern coast of France. At the same time, German industry, supplied with the natural resources of Ukraine and the Caucases, would have shifted production to naval and aviation output to more effectively oppose the United States and Britain in the waters of the Atlantic and Mediterranean. In the Far East, Japan would have been able to source natural resources from deep in Soviet territory and drill aggressively for oil in the northern half of Sakhalin Island. Its troops would have been able to advance to Lake Baikal and Irkutsk and set up a defensive line there, freeing up many divisions, aircraft, and armored vehicles of the *Kwantung* army for use in China or in the Pacific.

It is still possible that in such a scenario the Anglo-American alliance would have prevailed in World War II. After all, the overall Anglo-American GDP would have remained larger than that of the Axis empires, and the United States was the first to deploy atomic weapons. However, would the American and British electorates have shown the fortitude to suffer the sort of casualty lists required to win the war? Even Churchill admitted that, "it is the Russian Armies who have done the main work in tearing the guts out of the German army. In the air and on the oceans we could maintain our place, but there was no force in the world which could have been called into being, except after several more years, that would have been able to maul and break the German army unless it had been subjected to the terrible slaughter and manhandling that has fallen to it through the strength of the Russian Soviet Armies."[1]

The Germans had another glittering diplomatic opportunity to tilt the war in their favor after Japan attacked its enemies in the Pacific in the last month of 1941. Immediately after the disclosure of the US "Victory Plan" with its "Europe First" strategy, and then the attack on Pearl Harbor, the Japanese were extremely desirous of a German declaration of war on the United States. It seems quite possible that Germany could have demanded and received a Japanese blockade of Vladivostok in return for joining the war on the United States. Japan's rulers might worry that such a policy could lead to war with the USSR, but running such a risk was reasonable if it resulted in Germany volunteering to draw off most of the military might of the United States to the North Atlantic.

At the same time, there was an opportunity for Hitler to pressure the Finns to move against the railway line to Murmansk. Finland was not self-sufficient in food, fuel, or weapons in 1941. Poor harvests and the transfer of labor from the agricultural sector to the military aggravated the situation. Massive food deliveries from its larger ally were the difference between survival and starvation for the Finnish people during the war. Germany annually shipped an average of two hundred thousand tons of grain to Finland representing approximately one hundred pounds per Finn per year.[2]

Prior to the launch of Barbarossa, a quick victory over the USSR seemed possible. After the Battle of Moscow, the German situation was much more fraught. Had Hitler threatened a reduction in aid if the Finns refused to return to the offensive, his allies would have been left in an untenable situation. After all, how else could the Finnish government obtain the food to feed its people if not from a "friendly" Germany? The USSR did not have food to spare, and German control of the Baltic, Norway, and Petsamo precluded shipments from overseas. Without sufficient food, the Finnish armies on the front lines would have disintegrated and potentially so would have the Finnish state. Faced with the choice of food and the possibility of victory, or starvation and certain defeat, the Finns would have had a strong incentive to join with German forces to attack the railway leading to Murmansk and the siege of Leningrad.

Had the Finns and Japanese moved to close off the two most important ports of entry of Lend-Lease aid, the Red Army would have been denied many of the critical flows of supplies that made the victories at Stalingrad and Kursk possible. While the Germans' advance would not have been as advantaged as in a scenario where the Japanese attacked in the Far East in 1941, such a change in the flow of history would still have had massive implications on the course of World War II and its aftermath. Stalin's rule would have been that much more precarious, the turn of the tide at Stalingrad might not have taken place, and German forces could have made it to the shores of the Caspian to seize Soviet oil fields and cut off aid flows coming up from Iran. Hitler's empire could have defeated the Red Army and turned its attention to defending Western Europe.

We will never know if the Soviet people could have pushed back the Germans with a significantly curtailed flow of Lend-Lease aid. However, even if the Red Army gained the upper hand in such circumstances, its advance toward Berlin would have been slower. Less pressure on the *Ostheer* would have allowed OKW to shift resources west to fight the Anglo-American forces and accelerate the German jet fighter and ballistic missile projects or even its atomic weapon program. Such an increase in *Wehrmacht* strength would have forced the United States to send that much more of its military across the Atlantic rather than the Pacific. We certainly can conclude that without the flow of aid to Vladivostok and Murmansk, World War II would have lasted longer, casualties suffered by the USSR, Britain, and the United States would have been larger, and a final defeat of the Axis would have been less certain. By late 1945, President Truman would have been sworn in and forced to decide if his limited supply of atomic weapons should be used on Germany or Japan. The prevailing "Europe First" strategy likely means that a German city would have been the first to suffer a radioactive blast. If Hitler survived such an attack, the historical record implies that he never would have considered surrender as an option.

So in either counterfactual scenario considered, were Japan and/or Finland convinced to act more forcefully against the USSR, we can draw some significant conclusions as to the course of the war. In the case of a Japanese attack on Siberia in 1941, it is highly likely that the combined Axis militaries would have crushed the USSR in a giant vise of military power. In the case of a lesser effort where the Soviet Union lost the use of Vladivostok and Murmansk, the Red Army would have been relatively weaker at the end of 1944. It is possible it would have collapsed, or it may have been pushed further east by the Germans. Soviet casualties would have been higher and those of the Axis lower. Similarly, with a weaker USSR, the Anglo-American offensive in Europe would have been disadvantaged. The D-Day landing might still have gone forward, but just as likely would have been a *Wehrmacht* in control of most of Europe engaged in a resurgent aerial bombing and naval interdiction campaign against Britain. At the least, the United States and Britain would have suffered greater casualties and required more time to liberate Western Europe. In the east, a Japanese empire confronted by diminished US forces would have yielded territory more slowly. Millions more would have perished across its empire from starvation.

It is unlikely but possible that more evenly matched, the Allies and the Axis would have forged a temporary peace. Another possibility is a campaign of atomic bombings of increasing frequency and horror. Hopefully it would have been the United States dropping the atomic bombs and not the Nazis. A *Wehrmacht* that was able to shift resources away from the fight on the Eastern Front in 1942 would have presumably made more progress toward the development of their own atomic weapons. Even if the United States was the first to field nuclear weapons, Germany had stockpiles of deadly nerve agents to deploy via V-2 rockets in retaliation for an atomic bombing of Berlin or Munich. Would the Allies still have won such a conflict? We can only speculate. A German empire holding the upper hand in the east and surrounded by Allied and occupied nations would have been a terribly strong and resilient foe.

The Finns and Japanese declined to act against the Soviets, the massive output of the US economy flowed to the USSR, and the Red Army began to recover. Both Finland and Japan had viewed the USSR as their most dangerous enemy and the one most likely to rip away their territory in wars of conquest. However, while they had the means to assist Germany in destroying the Soviet state, they chose not to do so. In the end, the Red Army smashed the Finnish and Japanese armies in turn in 1944 and 1945, leading to bloody and humiliating defeats.

When Hitler launched the invasion of the USSR, he believed that a war of extermination for either communism or national socialism had begun. The barbaric orders he issued created a self-fulfilling prophesy and ensured the war became just as brutal as he had predicted. Thankfully, he played his diplomatic hand poorly with his two most militarily potent allies. If he had coordinated with them and jointly developed plans to destroy the Soviet Union, Germany would have had a much higher chance of achieving victory. As it was, Finland and Japan did less than they might have to assist the Nazis and paid a heavy price for their failure to act. Thus, Hitler's great mistake was not the invasion of the USSR that came so close to success. Rather, it was the German failure to persuade the allied governments of Finland and Japan that their best interests demanded greater efforts to cut off and strangle the Soviet Union.

In the years since the war, many theories have been advanced as to why Germany lost to the USSR in World War II. Historians have argued that slightly better weather, a thousand more tanks, different German priorities in its offensives, or a more enlightened occupation policy by the invaders would have led to the collapse of the Soviet Union. Under scrutiny, none of these reasons individually would have led to an Axis victory. However, forceful attacks on Soviet armies in the Far East and the Far North in 1941 to 1942 and interdiction of ten billion tons of crucial aid supplies would have stretched the USSR past the breaking point. The Red Army did the bulk of the fighting and the dying in World War II, but the United States and Britain supplied tens of millions of Soviet citizens and soldiers with what they required—food, trucks, ammunition, tanks, radios, planes, explosives, radars, ships, tractors, medicine, and chemicals—to win. Lend-Lease aid on its own did not win the war on the Russian Front, but without it, the USSR would have lost.

Finland and Japan had the means, the enmity, and the motivation to tie down upward of a million Red Army soldiers and cut both the Kirov and the Trans-Siberian railways. More forward-thinking German political efforts and tighter military coordination with its allies could have doomed the USSR in 1941 or 1942. The free people of the world can only be thankful that Hitler's diplomatic skills failed him in the end.

Notes

INTRODUCTION

1. See, for example, Bevin Alexander, *How Hitler Could Have Won World War II: The Fatal Errors That Led to Nazi Defeat* (New York: Three Rivers Press, 2000), or Ronald Lewin, *Hitler's Mistakes: New Insights into What Made Hitler Tick* (New York: William Morrow & Company, 1986).

2. Ian Kershaw, *Fateful Choices: Ten Decisions That Changed the World, 1940–1941* (New York: Penguin Press, 2007), 54.

3. Niall Ferguson, *The War of the World: Twentieth-Century Conflict and the Descent of the West* (New York: Penguin Press, 2006), 439.

4. Drew Middleton, "Hitler's Russian Blunder," *New York Times* Magazine, June 21, 1981.

5. Joachim C. Fest, *Hitler* (New York: Harcourt Brace Jovanovich, Inc., 1974), 642 and 646.

6. Norman Rich, *Hitler's War Aims: Ideology, the Nazi State, and the Course of Expansion* (New York: W. W. Norton & Company, 1973), 204.

7. William Shirer, *The Rise and Fall of the Third Reich* (New York: Ballantine Books, 1950), 1087.

CHAPTER 1

1. Wikimedia Commons, European Plain, CC BY-SA 3.0, https://commons .wikimedia.org/w/index.php?curid=1607793.

2. Bethmann-Hollweg Denkschrift [Memorandum by Bethmann-Hollweg], September 9, 1914, Bundesarchiv-Lichterfelde, Reichskanzlei, Grosses Hauptquartier 21, No. 2476, pages 1–2, downloaded from German History in

Documents and Images (GHDI), http://germanhistorydocs.ghi-dc.org/docpage .cfm?docpage_id=1811.

3. Notes by Industrial League Presidium Member Gustav Stresemann on the Audience of a Delegation of Large Economic Associations with Chancellor Theobald von Bethmann-Hollweg on May 17, 1915, on the Question of War Aims. Politisches Archiv des Auswärtigen Amtes [Political Archive of the Foreign Office], Nachlaß Gustav Stresemann, Vol. 146, page 2. Downloaded from German History in Documents and Images (GHDI), http://germanhistorydocs.ghi-dc .org/pdf/eng/1002_Indust%20Leaders-War%20Aims_189.pdf.

4. Ibid.

5. Wikimedia Commons, WWI Germany Goals, Ceha, CC BY-SA 4.0, https://commons.wikimedia.org/wiki/File:Ww1_germany_goals.GIF; https:// creativecommons.org/licenses/by-sa/4.0.

6. Bethmann-Hollweg Denkschrift [Memorandum by Bethmann-Hollweg], 2.

7. See Niall Ferguson, *The Pity of War* (New York: Basic Books, 1999), 295.

8. John Mosier, *The Myth of the Great War* (New York: HarperCollins, 2001), 5.

9. Andrew Price-Smith, *Contagion and Chaos: Disease, Ecology, and National Security in the Era of Globalization* (Cambridge, MA: MIT Press, 2009), 68–78.

10. Adolf Hitler, *Mein Kampf* (Boston: Houghton Mifflin Company, 1927), 643.

11. Ibid., 645–46.

12. Ibid., 649.

13. Ibid., 654.

14. Ibid., 273.

15. Robert Cecil, *Hitler's Decision to Invade Russia, 1941* (New York: David McKay Company, 1975), 100.

16. Frank McDonough, *Hitler, Chamberlain and Appeasement* (Cambridge: Cambridge University Press, 2002), 15.

17. Stephen Lee, *European Dictatorships 1918–1945* (London: Methuen & Company, 1987), 18–23.

18. McDonough, *Hitler, Chamberlain and Appeasement*, 14.

19. Chief of the Committee of Imperial Defense, General Sir Maurice Hankey, "Notes on Hitler's External Policy in Theory and Practice," *British Documents on Foreign Affairs, Germany 1933*, 339.

20. Clement Leibovitz and Alvin Finkel, *In Our Time: The Chamberlain-Hitler Collusion* (New York: Monthly Review Press, 1997).

21. Ibid., 33–34.

22. See Wolfgang Mommsen and Lothar Kettenacker, eds., *The Fascist Challenge and the Policy of Appeasement* (London: HarperCollins Publishers Ltd., 1983), 413–27.

CHAPTER 2

1. Angus Maddison, *The World Economy: Historical Statistics* (Paris: OECD Publishing, 2003), 82, 83, 38, 39, 96.

2. Source data for table 1: Angus Maddison, *The World Economy: Historical Statistics* (Paris: OECD Publishing, 2003), 50–51, 85, 98. Note that Geary-Khamis dollars are an estimate of purchasing power parity for nations across time in one base currency. It is not an exact measurement system but yields generally accurate information as to the relative size of different nations' economic output at the time of World War II.

3. See A. J. B. "Germany's Mineral Supplies. III—Iron, Nickel, and Copper," *Bulletin of International News* 16, no. 25, Royal Institute of International Affairs, London, 1939.

4. Charles Will Wright, *The Iron and Steel Industries of Europe* (Washington, DC: United States Department of the Interior, Bureau of Mines, 1939), 1.

5. Ibid., 12.

6. John Keegan, *The Second World War* (New York: Penguin Books, 1989), 146.

7. Craig Luther, *Barbarossa Unleashed* (Atglen, PA: Schiffer Publishing, Ltd., 2014), 106.

8. The USSR had more than 139 submarines in service by the middle of 1941, with more than seventy boats stationed in the Baltic and ninety additional vessels under construction. This compares to Germany with "only" fifty-seven in late 1940. See Roger Chesneau, *Conway's All the World's Fighting Ships, 1922–1946* (Annapolis, MD: Naval Institute Press, 1980); Lt. Colonel E. Bauer, *The History of World War II* (New York: The Military Press, 1984), 170; and Peter Doyle, *World War II in Numbers* (Buffalo: Firefly Books, 2013), 22–23.

9. Nick Holdsworth, "Stalin 'Planned to Send a Million Troops to Stop Hitler if Britain and France Agreed Pact,'" *Daily Telegraph*, October 18, 2008.

10. Nikita Khrushchev, *Khrushchev Remembers*, trans. and ed. Strobe Talbott (Boston: Little, Brown and Co., 1970), 128.

11. Andrew Nagorski, *The Greatest Battle: Stalin, Hitler and the Desperate Struggle for Moscow That Changed the Course of World War II* (New York: Simon and Schuster, 2007), 20.

12. Raymond James Sontag and James Stuart Beddie, eds., *Nazi-Soviet Relations, 1939–1941: Documents from the Archives of the German Foreign Office*. Originally published by the United States Government for the Department of State, 1948. Reprinted in 1976 by Greenwood Press, Westport, CT, 50–61.

13. Krushchev, *Khrushchev Remembers*, 128.

14. Wikimedia Commons, Occupation of Poland 1939, https://commons.wikimedia.org/wiki/File:Occupation_of_Poland_1939_(b%26w).png, Author: Lonio17, reformatted as B&W by Poeticbent.

CHAPTER 3

1. Egbert Kieser, *Operation Sea Lion, The German Plan to Invade Britain, 1940* (London: Cassel & Co., 1999), 82.

2. Chris Mann and Christer Jorgensen, *Hitler's Arctic War: The German Campaigns in Norway, Finland and the USSR, 1940–1945* (New York: St. Martin's Press, 2003), 61.

3. Basil Collier, *The Defense of the United Kingdom* (London: Naval and Military Press, 1957), 440 (note "Capital Ships" here include battleships and battlecruisers—the *Nelson*, *Rodney*, *Renown*, *Repulse*, and *Barham*. At this point in the war the Germans had no ships in seaworthy operation that could match any of these five British vessels).

4. Winston Churchill, *The Second World War, Volume I* (New York: Time Incorporated, 1959), 108.

5. Collier, *The Defense of the United Kingdom*, 135–36.

6. Raeder quoted in late 1939. Source: Britishonlinearchives.co.uk, under the heading "German Naval Policy."

7. Geoff Hewitt, *Hitler's Armada: The German Invasion Plan, and the Defense of Great Britain by the Royal Navy, April–October 1940* (Barnsley, UK: Pen & Sword Maritime, Kindle Edition, locations 736 and 1178).

8. Ibid., location 659.

9. Ibid., location 2281.

10. Ibid., location 3042.

11. Churchill, *The Second World War, Volume I*, 107–8.

12. Robert Jackson, *Churchill's Moat* (Shrewsbury, UK: Airlife Publishing Ltd., 1995), 51.

13. Collier, *The Defense of the United Kingdom*, 105, 131–32.

14. Field Marshal Lord Alanbrooke, *War Diaries 1930–1945*, entry for July 22, 1940 (Berkeley and Los Angeles: University of California Press, 1957), 94.

15. Robert Harris and Jeremy Paxman, *A Higher Form of Killing: The Secret Story of Chemical and Biological Warfare* (New York: Hill and Wang, 1982), 111.

16. Rick Atkinson, *The Day of Battle: The War in Sicily and Italy, 1943–1944* (New York: Henry Holt and Co., 2007), 271–78.

17. Harris and Paxman, *A Higher Form of Killing*, 54.

18. William Shirer, *The Rise and Fall of the Third Reich* (New York: Simon & Schuster, 1960), 762.

19. Kieser, *Operation Sea Lion*, see chapter XII, "Kriegsmarine and Heer at Odds."

20. Hewitt, *Hitler's Armada*, location 1305.

21. Ibid., location 3051.

22. Peter Doyle, *World War II in Numbers* (Ontario: Firefly Books, 2013), 52.

23. Winston Churchill, *Their Finest Hour, The Second World War* (Boston: Houghton Mifflin, 1949), 102.

24. Grand Admiral Erich Raeder, *Struggle for the Sea* (London: William Kimber, 1959), 182–83.

25. Kieser, *Operation Sea Lion*, 156.

26. Jackson, *Churchill's Moat*, 106.

27. Marvin Perry, *Sources of the Western Tradition Volume II: From the Renaissance to the Present* (Boston: Wadsworth Publishing, 2012), 399.

28. Raeder, *Struggle for the Sea*, 188–89.

29. Shirer, *The Rise and Fall of the Third Reich*, 761.

CHAPTER 4

1. Grand Admiral Karl Doenitz, *Memoirs: Ten Years and Twenty Days* (Annapolis, MD: Naval Institute Press, 1958), 55 and 71.

2. Erich Raeder, *Struggle for the Sea* (London: William Kimber, 1959), 174–75.

3. Doenitz, *Memoirs: Ten Years and Twenty Days*, 109.

4. Ibid., 148.

5. John Keegan, *The Second World War* (New York: Penguin Books, 1989), 147.

6. Stephen Howarth and Derek Law, eds., *The Battle of the Atlantic, 1939–1945, the 50th Anniversary International Naval Conference* (Annapolis, MD: Naval Institute Press, 1994), 334.

7. Doenitz, *Memoirs: Ten Years and Twenty Days*, 146.

8. Ibid., 116.

9. Geoff Hewitt, *Hitler's Armada: The German Invasion Plan, and the Defense of Great Britain by the Royal Navy, April–October 1940* (Barnsley: Pen & Sword Maritime, Kindle Edition), location 2468.

10. Office of War Information, Washington, D.C., November 28, 1944. See: www.usmm.org/wsa/shiploss.html.

11. John Keegan, ed., *HarperCollins Atlas of the Second World War* (Ann Arbor: Borders Press, 1999), 46–47.

12. Lizzie Collingham, *The Taste of War: World War II and the Battle for Food* (New York: Penguin Press, 2012), 90.

13. Ibid., 89 and 91.

14. Howarth and Law, *The Battle of the Atlantic*, 586.

15. Raeder, *Struggle for the Sea*, 205–6.

16. Officially authorized under US congressional legislation tellingly titled, "An Act to Promote the Defense of the United States" of March 11, 1941. See *77th Congressional Record*, 1st session, Chapter 11, page 31.

17. Doenitz, *Memoirs, Ten Years and Twenty Days*, 127–28.

18. Peter Doyle, *World War II in Numbers* (Buffalo: Firefly Books, 2013), 190–91.

19. Howarth and Law, *The Battle of the Atlantic*, 131–32.

20. Raeder, *Struggle for the Sea*, 194–95.

21. See Robert Crowley, ed., *What If?* (New York: G. P. Putnam's Sons, 1999), 295–305.

22. Doenitz, *Memoirs, Ten Years and Twenty Days*, 115.

23. Martin van Creveld, *Supplying War: Logistics from Wallenstein to Patton* (Cambridge: Cambridge University Press, 1977), 201.

24. Ibid., 197.

25. Crowley, *What If?* 303.

26. Ibid., 297.

27. Ibid., 304.

28. Note that the United States had oil and tankers to spare and sent millions of barrels of refined fuels to the USSR via Lend-Lease shipments from 1941 to 1945.

CHAPTER 5

1. Baron Carl Mannerheim, *The Memoirs of Marshal Mannerheim* (New York: E. F. Dutton & Company, 1954), 312–13.

2. https://commons.wikimedia.org/wiki/File:Ribbentrop-Molotov.svg, by Peter Hanula [GFDL (http://www.gnu.org/copyleft/fdl.html) or CC-BY-SA-3.0 (http://creativecommons.org/licenses/by-sa/3.0/)], from Wikimedia Commons.

3. Nikita Khrushchev, *Khrushchev Remembers*, trans. and ed. Strobe Talbott (Boston: Little, Brown and Co., 1970), 134 and 166.

4. Norman Rich, *Hitler's War Aims: Ideology, the Nazi State, and the Course of Expansion* (New York: W. W. Norton & Company, 1973), quote from November 23, 1939, 204–5.

5. Colonel General Franz Halder, *The Halder Diaries Volume IV*, reprinted from the translation prepared by the Office of the Chief of Counsel for War Crimes, Office of Military Government, United States (Boulder, CO: Westview Press, 1976), 50.

6. Chris Mann and Christer Jorgensen, *Hitler's Arctic War: The German Campaigns in Norway, Finland, and the USSR 1940–1945* (New York: St. Martin's Press, 2003), 66.

7. Mannerheim, *The Memoirs of Marshal Mannerheim*, 66.

8. Mann and Jorgensen, *Hitler's Arctic War: The German Campaigns in Norway, Finland and the USSR, 1940–1945*, 67.

9. Joachim von Ribbentrop, *The Ribbentrop Memoirs* (London: Weidenfield and Nicolson, 1954), 147–48.

10. Alan Bullock, *Hitler: A Study in Tyranny* (New York: Harper & Row, 1962), 611.

11. Robert Cecil, *Hitler's Decision to Invade Russia, 1941* (New York: David McKay Company, 1975), 106.

12. Ribbentrop, *The Ribbentrop Memoirs*, 155.

13. Raymond James Sontag and James Stuart Beddie, eds., *Nazi-Soviet Relations, 1939–1941: Documents from the Archives of the German Foreign Office* (Honolulu: University Press of the Pacific, 2003), 240.

14. Ibid., 240.

15. Ibid., 240.

16. Ibid., 244.

17. Ibid., 255–57.

18. Ribbentrop, *The Ribbentrop Memoirs*, 150.

19. Halder, *The Halder Diaries Volume V*, 84.

CHAPTER 6

1. Joel Hayward, "Hitler's Quest for Oil: The Impact of Economic Considerations on Military Strategy, 1941–1942," *Journal of Strategic Studies* 18, no. 4 (December 1995): 99 (Hitler's quote is from January 20, 1941).

2. Joachim von Ribbentrop, *The Ribbentrop Memoirs* (London: Weidenfield and Nicolson, 1954), 154.

3. United States Department of State, *Documents on German Foreign Policy: From the Archives of the German Foreign Ministry* (Washington: United States Government Printing Office, 1957–1964). Series D (1939–1945), *The War Years, Volume 11*: February 1–June 22, 1941. Document 532, 899–902. (English translation accredited to US Department of State Division of Language Services.)

4. Ibid.

5. See for example, Ian Kershaw, *Fateful Choices: Ten Decisions That Changed the World, 1940–1941* (New York: Penguin Press, 2007), 269–70, 275–76.

6. Mannerheim, *The Memoirs of Marshal Mannerheim*, 403–4.

7. Gabriel Gorodetsky, *Stafford Cripps' Mission to Moscow, 1940–1942* (Cambridge: Cambridge University Press, 1984), 58.

8. Raymond James Sontag and James Stuart Beddie, eds., *Nazi-Soviet Relations, 1939–1941: Documents from the Archives of the German Foreign Office*. Originally published by the United States Government for the Department of State, 1948. Reprinted in 1976 by Greenwood Press, Westport, CT, 268–69.

9. Ibid., 273.

10. Paul Hehn, *A Low, Dishonest Decade: The Great Powers, Eastern Europe, and the Economic Origins of World War II, 1930–1941* (New York: Continuum International Publishing Group, 2002), 391–92.

11. Sontag and Beddie, *Nazi-Soviet Relations*, 317.

12. See: http://serbianna.com/analysis/archives/3510 and Heinz Magenheimer, *Hitler's War: Key Strategic Decisions 1940–1945* (New York: Barnes & Noble Books, 2003), 47.

13. Hein, *A Low Dishonest Decade*, 392.

14. Norman Rich, *Hitler's War Aims: Ideology, the Nazi State, and the Course of Expansion* (New York: W. W. Norton & Company, 1973), 208.

CHAPTER 7

1. David Glantz, *Stumbling Colossus* (Lawrence, KS: University Press of Kansas, 1998), 260.

2. Robert Conquest, *The Harvest of Sorrow* (New York: Oxford University Press, 1986), 4, 337.

3. Willamson Murray and Allan Millett, *A War to Be Won: Fighting the Second World War* (Cambridge: Harvard University Press, 2000), 110.

4. Ibid., 112.

5. Peter Doyle, *World War II in Numbers* (Buffalo: Firefly Books, 2013), 62.

6. Angus Maddison, *The World Economy: Historical Statistics* (Paris: OECD Publishing, 2003), 50–51, 60–61, and 98.

7. Peter Zeihan, *The Absent Superpower* (Austin, TX: Zeihan on Geopolitics, 2017), 133.

8. Tsutsui Kiyotada, ed., *Fifteen Lectures on Showa Japan: Road to the Pacific War in Recent Historiography*, from Lecture #10, Hanada Tomoyuki, "The Nomonhan Incident and the Japanese-Soviet Neutrality Pact," Japan Publishing Industry Foundation for Culture, Tokyo, Japan, 2016, 177.

9. Chris Bellamy, *Absolute War: Soviet Russia in the Second World War* (New York: Alfred A. Knopf, Inc., 2007), 82–83.

10. John Erickson, *The Soviet High Command: A Military-Political History 1918–1941* (London: Frank Cass Publishers, 1962), 522.

11. Conquest, *The Harvest of Sorrow*, 4.

12. Ibid., 301.

13. Robert Conquest, *The Great Terror, a Reassessment* (Oxford: Oxford University Press, 1990), 485.

14. Ibid., 450.

15. Ibid., 450.

16. Alan Clark, *Barbarossa: The Russian-German Conflict, 1941–1945* (New York: William Morrow and Company, 1965), 43.

17. Conquest, *The Great Terror*, 451.

18. Lt. Colonel E. Bauer, *The History of World War II* (New York: The Military Press, 1984), 41.

19. Baron Carl Mannerheim, *The Memoirs of Marshal Mannerheim* (New York: E. F. Dutton & Company, 1954), 350.

20. Richard Condon, *The Winter War: Russia against Finland* (New York: Ballantine Books, 1972), 153–54.

21. John Erickson, *The Soviet High Command: A Military-Political History 1918–1941* (London: Frank Cass Publishers, 1962), 548.

22. William Manchester, *The Last Lion: Winston Spencer Churchill: Alone, 1932–1940* (New York: Bantam Books, 1988), 59.

23. Condon, *The Winter War*, 154.

24. Bellamy, *Absolute War, Soviet Russia in the Second World War*, 80.

25. *Foreign Relations of the United States Diplomatic Papers, 1941, General, The Soviet Union, (1941)* (Washington: United States Government Printing Office, 1959), 620.

CHAPTER 8

1. Robert Kirchubel, *Operation Barbarossa 1941: Army Group South* (Westport, CT: Praeger Publishers, 2004), 15.

2. Michael Olive and Robert Edwards, *Operation Barbarossa 1941* (Mechanicsburg, PA: Stackpole Books, 2012), vii.

3. Stephen Van Evera, *Causes of War: Power and the Roots of Conflict* (Ithaca: Cornell University Press, 1999), 21.

4. Ibid., 21.

5. Craig Luther, *Barbarossa Unleashed* (Altglen, PA: Schiffer Publishing, Ltd., 2013), 198–99.

6. Willy Peter Reese, *A Stranger to Myself: The Inhumanity of War: Russia, 1941–1944*, from the Forward by Max Hastings (New York: Farrar, Straus and Giroux, 2003), vii.

7. Niall Ferguson, *The War of the World: Twentieth-Century Conflict and the Descent of the West* (New York: Penguin Press, 2006), 439.

8. Norman Ohler, *Blitzed: Drugs in Nazi Germany* (London: Penguin Books, 2011; first English translation 2015), 141–43.

9. Peter Doyle, *World War II in Numbers* (Buffalo: Firefly Books, 2013), 60–63. Note that only about eleven thousand of the Soviet's military aircraft were actually serviceable on June 22, 1941. Many Soviet tanks were obsolete, not equipped with radios, and of questionable operational value. See Sir Alistair Horne, *Hubris* (New York: Harper), 200.

10. *The War of the World*, 435.

11. Colonel General Franz Halder, *The Halder Diaries Volume VI*, reprinted from the translation prepared by the Office of the Chief of Counsel for War Crimes, Office of Military Government, United States (Boulder, CO: Westview Press, 1976), 196.

12. Halder, *The Halder Diaries, Volume VII*, 36.

13. Alvin Coox, *Nomonhan, Japan Against Russia 1939, Volume Two* (Stanford: Stanford University Press, 1985), 1043–44.

14. Winston Churchill, *The Second World War, Volume I* (New York: Time Incorporated, 1959), 185.

15. Winston Churchill, *Secret Session Speeches*, from his speech to a closed session of House of Commons, June 25, 1941 (London: Cassell and Company, Ltd., 1946), 37.

16. Ibid., 316.

17. *Foreign Relations of the United States Diplomatic Papers, 1941, General, the Soviet Union, Volume 1*, document 622, Office of the Historian, United States Department of State, Washington, DC, 627.

18. Susan Butler, *My Dear Mr. Stalin: The Complete Correspondence of Franklin D. Roosevelt and Joseph V. Stalin* (New Haven, CT: Yale University Press, 2005), 4.

19. Ibid., 4.

20. Winston Churchill, *The Second World War, Volume III The Grand Alliance* (Boston: Houghton Mifflin Company, 1950), 331.

21. Ibid., 332.

22. Butler, *My Dear Mr. Stalin*, 11.

23. Christian Hartmann, *Operation Barbarossa: Nazi Germany's War in the East, 1941–1945* (Oxford: Oxford University Press, 2013), 98.

24. Laurence Rees, *War of the Century: When Hitler Fought Stalin* (New York: The New Press, 1999), 71.

25. David Glantz, *Stumbling Colossus* (Lawrence, KS: University Press of Kansas, 1998), 260.

26. B. H. Liddell Hart, *The German Generals Talk* (New York: William Morrow and Company, 1948), 181.

27. Heinz Magenheimer, *Hitler's War: Key Strategic Decisions 1940–1945* (New York: Barnes & Noble Books, 2003), 105.

28. Michael Olive and Robert Edwards, *First Winter on the Eastern Front 1941–1942* (Mechanicsburg, PA: Stackpole Books, 2013), XVI.

29. Luther, *Barbarossa Unleashed*, 647.

30. Stuart Goldman, *Nomonhan, 1939: The Red Army's Victory That Shaped World War II* (Annapolis, MD: Naval Institute Press, 2012), 177, and John Erickson, *The Soviet High Command, A Military-Political History 1918–1941* (London: Frank Cass Publishers, 1962), 631–32.

31. Andrew Nagorski, *The Greatest Battle: Stalin, Hitler and the Desperate Struggle for Moscow That Changed the Course of World War II* (New York: Simon and Schuster, 2007), 217–18.

32. https://commons.wikimedia.org/wiki/File:Eastern_Front_1942-05_to_1942-11.png, By User:Gdr [GFDL (http://www.gnu.org/copyleft/fdl.html) or CC-BY-SA-3.0 (http://creativecommons.org/licenses/by-sa/3.0/)], from Wikimedia Commons.

CHAPTER 9

1. Craig Luther, *Barbarossa Unleashed* (Atglen, PA: Schiffer Publishing, Ltd., 2014), 27.

2. Website of the Imperial War Museums, see: http://www.iwm.org.uk/history/operation-barbarossa-and-germanys-failure-in-the-soviet-union.

3. David Stahel, *Kiev 1941: Hitler's Battle for Supremacy in the East* (Cambridge: Cambridge University Press, 2012), 4–5.

4. Laurence Rees, *War of the Century: When Hitler Fought Stalin* (New York: The New Press, 1999), 52–56.

5. Luther, *Barbarossa Unleashed*, 609.

6. Susan Butler, *My Dear Mr. Stalin: The Complete Correspondence of Franklin D. Roosevelt and Joseph V. Stalin* (New Haven, CT: Yale University Press, 2005), 40.

7. Sir Alistair Horne, *Hubris* (New York: Harper, 2015), 200.

8. Ibid., 222.

9. John Erickson, *The Soviet High Command: A Military-Political History 1918–1941* (London: Frank Cass Publishers, 1962), 631.

10. Ibid., 628.

11. Georgy Zhukov, *Memoirs of Marshal Zhukov* (New York: Delacourt Press, 1971), 323.

12. Ibid., 278.

13. Niall Ferguson, *The Pity of War* (New York: Basic Books, 1999), 148.

14. G. F. Krivosheev, *Soviet Casualties and Combat Losses in the Twentieth Century* (Barnsley: Greenhill Books, 1997), 86, 97.

15. Data from the German historian Rüdiger Overman, "Deutsche Militärische Veluste in Zweiten," 2000. See the Wikipedia entry "German Casualties in World War II" for additional detail.

16. Peter Doyle, *World War II in Numbers* (Buffalo: Firefly Books, 2013), 65.

17. David Glantz, "The Struggle for Stalingrad City: Opposing Orders of Battle, Combat Orders and Reports, and Operational and Tactical Maps, Part 2: The Fight for Stalingrad's Factory District—14 October–18 November 1942," *Journal of Slavic Military Studies* 21, no. 2 (2008): 377–471, 468.

18. Ibid., 64–65.

19. Ibid., 38–39.

20. Ibid.

CHAPTER 10

1. R. H. S. Stolfi, *Hitler's Panzers East: World War II Reinterpreted* (Norman: University of Oklahoma Press, 1991), 140.

2. Andrew Roberts, *The Storm of War: A New History of the Second World War* (New York: HarperCollins Publishers, 2001), 175.

3. Theodore Ropp, *War in the Modern World* (Westport, CT: Greenwood Press, 1959), 315 and 318.

4. Martin van Creveld, *Supplying War: Logistics from Wallenstein to Patton* (Cambridge: Cambridge University Press, 1977), 157.

5. Ibid., 168–69.

6. Ibid., 176.

7. David Glantz, "The Soviet-German War 1941–1945: Myths and Realities: A Survey Essay," The 20th Anniversary Distinguished Lecture at the Strom Thurmond Institute of Government and Public Affairs, Clemson University, Clemson, SC, October 11, 2001, 24.

8. Georgy Zhukov, *Memoirs of Marshal Zhukov* (New York: Delacourt Press, 1971), 344–45.

9. See Pavel and Anatoli Sudoplatov, *Special Tasks: The Memoirs of an Unwanted Witness—A Soviet Spymaster* (Boston: Little, Brown and Co., 1994), 133–35, Central Intelligence Agency's website: see https://www.cia.gov/library/center-for-the-study-of-intelligence/csi-publications/csi-studies/studies/vol48no2/article12.html#rfn11, and Andrew Nagorski, *The Greatest Battle: Stalin, Hitler and the*

Desperate Struggle of Moscow That Changed the Course of World War II (New York: Simon and Schuster, 2007), 195, 202, and 207.

10. Ben Shepherd, *Hitler's Soldiers, The German Army in the Third Reich* (New Haven, CT: Yale University Press, 2016), 185.

11. Robert Kirchubel, *Operation Barbarossa: The German Invasion of Soviet Russia* (Oxford: Osprey Publishing, 2013), 363.

12. Laurence Rees, *War of the Century: When Hitler Fought Stalin* (New York: The New Press, 1999), 73.

13. *Statistics of the Military Effort of the British Empire during the Great War 1914–1920* (London: The War Office, 1922), 353.

CHAPTER 11

1. B. H. Liddell Hart, *The German Generals Talk* (New York: William Morrow and Company, 1948), 175–76.

2. Harald Lejenas, "The Severe Winter in Europe 1941–42: The Large-Scale Circulation, Cut-Off Lows and Blocking," *Bulletin of the American Meteorological Society*, March 1, 1989, 271, 279.

3. Winston S. Churchill, ed., *Never Give In!: Winston Churchill's Speeches* (London: Bloomsbury Academic, 2013), 276.

4. Trumbull Higgins, *Hitler and Russia: The Third Reich in a Two-Front War 1937–1941* (London: Macmillan Publishers, 1966), 151.

5. Martin van Creveld, *Supplying War: Logistics from Wallenstein to Patton* (Cambridge: Cambridge University Press, 1977), 174.

6. Andrew Nagorski, *The Greatest Battle: Stalin, Hitler and the Desperate Struggle of Moscow That Changed the Course of World War II* (New York: Simon and Schuster, 2007), 227.

7. Heinz Guderian, *Panzer Leader* (Boston: Da Capo Press, 1996), 266–67.

8. Ibid., 15.

9. Hart, *The German Generals Talk*, 167.

10. Richard Ovary, *Why the Allies Won* (New York: W.W. Norton, 1996), 217.

11. Martin van Creveld, *Supplying War: Logistics from Wallenstein to Patton* (Cambridge: Cambridge University Press, 1977), 151.

12. See Lutz Unterseher, "Wheels or Tracks? On the 'Lightness' of Military Expeditions," *Project on Defense Alternatives*, Washington, DC, July 2000: http://www.comw.org/pda/0007wheels.html.

13. Eric Schmitt, "Iraq-Bound Troops Confront Rumsfeld over Lack of Armor," *New York Times*, December 8, 2004.

14. van Creveld, *Supplying War*, 180.

15. Georgy Zhukov, *Memoirs of Marshal Zhukov* (New York: Delacourt Press, 1971), 344–45.

CHAPTER 12

1. William Shirer, *The Rise and Fall of the Third Reich* (New York: Ballantine Books, 1950), 824.

2. Chris Bellamy, *Absolute War: Soviet Russia in the Second World War* (New York: Alfred A. Knopf, Inc., 2007), 100.

3. Winston Churchill, *The Second World War, Volume I* (New York: Time Incorporated, 1959), 180.

4. Craig Luther, *Barbarossa Unleashed* (Atglen, PA: Schiffer Publishing, Ltd., 2014), 102–3.

5. Churchill, *The Second World War*, 174.

6. Sir Alistair Horne, *Hubris* (New York: Harper, 2015), 200, and Andrew Nagorski, *The Greatest Battle: Stalin, Hitler and the Desperate Struggle of Moscow That Changed the Course of World War II* (New York: Simon and Schuster, 2007), 228.

7. Bryan Fugate, *Operation Barbarossa, Strategy and Tactics on the Eastern Front, 1941* (Novato, CA: Presidio Press, 1984), 272 and 285.

8. Luther, *Barbarossa Unleashed*, 610.

9. Hubert van Tuyll, *Feeding the Bear: American Aid to the Soviet Union, 1941–1945* (New York: Greenwood Press, 75).

CHAPTER 13

1. Willy Peter Reese, *A Stranger to Myself: The Inhumanity of War: Russia, 1941–1944*, from the Foreword by Max Hastings (New York: Farrar, Straus and Giroux, 2003), ix–x.

2. Christian Hartmann, *Operation Barbarossa: Nazi Germany's War in the East, 1941–1945* (Oxford: Oxford University Press, 2013), 150–51.

3. Richard Ovary, *Why the Allies Won* (New York: W.W. Norton, 1996), 187.

4. Ibid., 187–88.

5. Andrew Nagorski, *The Greatest Battle: Stalin, Hitler and the Desperate Struggle of Moscow That Changed the Course of World War II* (New York: Simon and Schuster, 2007), 73.

6. Andrew Roberts, *The Storm of War: A New History of the Second World War* (New York: HarperCollins Publishers, 2001), 181.

7. See Daniel Goldhagen, *Hitler's Willing Executioners* (New York: Random House, 2007), or Christopher Browning, *Ordinary Men: Reserve Police Battalion 101 and the Final Solution in Poland* (New York: Harper Perennial, 1998), and Andrew Roberts, "The Genocide Generals: Secret Recordings Explode the Myth They Knew Nothing about the Holocaust," *The Daily Mail*, London, UK, July 21, 2007.

8. Jonathan Smele, *The "Russian" Civil Wars, 1916–1926: Ten Years That Shook the World* (New York: Oxford University Press, 2015), 14–15.

9. Chris Bellamy, *Absolute War: Soviet Russia in the Second World War* (New York: Alfred A. Knopf, Inc., 2007), 27.

10. Laurence Rees, *War of the Century: When Hitler Fought Stalin* (New York: The New Press, 1999), 57.

11. Bellamy, *Absolute War, Soviet Russia in the Second World War*, 456.

12. Antony Beevor, *Stalingrad: The Fateful Siege: 1942–1943* (New York: Penguin Books, 1998), 67.

13. See M. T. Anderson, *Symphony for the City of the Dead: Dmitri Shostakovich and the Siege of Leningrad* (Somerville, MA: Candlewick Press, 2015), 226–27.

14. Roger Reese, *Why Stalin's Soldiers Fought: The Red Army's Military Effectiveness in World War II* (Lawrence, KS: University Press of Kansas, 2001), 18.

15. Georgy Zhukov, *Memoirs of Marshal Zhukov* (New York: Delacourt Press, 1971), 290.

16. Reese, *Why Stalin's Soldiers Fought*, 185.

17. See the Holocaust Encyclopedia of United States, Holocaust Memorial Museum Website, under the entry *Lebensraum*: https://www.ushmm.org/wlc/en/article.php?ModuleId=10008219.

18. Ibid., 45.

19. Alex Alexiev, "Soviet Nationalities in German Wartime Strategy, 1941–1945" (Santa Monica, CA: Rand Institute, 1982), vi.

CHAPTER 14

1. Michael Barnhart, *Japan Prepares for Total War: The Seach for Economic Security, 1919–1941* (Ithaca, NY: Cornell University Press, 1987), 89.

2. https://commons.wikimedia.org/wiki/File:Hokushin-ron-Map.svg, by Hokushin-ron-Map.png: *Pacific_Area_-_The_Imperial_Powers_1939_-_Map.svg: Emok*derivative work: Emok (talk)World2Hires_filled_mercator.svg: EmokImage:Pacific_Area_-_The_Imperial_Powers_1939_-_Map.jpg [CC BY-SA 3.0 (https://creativecommons.org/licenses/by-sa/3.0)], via Wikimedia Commons.

3. Philip Jowett, *The Japanese Army 1931–1945*, volume 1 (Oxford: Osprey Publishing, 2002), 7, 15.

4. Ernst Presseisen, *Germany and Japan: A Study in Totalitarian Diplomacy 1933–1941* (New York: Howard Fertig, Inc., 1969), 48 and 52.

5. Soviet Pacific Fleet data is for June 1941 from J. Rohwer and M. S. Monakov, *Stalin's Ocean-Going Fleet: Soviet Naval Strategy and Shipbuilding Programmes, 1935–1953* (London: Frank Cass Publishers, 2001), 138, and does not include thirty-seven small submarines. Other naval strengths data is for September 1941 from John Keegan, ed., *HarperCollins Atlas of the Second World War* (Ann Arbor: Borders Press, 1999), 67.

6. https://commons.wikimedia.org/wiki/File:Second_Sino-Japanese_War_WW2.png, by US Army [Public domain], via Wikimedia Commons.

CHAPTER 15

1. Michael Barnhart, *Japan Prepares for Total War: The Search for Economic Security, 1919–1941* (Ithaca, NY: Cornell University Press, 1987), 95.

2. Ibid., 102–3.

3. Daniel Yergin, *The Prize: The Epic Quest for Oil, Money & Power* (New York: Simon & Schuster, 1991), 309.

4. Graeme Heard and Anne Aldis, eds., *Russian Regions and Regionalism: Strength through Weakness* (London: RoutledgeCurzon, 2003), 145.

5. Alexander Igolkin, "The Sakhalin Anomaly," *Oil of Russia Magazine*, Moscow, Russian Federation, No. 1, 2004.

6. Ibid.

7. Yergin, *The Prize*, 308.

8. Stephen Roskill, *Hankey: Man of Secrets, Volume III 1931–1963* (New York: St. Martin's Press, 1974), 73.

9. Charles Maechling, "Pearl Harbor: The First Energy War," *History Today*, Volume 50, Issue 12, December 2000.

10. Yergin, *The Prize*, 311.

11. Franklin Delano Roosevelt, *F.D.R.: His Personal Letters: 1928–1945*, vol. 2 (New York: Duell, Sloan and Pearce, 1950), 1077.

12. Ulrich Mohr, *Ship 16: The Story of the Secret German Raider Atlantis* (New York: The John Day Company, 1956), 153–55.

13. *Trial of the Major German War Criminals Before the International Military Tribunal*, Nuremberg 1945–1946. Evidence entered by the USA against Ribbentrop #129: extract from minutes of discussion between Von Ribbentrop and the Japanese Ambassador Oshima, 23 February 1941, volume III, 329, 372, 274. See: https://www.loc.gov/rr/frd/Military_Law/pdf/NT_Vol-XXIV.pdf.

14. Ernst Presseisen, *Germany and Japan: A Study in Totalitarian Diplomacy 1933–1941* (New York: Howard Fertig, Inc., 1969), 287.

15. Kazuo Yagami, *Konoe Fumimaro and the Failure of Peace in Japan 1937–1941* (Jefferson, NC: McFarland & Co., Inc., 2006), 101.

16. Yale Law School, Lillian Goldman Law Library, The Avalon Project. See: http://avalon.law.yale.edu/wwii/s2.asp and http://avalon.law.yale.edu/wwii/s1.asp.

17. David Lu, *The Agony of Choice: Matsuoka Yosuke and the Rise and Fall of the Japanese Empire, 1880–1946* (Lanham, MD: Lexington Books, 2002), 206.

18. Ibid., 208.

19. Kazuo Yagami, *Konoe Fumimaro and the Failure of Peace in Japan, 1937–1941: A Critical Appraisal of the Three-Time Prime Minister* (Jefferson, NC: McFarland & Company, Inc., 2006), 102.

20. *The "Magic" Background of Pearl Harbor, Volume 1* (Washington, DC: United States Department of Defense, 1977), A-191.

21. Ibid., A-192.

22. Ibid., A-196.

23. Ibid., A-196.

24. Bernd Wegner, ed., *From Peace to War: Germany, Soviet Russia and the World, 1939–1941* (Providence, RI: Berghahn Books, 1993), 547–49.

CHAPTER 16

1. Bernd Wegner, ed., *From Peace to War: Germany, Soviet Russia and the World, 1939–1941* (Providence, RI: Berghahn Books, 1993), 235.

2. For example, see: Michael Barnhart, *Japan Prepares for Total War: The Search for Economic Security, 1919–1941* (Ithaca, NY: Cornell University Press, 1987), 34.

3. Nobutaka Ike, ed., *Japan's Decision for War: Records of the 1941 Policy Conferences*, 32nd Liaison Conference, June 25, 1941 (Stanford: Stanford University Press, 1967), 59.

4. Ibid., 67.

5. Ibid., 71.

6. Ibid., 74.

7. Ibid., 76–88.

8. Ernst Presseisen, *Germany and Japan: A Study in Totalitarian Diplomacy 1933–1941* (New York: Howard Fertig, Inc., 1969), 307.

9. Herbert Bix, *Hirohito, and the Making of Modern Japan* (New York: HarperCollins, 2000), 398.

10. Alvin Coox, *Nomonhan, Japan Against Russia 1939, Volume Two* (Stanford: Stanford University Press, 1985), 1037, 1040, 1042.

11. https://commons.wikimedia.org/w/index.php?curid=56603453, by 2Q [CC BY-SA 4.0 (https://creativecommons.org/licenses/by-sa/4.0)], from Wikimedia Commons.

12. Ike, *Japan's Decision for War: Records of the 1941 Policy Conferences*, 292.

13. David Lu, *The Agony of Choice: Matsuoka Yosuke and the Rise and Fall of the Japanese Empire, 1880–1946* (Lanham, MD: Lexington Books, 2002), 238.

14. Kazuo Yagami, *Konoe Fumimaro and the Failure of Peace in Japan 1937–1941* (Jefferson, NC: McFarland & Co., Inc., 2006), 115–16.

15. Ibid., 117.

16. Bix, *Hirohito, and the Making of Modern Japan*, 399.

CHAPTER 17

1. Albert Weeks, *Russia's Life-Saver: Lend-Lease Aid to the U.S.S.R. in World War II* (Lanham, MD: Lexington Books, 2004), ix.

2. Ibid., x.

3. Ibid., 8.

4. Hubert van Tuyll, *Feeding the Bear: American Aid to the Soviet Union, 1941–1945* (New York: Greenwood Press, 1989), 74.

5. Igor Miecik, "Great War of Myths, or How the USSR Hid the Truth about World War II," *Polska Newsweek*, July 8, 2017, see link: http://www.newsweek.pl/wiedza/historia/zsrr-i-ii-wojna-swiatowa-jak-zsrr-zbudowal-mit-wielkiej-wojny-ojczyznianej,artykuly,341979,1.html.

6. van Tuyll, *Feeding the Bear*, 164.

7. Ibid., 152, 157, 158.

8. Ibid., 152, 157, 158.

9. Nikita Khrushchev, *Khrushchev Remembers*, trans. and ed. Strobe Talbott (Boston: Little, Brown and Co., 1970), 225–26.

10. Roderick Stackelberg and Sally Winkle, *The Nazi Germany Sourcebook: An Anthology of Texts* (New York: Routledge, 2002), 283.

11. Alla Paperno, "The Unknown World War II in the Northern Pacific," based on a presentation at the International Scientific and Practical Conference at the St. Petersburg House of Friendship and Peace, April 27, 2000. See http://lend-lease.airforce.ru/english.articles/paperno/index.htm.

12. Thomas Fleming, "The Big Leak," *American Heritage Magazine* 28, no. 8 (December 1987), Rockville, MD.

13. Data from http://sea-distances.org, travel time calculated using Liberty ship speed of eleven knots.

14. Ibid.

CHAPTER 18

1. Paul Carell, *Hitler Moves East, 1941–1943* (Boston: Little, Brown and Co., 1964), 413–14.

2. Richard Pipes, *The Russian Revolution* (New York: Vintage Books, 1991), 598.

3. Olli Vehvilainin, *Finland in the Second World War: Between Germany and Russia* (New York: Palgrave Publishers, Ltd., 2002), 86–87, 90.

4. C. Leonard Lundin, *Finland in the Second World War* (Bloomington: Indiana University Press, 1957), 175.

5. Henrik Lunde, *Finland's War of Choice* (Havertown, PA: Casemate Publishers, 2011), 49.

6. Vehvilainin, *Finland in the Second World War*, 89.

7. Waldemar Erfurth, *The Last Finnish War* (Washington: University Publications of America, Inc., 1979), 17.

8. Henrik Lunde, *Finland's War of Choice* (Havertown, PA: Casemate Publishers, 2011), 56 and 187.

9. Ibid., 43–44.

10. Ibid., 381.

11. https://commons.wikimedia.org/wiki/File%3AContinuation_War_De-cember_1941_English.jpg, by Peltimikko [CC BY-SA 3.0 (https://creativecommons.org/licenses/by-sa/3.0) or GFDL (http://www.gnu.org/copyleft/fdl.html)], from Wikimedia Commons.

12. *Documents Concerning the Relations Between Finland, Great Britain and the United States of America during the Autumn of 1941*, Publication of the Ministry of Foreign Affairs of Finland, Helsinki, Finland, 1942, 13.

13. Ibid., 24–25. Note that originally the note read December 3, but after its delivery the British changed this to the 5th.

14. Vehvilainin, *Finland in the Second World War*, 96–100.

15. Lunde, *Finland's War of Choice*, 129–30 and 143.

16. Baron Carl Mannerheim, *The Memoirs of Marshal Mannerheim* (New York: E. F. Dutton & Company, 1954), 298–300.

17. Lundin, *Finland in the Second World War*, 100.

18. Lunde, *Finland's War of Choice*, 249.

19. Carell, *Hitler Moves East, 1941–1943*, 425.

20. Ibid., 424.

21. Lunde, *Finland's War of Choice*, 59.

22. Lundin, *Finland in the Second World War*, 200.

23. Lunde, *Finland's War of Choice*, 271.

CONCLUSION

1. From a speech given in the House of Commons August, 2, 1944: Sir Winston Churchill, *The Dawn of Liberation* (London, UK: Cassell and Company, Ltd., 1945), 155.

2. Olli Vehvilainin, *Finland in the Second World War: Between Germany and Russia* (New York: Palgrave Publishers, Ltd., 2002), 101.

Index

Note: The photo insert images are indexed as p1, p2, p3, etc.